For God Alone

For God Alone

A Primer on Prayer

BONNIE THURSTON

DARTON·LONGMAN+TODD

First published in 2009 by
Darton, Longman and Todd Ltd
1 Spencer Court
140–142 Wandsworth High Street
London SW18 4JJ

© 2009 Bonnie Thurston

The right of Bonnie Thurston to be identified as the Author
of this work has been asserted in accordance with the
Copyright, Designs and Patents Act 1998.

ISBN 978-0-232-52760-5

A catalogue record for this book is available from the British Library.

Typeset by YHT Ltd, London
Printed and bound in Great Britain by
Athenaeum Press, Gateshead, Tyne & Wear

Table of Contents

Dedication

For my brother Alfred V. Bowman on his 50th birthday.

Thanksgivings

So many parishes, people and places have nourished my life of prayer.

I am profoundly grateful for the parish of my childhood, First Christian Church, Beckley, WV; Christ Church, Oxford where I attended Evensong most term days in 1972; St. Paul's Memorial Episcopal Church, Charlottesville, VA which carried me through graduate study and into adult life; the noon Eucharist and Healing Service at St. Matthew's Episcopal Church, Wheeling, WV; and for the parishes that have tolerated my attempts at ministry: Knoxville Christian Church, Pittsburgh, PA; Taylorstown Christian Church, Taylorstown, PA; McMechan Christian Church, McMechan, WV; Chapel Hill Christian Church, Wellsburg, WV; and First Christian Church, Wheeling, WV.

I have learned prayer from everyone with whom I have prayed and who has prayed for me, but especially from my mother, Eleanor King Bowman, my late husband, Burton B. Thurston, Sr., Br. David Steindl-Rast, O.S.B., Fr. Daniel J. O'Hanlon, S.J. (of blessed memory), Marilyn Barton, and my extended "Thomas Merton family."

My life of prayer has been nourished by many monasteries and retreat houses, but especially All Saints Sisters of the Poor, Catonsville, MD; Our Lady of the Angels Monastery, Crozet, VA; The Abbey of Gethsemani, Trappist, KY; Mount St. Joseph, Wheeling, WV; Paul VI Pastoral Center, Wheeling, WV; Kearns Spirituality Center, Allison Park, PA; the Great

Britain and Ireland Province of the Daughters of Wisdom, and the Society of the Sacred Cross, Tymawr Convent, Wales.

A good deal of the material in this book was first presented as talks in various venues and places, and I benefited a great deal from those who attended and responded.

Finally, hearty thanks to editor Brendan Walsh, who was enthusiastic about this book from the start, to the wonderful staff at Darton, Longman, Todd in London (thank you Claudine, Helen and Georgina) who were immensely patient with me, negotiated translation between the two languages we speak(!), and brought the book to the attention of the University of Notre Dame Press where Barbara Hanrahan and her associates (especially Susan Roberts and Wendy McMillen) have been equally patient, helpful and kind. I wish every author the joy of editors like these.

The Anchorage, Wheeling, WV, USA
Feast of All Saints, 2008

Before, I wanted
to have an oratory.

Then, I wanted
to be an oratory.

A small shift
of infinitives,
omitted verb,
obliterated pronoun,
mark a cosmic *transitus,*
an ontological change:

From praying
to being prayer.

From burning
to being fire.

Introduction

"Lord, teach us to pray. . ." (Luke 11:1)

I am not an expert on prayer. Nobody is. We are all beginners in the life of prayer, and will always be so, because God is so vast and God's gift of prayer has infinite dimensions for exploration. The more prayer territory we explore, the more we find there is to explore. And often, after we develop an exploratory method, a prayer practice or habit that works for us, it breaks, doesn't "take us there" any more, so we have to begin all over again. Teresa of Avila said, "no one is so advanced in prayer that they do not often have to return to the beginning."[1] A lot of people who think they can't pray just haven't found their own language for or mode of prayer. And a lot of people who think their prayer life has dried up need to try another *way* of praying. But that is getting ahead of myself.

I am not an expert on prayer; I am like the father with the sick son who said to Jesus, "I believe. Help my unbelief." (Mark 9:24) I say, "Lord, I want to pray. Help me pray." And that is itself prayer. The desire to pray is already prayer. Although not an expert, I spent a large part of my life writing and teaching about prayer (which was certainly an example of the blind leading the blind!) before I made the decision to stop talking about it and start doing more of it. Liturgically and informally I was often in the position of leading prayer. I gave retreats and spent time talking with people about prayer. I observed that people sincerely desire prayer. But they seldom know what it is or how to do it. Christian leaders and authority figures repeatedly tell people to pray, but seldom teach about what prayer is or how one might do it.[2] This makes me suspicious that perhaps they don't know themselves. We tell people to pray, not how to pray, as if they could "catch prayer" or "pick up prayer" like the current virus!

So after a number of years considering it, I have the audacity to write a book on prayer—as if we needed another book. Really, if you want to learn to pray, you have to commit the time and do it. In a conference he gave to men and women seeking renewal in religious life after Vatican II Thomas Merton asked rhetorically, "What do we want, if not to pray? O.K., now, pray." This he followed with the haunting question, "What is keeping us back from living lives of prayer? Perhaps we don't really want to pray. This is the thing we have to face."[3] If you want to pray, you have to understand that prayer is an experimental project. You try something, and if it works, you keep doing it for a while. If it doesn't work, you try something else. When it stops working, you try something else. You keep alive the deep desire for prayer, for sharing God's inner life. Thomas Merton has written that "the secret of prayer is a hunger for God", that "the will to pray . . . is the essence of prayer."[4] That desire to pray is God's great gift to you in the first place. You keep that spark alive in any way you can and in the process discover yourself mysteriously going deeper and higher and wider, as if *you* weren't doing it at all. Which you aren't. Real prayer is gift, just as desire for it is gift. If you want to pray (and you must, as you are reading this book), then know that God has already gifted you with prayer and is drawing you to the Divine Self.

Most sincere Christians have a deep desire for prayer. But most of us have a pump that needs a little priming. That's an old-fashioned image, so let me explain it. My late husband and I had a big vegetable garden on a piece of flat land by a small river. Usually it got dry in August, and we needed to water the garden. So we'd attach an ordinary garden hose to a pitcher pump (one you pumped by hand with a handle) and run the hose down to the river. In order to get the pump to suck up the water, you had to prime the pump, put some water (carried in an old pitcher?) in it to get it going. Then, *voilà!* River water gushed out for the thirsty plants.

Perhaps you can think of this book as the water carried up from the river in an old, cracked pitcher to prime your pump. It won't be nearly enough to slake your thirst, but it might get you going. What you want is the river water, not the pump or the hose. Rumi, a Persian master of prayer, exclaimed, "smash the jug/and come to the river!"[5] But most of us have to start with a jug, a pump, a hose. The types of prayer that are presented in this book are like the pump and the hose and the pitcher. They give form to your desire to pray. They are the conduits for your prayer. If your pump doesn't work, try another one. If your hose springs a leak, replace it. Don't confuse the jug with the water. Remember that the Living Water you are so thirsty for will always be there. The water won't dry up and the spring won't run dry no matter how many false starts you make or how many pumps and hoses you go through! And there is more than enough for everyone. Abundance characterizes God as much as do theology's traditional "omnis" (omnipotent, omnipresence, omniscient, etc.). And, as Rumi says, "...water is crying for a thirsty man."[6] More on that in a moment.

I wanted to write, not a tome, but a reasonably short book on prayer, one whose size and approach would be portable, practical and accessible. As the previous illustration indicates, "primer" in all its definitions seemed the appropriate word. As a book a primer is a brief introduction to a subject. In painting, the primer is the material used to prepare the surface *before* the paint is applied; it gets the material ready for the real thing. In genetics the primer is the molecule (of RNA or DNA) required for the longer chain of DNA to form. In explosives, the primer contains the compound used to ignite the explosive charge. This is a beginner's book, but it might well be a dangerous one!

In this little book I decided to deal almost exclusively with personal or "private" prayer (though I doubt any Christian prayer is really solitary), knowing it is influenced by one's common prayer and public worship. What I intended to do in my "prayer book", as I've thought of it during its gestation, was to present a variety of methods of prayer that have endured through Christian history. I make no attempt to be comprehensive. My principle of inclusion was to introduce only forms of prayer I myself have used and found helpful so that I can speak personally and existentially about them. There are many, many other, beautiful ways to pray.

I wanted to write a "how to" book that would be "homey," comfortable in tone. The title "For God Alone" comes from the opening words of Psalm 62:1, "For God alone my soul waits in silence; from him comes my salvation." I believe that the deepest motivation and end of prayer is, indeed, God alone. Presented here are a variety of methods of Christian prayer and how to do them. Some will be fruitful for you. Some probably won't. Fiddle around until you find what is most authentic for you. Feel free to change and adapt the methods to suit yourself. For each method I suggest sources for further exploration. Read them and do what those authors suggest if they help you. If these are not helpful, seek out other methods not covered here.

But here's the thing. Doing practices and "saying prayers" isn't necessarily praying, as anyone who prays with a set form like morning or evening prayer in the Anglican tradition or the Liturgy of the Hours in the monastic tradition knows. One can be saying the prayers and thinking about something quite other. In the chapter "Prayers and Prayerfulness" in *Gratefulness: the Heart of Prayer*, Br. David Steindl-Rast, O.S.B. suggests that prayer is a "special kind of mindfulness." Traditionally it is called "recollection" and is made up of concentration and what Br. David calls "wonderment," "a kind of sustained surprise."[7] So I felt this book had to do three things in addition to presenting methods. First, it had to speak a bit about what prayer *is*. You will discover I think prayer is a mode of being and a quality of attention. I hope that in seeing how I came to that understanding, you might undertake your own definition or understanding of prayer. Second, since it's people who pray, a general book on prayer has to have an anthropology, a view of the human person. So you will find herein material on the nature of human beings as persons of body and mind and psyche and spirit. These "theological bits" are intended as road maps of an interior landscape which is real, although our extroverted and externally oriented world is largely unfamiliar with it.

Third, since I believe prayer is a mode of being, I had to try to present how one moves from "saying prayers" or "doing prayers" to "praying," to prayer itself. That is, I had to provide functional material (how do I do it?) and essential material (what is it in itself?). This last task proved to be the most difficult, in part because of how individuated prayer is. For each of us, prayer is as individuated as our fingerprint or our DNA. Perhaps the primary task of Christian spiritual maturity is to find one's own language of prayer, one's own way of praying. Verbal, intercessory prayer will be *the* mode of prayer for some of us. For others it will be some form of wordless prayer, a kind of attention. However, most of the great works on prayer in the Christian tradition do suggest there is a progression. The image of a ladder or of stairs is often used by masters like John Climacus (John of the Ladder) and St. Teresa of Avila. Thus there is a reason for my order of presentation of methods (pumps and hoses and pitchers!) of prayer: various methods of vocal prayer, praying with Scripture, the Jesus Prayer, praying with the body, and contemplative ways of praying (called here "the prayer of waiting"). This book wanders through the three historic Christian modes of prayer: *oratio* (praying with words); *meditatio* (praying with the mind and thought) and *contemplatio* (the prayer of rest or "the prayer of waiting"). However, each chapter in this book is self-contained, and you can read them in any order, using what is helpful at this stage of your journey and either ignoring or saving for another time what seems useless (or incomprehensible) now. Don't worry too much about where in the river you put your hose or which hose you use. Just get to the water!

How we pray is who we are. How I pray (and who I am) is shaped by the Christian communities in which I was raised, the various churches of the American Protestant Campbell-Stone Movement and the Anglican tradition, particularly its more Catholic manifestations. My working environment for some years has been or included the Roman Catholic Church, to which I have reason for profound gratitude, and a Presbyterian seminary. Let me be clear at the outset that I am a Christian, and I pray as a Christian. In terms of method, I do not have a narrow interpretation of what this means, and you will find reference here to prayer practices and insights from other religions, particularly Buddhism and Islam, with which I have familiarity and for which I have great respect. Allegiance to Jesus Christ and life in the matrix of the Holy Spirit frees me to use the prayer *methods* of other religious traditions to the degree that they do not compromise what for me is exclusive allegiance to Jesus.[8] As a follower of Jesus Christ, not every prayer option is open to me, but a lot are, enough are. So, this is a Christian book and in some sense a biblical book since it uses the Jewish and Christian scriptures extensively. I sincerely hope it isn't a narrow or mean-spirited book because I do not serve a narrow or mean-spirited God, but One Whom, as Matthew's Jesus says, "makes his sun rise on the evil and on the good, and sends rain on the righteous and on the unrighteous." (Matthew 5:45) To use the earlier metaphor, the Christian's God is the River Water available for everybody to plunge right into.

Since I don't want my own take or slant on prayer to be a mystery (we will encounter mystery enough in our journeys into prayer), let me briefly here introduce my four basic premises about prayer, premises you will encounter at various places in the material that follows, and especially in chapter 1. Basically, I think prayer is the practice of attending to God's presence. Therefore my first premise is that prayer (like playing the piano or playing baseball) requires practice. We learn to pray by praying. Reading books about and going to talks on prayer are no substitute for praying. Second, prayer is a relationship; to be sure, a relationship that has been initiated with us, but a relationship that requires attention. Relationships take attending to; they take time and patience. If one is serious about prayer, one gives time to it just as one would to a serious relationship with a lover or a friend which, in fact, is what prayer, in part, is.

We live in a culture that is performance-oriented, beginning with potty training and moving right on through schooling and work. It is deeply ingrained in most of us to "do it right" or "get it right." But prayer is a subject in which everybody gets an "A." You don't have to be Albert Einstein to get a Nobel Prize in prayer. Indeed, exclusive reliance on intellect will become a hindrance. Prayer is not really about our own intelligence or skill, and so we can't do it wrongly. My third premise is there may be more and less effective modes of prayer at any given time in your journey, but at root the desire to pray at all (even the lament that you "can't pray") is a gift from God who has called you and waits for you. Fear of failure in prayer is a particularly pernicious and groundless fear. As those in the river will tell you, "come on in; the water's fine."

Fourth, because prayer is a response to Divine initiative, God is always present and always waiting for you. Presence is the nature of God; attending to that Presence is the nature of prayer. Much of the Christian story is built on this simple fact, from the angel who tells Joseph that Mary's unborn child is "'Emmanuel,' which means, 'God is with us,'" (Matthew 1:23), to Jesus' parable of the Prodigal Son which is really the story of the Faithful Father looking up the road for the son to come home (Luke 15:20), to the arms of Jesus open on the Cross, to the Risen Christ's promise, "I am with you always." (Matthew 28:20) The Divine embrace is prepared and waiting; we need only walk into it.

We learn to pray by praying. Prayer is a relationship that takes time, but you can't do it wrongly. God is "with us" even when God seems absent since, as Canadian scholar, Lynn Szabo says, "silence is the language of the seemingly absent God."[9] God is waiting for us to notice the Divine presence. If the essence of "practicing prayer" is open-ness to God's presence, prayer's essential attitude must be gratitude. In his important book previously mentioned, Br. David Steindl-Rast, O.S.B. teaches that gratefulness is the heart of prayer. He is so right.

My final introductory word is about language. In my own writing, I try very hard to be inclusive. Sometimes, in this book for the sake of simplicity I use the masculine pronoun for God, and I apologize at the outset to those of you whom this will offend. I hope it won't prevent your use of the book. When I quote another writer, I am enough of a pedant to think it is wrong to "doctor" the sources, so I reproduce the copy as it is in the original. I don't like it when someone puts words in my mouth, and I don't want to do it to others.

And so this book begins with the request of that first disciple, "Lord, teach us to pray." It is a subject that God alone can teach us. May we be receptive and eager students.

Chapter 1

Prayer: Toward a Definition[1]

God saw everything that he had made, and indeed, it was very good. (Genesis 1:31)

...pray without ceasing...
(1 Thessalonians 5:17)

An Introductory Exercise

This chapter is theoretical. It presents one definition and theology of prayer. I hope it won't be too heavy and boring, but if starting with theology seems burdensome to you, perhaps you should begin with another chapter. In any case, before I impose on you my theology and definition of prayer, it would be helpful if you paused to think for a few minutes about your own definition and understanding. If you had to define prayer, what would you say? If someone asked you what prayer is, how would you answer? You might want to jot your responses down in a notebook, or inside the back cover of this book. Just for fun, date your definition. You may find that in the course of reading this book or over time as you develop your practices and life of prayer, your definition will change.

To "prime your pump" (see the Introduction if you didn't read it!) I've provided a rather long list of definitions of prayer.

Some are general, and some are attributable to a particular person and so are footnoted in case you are intrigued and want to learn more about that idea. It's useful to note with which of these definitions you are most comfortable, which seem most unfamiliar, which seem incomprehensible. If you have a strong negative reaction to one of the statements, stop and think about why that might be the case. What does it trigger in you and why? Here are the definitions:

- Prayer is talking to God.
- Prayer is conversation with God in which both parties talk and listen.
- Prayer is a response to God in thought and deed, with or without words.
- Prayer is listening to God.
- Prayer is a state of "pure beholding," pure perception of What Is, of Reality.
- Prayer is a love affair between two free agents. (Metropolitan Anthony[2])
- Prayer is an encounter and a relationship that cannot be forced. (Metropolitan Anthony[3])
- Prayer is descending with the mind into the heart and resting there in God's presence.
- Prayer is a process of learning to be empty and passive in order to receive and respond to God's will.
- Prayer is saying to God: "Here I am. Send me." Or "Here I am. Find me." Or "Where *are* YOU?!?"
- Prayer is focused inactivity.
- Prayer is the expression of our fundamental relationship to God. (Jean Danielou[4])
- Prayer is to "discover what God is in Himself and wonder at it." (Jean Danielou[5])
- Prayer is "a cry for the Kingdom," an admission things are not as they should be, not as God intends them to be. (Stanley Grenz[6])

- Prayer is any expression of the realization of one's dependence upon God.
- Prayer is "primary speech." (Ann and Barry Ulanov[7])

Having presented others' thoughts on prayer, let me tell you what I think prayer is: prayer is the attentiveness to God's presence that restores God's original image in and intention for us, for human beings. Prayer is a mode of being. Here is a very dense summary of what I want to say and of what I will unpack in the remainder of this chapter: prayer, as a response to Divine initiative, is placing the Self in God's presence in order to restore its original nature, to be re-made in the Divine image, and, ultimately, to rest in God's presence in loving adoration. Generally this process begins by descending with the mind (*nous*) into the heart (*kardia*).

Prayer: A Mode of Being

Like everything else, prayer begins in the beginning. For biblical Christians this means we open our inquiry with the book of Genesis. Genesis tells us two very important things about prayer. First, human beings are made in God's image, and, second, the God in whose image we are made wants to be in relationship with us. Genesis makes it very clear that the prototype for the human person is the Divine One. Human beings are made in God's image. "Then God said, 'Let us make humankind (*adam*) in our image, according to our likeness ... So God created humankind in his image, in the image of God he created them; male and female he created them." (1:26–27) This astonishing statement, that it takes man *and* woman to have a full image of God, is followed by an even more thrilling one: "God saw everything that he had made, and indeed, it was very good." (1:31) This was the sixth point in Julian of Norwich's vision, "that God is all that is good, and the good that is in all things, that is he..."[8] And, although, as Mother Teresa of Calcutta frequently noted, some of us wear unfortunate disguises, we humans are made in God's image, "good." The image of divinity that God formed and breathed into us is always longing to return to its source. We were made for relatedness to God. Prayer is first and foremost a natural expression of that longing.

Second, God did not create us and flick us off into the universe like so many annoying insects. God wants to be in relationship to us. The paradigmatic story that demonstrates this is found in Genesis 3, and it isn't the sad bit about that piece of fruit. The paradigmatic story is not that of "the Fall" but of "the Longing" of God for humanity. Adam and Eve (male and female, thus the human family *in toto*) "heard the sound of the Lord God walking in the garden at the time of the evening breeze, and the man and his wife hid themselves from the presence of the Lord God among the trees of the garden. But the Lord God called to the man, and said to him, 'Where are you?' He said, 'I heard the sound of you in the garden, and I was afraid, because I was naked; and I hid myself." (3:8–10) We have been beaten down with the judgement that follows the human beings' poor choices. But, what I want to point out in regard to prayer is that God "comes down" and wants to be with us in the garden, that Ancient Near Eastern image for paradise, that God has created for us. And we human beings hide in the bushes. Even when God calls out to us, our response is not delight, but fear. From time immemorial we have hidden from a good and loving and generous God. The problem is with us, not God. Why do we hide from the One who loves us and wants to be in relationship with us? In the context of prayer, note that God takes the initiative to be with us. And even when God finds us in disobedience, and must respond with judgement, God also responds with practical care. "The Lord God made garments of skins for the man and for his wife, and clothed them." (Genesis 3:21)

Here is the first bit of good news. Each human being is created in God's likeness and for relationship to God. That is our identity, who we are in the truth of our being. In a very direct and literal way, we are, as many of my generation were taught in Sunday School, children of God, made of and for God's own Self. Our True Self, who we really are, is a reflection of God's Self within us. (There will be a good deal more discussion of the True Self in chapters 4 and 7.) Each of us is unique, a manifestation of God which could not exist if we didn't. "Every human person," wrote Karl Rahner, s.j., "is an event of the free, unmerited, radical, and absolute self-communication of God." "Each man or woman is a unique and unrepeatable term of God's creative love. Each must find their path to God in a way that is proper to themselves."[9] We not only find our way to God Whose image we bear by prayer: prayer itself is the path to God.

Unfortunately, there is some not-so-good news, and it is that we generally live out of our false self, our "little s" self, rather than from our True Self, our "big S" self. That is, we live like carbon copies of a socially or culturally determined pattern rather than as unique, free creations of and mirrors of God. We don't exercise the power of choice that God gave us, but accept passively the assumptions of the cultures in which we live. We in the West have been socialized by advertising and commerce (the goal of which is to sell stuff) rather than by Holy Writ. When we abrogate ourselves to the prevailing cultural myth, we give up our freedom, the freedom Christ died to give us according to Galatians 5:1. We submit to a yoke of the most terrible kind of slavery, the slavery to unexamined custom, "the way things are here." An unexamined and unquestioning way of living is seldom a life of prayer.

In the spiritual classic, *New Seeds of Contemplation*, Thomas Merton writes helpfully and persuasively about the True and False Self. He defines the false self, the "little s" self: "My false and private self is the one who wants to exist outside the reach of God's will and God's love—outside of reality and outside of life. And such a self cannot help but be an illusion." He continues, "All sin starts from the assumption that my false self, the self that exists only in my own egocentric desires is the fundamental reality of life to which everything else in the universe is ordered."[10]

Prayer and sin and identity are all deeply connected, but I want our focus to remain on prayer and identity. So here is some more good news. God eternally takes the initiative to call us back to our True Selves, our "big S" Selves." From the very beginning, God has been gently calling, "Where are you?" God's initiative in reaching toward us is the fundamental datum of reality. God created us. God loved us first, as 1 John 4:19 puts it. God chose us in Abraham and Sarah, liberated us in Moses and Miriam, gifted us by means of the Torah, and when we ignored it, called us back by means of the prophets. Finally, we Christians believe that God came down among us to restore us to relationship. When there is a breach in relationship, only the wronged party can restore it because only the wronged party can forgive. That is what God did for us. We broke the relationship; God forgave us. This is the practical meaning of what Paul wrote in Romans, "While we were yet sinners, Christ died for us." (Romans 5:8)

So what does this have to do with prayer? Prayer is our response to the God Who is constantly taking the initiative to be in relationship to us. As such, it is the way we restore our original, Godly nature, the way we become the Selves God intended us to be. In *New Seeds of Contemplation*, Thomas Merton describes the process this way:

> There exists some point at which I can meet God in a real and experimental contact with His infinite actuality. This is the "place" of God ... it is the point where my contingent being depends upon His love. Within myself is a metaphorical apex of existence at which I am held in being by my Creator. God utters me like a word containing a partial thought of Himself. A word will never be able to comprehend the voice that

utters it. But if I am true to the concept that God
utters in me, if I am true to the thought of Him I was
meant to embody, I shall be full of His actuality and
find Him everywhere in myself, and find myself
nowhere. I shall be "saved."[11]

Prayer is the "point" where we meet God and the means by
which we restore our original nature, or reclaim, or perhaps
even discover for the first time, the relatedness to God which
is the very core of our being. Prayer is our Divine mode of
being. As Jean Danielou has written, "prayer is the expression
of our fundamental relationship to God." "Prayer is the
expression of an ontological bond that exists between God and
us. It is the outward manifestation of a fundamental reality: we
continuously receive ourselves from God, and we continuously
refer back to him." ". . .our existence [is] the unceasing gift
that God makes of ourselves to ourselves." As an expression of
our basic relationship to God, then, prayer is in Danielou's
deathless phrase "a mode of being."[12] This idea, that prayer is a
"mode of being," may well be what St. Paul had in mind when
he charged the Thessalonians to "pray without ceasing." (1
Thessalonians 5:17) Paul didn't mean "say prayers all the
time" (which, as we noted in the Introduction, might or
might not be praying), but "*be* prayer all the time." This is a
goal of Christian maturity to which we aspire, to live from our
God-made-good and God-reflecting center, in the presence of
God and in love with other human beings.

I recognize that this is not the way we usually talk about
prayer, if, in fact, we talk about prayer at all. We usually talk
about prayer as talk. And therein, I suggest, we begin to go
wrong if we are defining prayer in an essential rather than a
functional way. Prayer first of all "consists in making ourselves
present to him who is present to us . . . . To pray is to become
aware of his presence."[13] Thus prayer is more a matter of
attention than it is of any particular thing we say or do. In the
most profound possible prayer, we don't say anything at all. (I

will say more about this in chapters 8 and 9.) Would that Job's so-called friends had understood this! It was certainly the teaching of the Rabbis at the time of Jesus. They taught that "the essential thing in prayer ... is the direction of the thoughts and desires."[14] Maimonides said that one "should clear out his mind of all thought of his own, and regard himself as if he were standing before the Shekinah (in the manifest presence of God). Without this a prayer is no prayer."[15] The Syriac Father, Evagrius, in his essay "Admonitions on Prayer," said that "a single word said with an attentive mind is better than a thousand when the mind is far away."[16] Perhaps this is why in the Sermon on the Mount Jesus warned us against wordy prayers, which he described as "pagan." (Matthew 6:7) More words can indicate less meaning, less focus.

What I am suggesting is that prayer is a matter of ontology, of who we are, of the very nature of our being, and of our attentiveness to life. When we place ourselves in God's presence, we reconnect with who we are. When we are attentive to God, we become who we were meant to be. The image I have of this is a very homely one: it's like putting the plug in the socket to make the light go on. One doesn't have to understand electricity to receive its benefits, and the most beautiful lamp in the world doesn't give light until it's plugged in.

Another way to say this is to say that, in the Christian tradition, prayer is for transformation. Prayer re-forms us in the Divine image. Orthodox Christianity has a term for this: "deification in Christ." No matter what prayers we say or what prayer practices we engage in, this transformation is occurring. Whether I "say prayers" (petition God on behalf of my concerns, or repeat the Jesus Prayer, or pray the daily monastic offices) or sit wordlessly (that is, practice meditation or "centering prayer" or the prayer of waiting), I have brought myself into God's presence and that, in and of itself, changes me. My own sense is that a good deal of what "happens" in prayer is this change in me which might be more important than what happens "out there" as a result of my prayer. In any case, I don't know how prayer works, and I hope you are not reading this book to find out because if you are, you will be disappointed. Ideally, we pray not to receive Divine favors (although they are likely to be given), but to be in loving relationship with God.

So let me come back to and repeat my opening statement about prayer: "Prayer is the attentiveness to God's presence that restores God's original image in and intention for us." Prayer is attentiveness to God's presence (ideally, resting there in loving adoration) in order to restore our original image. For most of us this will mean descending with the mind (Greek *nous*) into the heart (Greek, *kardia*). As Pascal noted, "it is the heart which experiences God, and not the reason."[17] Years earlier in a letter on "moderation in spiritual impulses," an anonymous writer (perhaps author of *The Cloud of Unknowing*) noted "...if you try to see God through the eyes of reason, you will see nothing ... Reason can tell us how powerful, wise and good God is through the evidence of his creatures, but not in himself; once reason fails, then the exercise of love comes into play, because through love alone can we feel ... and find ... God himself."[18] Mostly what I have been calling the false self or the "little s" self, the self which distances us from God and thus from each other, is centered in our intellectual ego. That other seventeenth-century Frenchman, René Descartes, I think was quite wrong, and to him we owe a long detour in the history of the evolution of Christian interior life. *Cogito ergo sum*, "I think, therefore I am," is distinctly un-Christian, manifestly *not* who we are. Post-Descartes, we became enamored of reason, the intellectual function, and the so-called "Enlightenment." While it led to many technical advances and material progress (for which we can be grateful), in effect *cogito* put out the lights of prayer for a lot of people.

As indicated, I believe I am because God breathed the breath of life into me by means of the love my parents had for each other. I am because of God's initiative and love, not

because of my own mental cleverness and constructs, no matter
how acute or even helpful and pragmatic they are. Reason can
distance us from God because Who God IS and what God does
is often so, well, *unreasonable*. In the words of the Psalmist,
God's "greatness is unsearchable." (145:3) God does not ask
either intellectual understanding or reason of us. God asks for
faith, trust, obedience. But not faith as a noun, a collection of
abstract constructs, propositions or creeds, but faith as a verb,
faith *in*, in One Who is trustworthy and faith-full. Which is
all to say that becoming too cerebral, too rational, about prayer
is a great danger because prayer is a "heart thing." In biblical
anthropology mind, *nous*, is the faculty of intellectual perception. *Nous* was used by the Greek philosophers for "reason."
But the heart, *kardia*, is the whole inner self, the source of the
inner life, thinking and feeling and volition. For the biblical
writers, the heart was the central bodily organ and the religious center of the person, the space, if you will, that God
inhabits. The Psalmist asks God to create in him a clean *heart*.
(Psalm 51:10) Proverbs says "Trust in the Lord with all your
heart." (Proverbs 3:5) Through the prophet Joel God pleads
"return to me with all your *heart*." (Joel 2:12) You get the
idea. As one biblical scholar has noted, "...the heart is
understood as the center of the human capacity for emotion-
fused thinking ... . The heart is central to how one thinks,
feels, arbitrates, and evaluates."[19] In the properly ordered
Christian person, mind is subject to heart. And this is because,
as St. Paul reminded the Corinthians, "knowledge puffs up but
love builds up." (1 Corinthians 8:1) There will be much more
on this distinction in chapter 4.

In order to be re-made in the image of God, I pray. And
whatever else it is, my prayer is placing myself in the presence
of God. Most of us have trouble finding God's presence
because we have not been taught where or how to find it, or,
more properly, to notice it, because the presence of God is, in
fact, the matrix in which we "live and move and have our
being." (Acts 17:28) And remember the quotation from Julian

of Norwich who found God in all. We search for God like the fish search for water. Most of us think that in order to pray we have to get busy and do something, when, in fact, to pray most deeply we may need to stop doing altogether. And one of the things we may have to stop doing is talking. As John Kirvan says in his book *Raw Faith,* it is high time "to stop talking about ourselves and calling it prayer."[20]

In the world in which we live, in order to put ourselves in the presence of God, most of us will have to seek some measure of silence and solitude. If we want to reconnect with our deepest selves, with the very Source of our being, we are going to have to be still. This is what Scripture says: "Be still and know that I am God." (Psalm 46:10) Please note that in this verse, God-knowledge arises from silence. I expect this is why the gospels are careful to point out that Jesus "went out to a deserted place, and there he prayed." (Mark 1:35) Part of the reason Jesus was the perfect human being was that He knew how just "to be" as well as how "to do." Jesus knew and nurtured His connection with the Source of His being. I am profoundly convinced that the lack of interiority, the inability to "be still and know," is the most dangerous element of contemporary society and culture. We are entertaining ourselves to perdition. Ours is a society that makes too much noise. Noise pollution may be the most deadly toxin we face. We are a people who talk too much (and here I am doing it!) in an economy where an excess of anything devalues it. Dale Allison has remarked that "artificial noise has become an unholy liturgy that unites all in the aimless rush towards collective amnesia and banality, away from nature's God and his self-imposed muteness of love."[21]

Once we understand prayer as ontology, a way of being in the world, then we can begin to understand the difference between prayers and prayerfulness, between saying prayers and praying. Br. David Steindl-Rast in his wonderful book *Gratefulness: The Heart of Prayer* puts it this way: "We must distinguish prayer from prayers. Saying prayers is one activity among others. But prayer is an attitude of the heart that can transform every activity." "...prayers are the poetry of prayerful living."[22] What is the great difficulty that keeps us from this sort of poetic life? St. Teresa of Avila is reputed to have said that all our difficulties in prayer begin with the assumption that God is somewhere else. St. Teresa's analysis cuts right to the heart of our normal understanding of praying. "Praying," we think, consists of firing little rockets of language up into the stratosphere somewhere out there where God "lives." This is poor theology and worse christology.

One of the people who has most assisted me in the spiritual life was (ironically) an Enlightenment period Jesuit, Jean-Pierre de Caussade. On the subject of God's presence with us he wrote:

> You seek for God, beloved soul, and he is everywhere, everything speaks of him, everything offers him to you, he walks beside you, he surrounds you and is within you. He lives with you and yet you try to find him. You seek your own idea of god, although you have him in his reality. You seek perfection and you meet it in all that happens to you. All you suffer, all you do, all you inclinations are mysteries under which God gives himself to you..."[23]

If the Incarnation means anything at all, it means that God is *with* us. St. Matthew takes this so seriously that he opens his gospel by reminding us that the child of the virgin is called "Emmanuel," which means "God is with us." (Matthew 1:23) St. John tells us that "the Word became flesh and dwelt among us" (John 1:14), and John's Jesus in the Farewell Discourse of chapters 14–17 promises that He will never leave us "comfortless" or "orphaned," that is, without His presence. Jesus may be going away, but He sends the Holy Spirit to be with His friends forever and to teach them everything they need to know. As Norman Pittinger wrote in *Praying Today*,

"...God is no absentee ruler but a present agent..."[24] The important question as we begin a study of prayer is, "do we believe these gospel teachings?" Because if we do, it will revolutionize our understanding and practice of prayer.

First, it will mean that prayer will become less a matter of what we say and more a matter of paying attention. And paying attention requires that we be present where we are. Multi-tasking may be okay for computers or in the business world (though I seriously doubt its long-term effectiveness), but it is the death of prayerfulness. If prayer is attentiveness to God-with-us, most of us need to slow down and quiet down and pay attention to one thing at a time. I didn't make this up. In fact, if we can trust the prophet Isaiah, God said something very like it. "For thus said the Lord God, the Holy One of Israel: In returning and rest you shall be saved; in quietness and in trust shall be your strength." And the next phrase is "But you refused..." (Isaiah 30:15) Medical science has now determined that overwork and stress are literally killing us. They are also preventing us from being who God created us to be. We need not only to rest, but to return, to go back to something we were created to be. And that is beloved children made in the image of and for the love of their Divine Parent. In this regard a remark made by the liberation theologian Gustavo Gutiérrez is helpful. "Prayer," he writes, "is an experience of gratuitousness. This 'leisure' action, this 'wasted' time, reminds us that the Lord is beyond the categories of useful and useless."[25]

In addition to slowing down and paying attention to the here and now, most of us also need to, excuse me for saying it this way, shut up for at least a little while every day. By this I mean not only that we should turn off all our noise-making toys and stop talking, saying words with our mouth (and we do need to do that, for how can we hear God if we don't give God a chance to get a word in edgewise?), but that we should quiet the constant chatter in our minds and hearts. We need to cultivate a certain interior quietude, a fallowness of mind and heart that allows the seeds of God to germinate within us.

Second, prayerfulness as I am using the term means that we will need to adopt a new attitude toward the body, to see it not as the great enemy of the spiritual life, but as its great helper and ally. The body is the means God gave us to find God. It is by means of the body that we are present. W.H. Auden's poem, "Precious Five," makes this point so clearly. He devotes a stanza of the poem to each of the five senses and concludes that their job is to "bless what there is for being." One of the reasons that prayer can go stale, can become something other than prayerfulness, is that we are no longer present because we have lost touch with our bodies, the goodness with which they were created, and the purpose for which they were created. We have substituted all manner of artificial stimulations for the treasures that God wanted us to have. There is a real and profound relationship between inner quietude and the body. If the body is restless, the mind will wander, too. Slowing down, sitting still, being still are all aspects of the same thing. The image in Psalm 131 of the soul calmed and quieted upon the mother's breast is a powerful picture of the sort of prayerfulness of which I am speaking. With practice, it becomes, not a separate activity (or maybe absence of activity!), but an attitude, what in Philippians Paul called a "mindfulness" (forms of this Greek root, *phronein,* appear frequently in Philippians) that pervades all of life.

So let me conclude this discussion of a definition and theology of Christian prayer. The impulse to pray is, itself, a result of Divine initiative. God formed us and breathed a Divine Spirit into us to give us life. In baptism Christians were "marked as God's own forever," and our impulse is, always, quite rightly, to "return to the source." We were made by God for God. As St. Augustine said, our hearts are restless until they find rest in God. Our most profound prayer is to turn our whole being, our hearts and minds and souls and strength, lovingly and attentively to God. This quiet and focused attention to God-with-us is profoundly Christian prayer. How ever we "do it," that turning attentively to God is the sort of prayer that transforms, indeed, reforms us in the image in which we were made.

And the best news of all comes via the parable of the Prodigal Son because it indicates that God is always looking for that turning and returning. Even when we are still far off in our inattentiveness and noisiness and distraction, even when we are in a foreign land dining from the pigs' trough, God is looking for us, filled with compassion for us, ready to run up the road to meet us and put the Divine arms around us and quiet us on the Divine breast and welcome us home and throw us a great, big party. God always and everywhere and in every moment offers the Divine embrace. To step into it is to pray and to be who we were created to be: God's eternally beloved ones.

For Further Reading and Exploration

Abhishiktananda (Henri le Saux, O.S.B.), *Prayer* (Norwich: Canterbury Press, 1989).

Anthony Bloom (Metropolitan Anthony), *Beginning to Pray* (New York: Paulist Press, 1970).

Jean Danielou, *Prayer: The Mission of the Church* (Grand Rapids, MI: Eerdmans, 1996).

Richard Foster, *Prayer: Finding the Heart's True Home* (San Francisco: HarperSanFrancisco, 1992).

David Steindl-Rast, O.S.B., *Gratefulness: The Heart of Prayer* (New York: Paulist Press, 1984).

Chapter 2

Oratio:
Praying with Words

>...*in everything by prayer and supplication
with thanksgiving let your requests be known to
God. (Philippians 4:6)*

>...*with gratitude in your hearts sing psalms,
hymns, and spiritual songs to God.
(Colossians 3:16b)*

>...*I urge that supplications, prayers, interces-
sions, and thanksgivings be made for everyone... (1 Timothy 2:1)*

It's been my experience that when I say "prayer" most people
think "intercession." The common view is that Christian
prayer is basically asking God for things. That is certainly an
aspect of voiced prayer, but it is far from the only way to pray
with words, as the chapter's opening quotations from the
Pauline tradition attest. This chapter begins with a few brief
assumptions about praying with words, raises some difficulties
faced in this way of praying and then introduces various types
of vocal prayer. It closes with some suggested patterns of vocal
prayer which incorporate several of these types and an excursus
on praying the Psalms.

Vocal Prayer: Some General Considerations

Prayer is a natural expression of the deepest possible yearning of the soul for God. It is a way of expressing intimacy with God. By vocal prayer we express our dependence upon God for everything, give thanks for God's benefits (and, if we are mature, for the difficulties that lead us to greater dependence upon God), intercede for others, pray for ourselves, confess our sins, express our penitence, and adore God for being God. Vocal prayer, then, assumes the reality of a living, active, present God, even if we don't continually feel that presence. In our life of prayer, feeling isn't of great importance, and the sooner we learn this, the smoother our life of prayer will be. Vocal or voiced (either aloud or silently) prayer suggests ours is not an absent God. The Holy Qur'an teaches that God is as close as our jugular vein. The Christian monk Theophane the Recluse is reported to have said, "The awareness of God shall be with you as clearly as a toothache." That's a vivid way of putting it!

Second, vocal prayer assumes our absolute dependence upon this God Who is present. We *can't* do it ourselves, whatever *it* is. We are contingent creatures. Put negatively, we are powerless. Put positively, everything is gift, which, I suppose, is why the circumstances of our lives are called "givens." This deep, if unarticulated, understanding of contingency is at the root of all vocal prayer. We need things, other people need things, and so we ask God. We receive things, and so we thank God. We make mistakes and disappoint God, and so we ask God's forgiveness. We realize God's generosity and greatness and glory, and so we praise and adore God. We want to give something back, and so we pray prayers of oblation. Prayer is not really about us; it's about God from start to finish. This is the point that the Pharisee missed in Jesus' parable in Luke 18:9–14. The religious leader, the Pharisee, stands up and harangues God about himself (four uses of the first person singular pronoun in two verses!). The figure whom we might

expect to be the negative example, the collaborator with
Rome, the tax collector, throws himself on God's mercy. The
subject of his prayers is God, and Luke's Jesus says, "this man
went down to his home justified." (18:14)

In the gospels, we frequently see Jesus at prayer and hear
Jesus' teaching about prayer. Jesus assumes that human beings
are free, have free will and choice. We can choose prayer,
choose relationship with God. Or not. Jesus doesn't force
anybody. He says, "behold, I stand at the door and knock"
(Revelation 3:20) not, "I'll huff and I'll puff and I'll blow your
house down." Jesus offers invitations like "follow me" (Mark
1:17) and "come and see" (John 1:39). Jesus takes the initiative to invite, then waits for the response. This is the basic
pattern of prayer: God initiates; humans respond. Prayer is a
response to an invitation.

Jesus also assumed that God is personal. Prayer is a relationship, and it is hard to have a relationship with an
abstraction like Goodness or Truth or Beauty. It's much easier
to have a relationship with a person. I think this is the root of
the Father language for God in the gospels. In Aramaic, the
common language of Roman Palestine, *abba* was the word for
"father," a familial word, if not a childish one (not "Daddy").[1]
Actually it occurs only three times in the New Testament:
Mark 14:36 (parallels Matthew 26:39, Luke 22:42), Galatians
4:6, and Romans 8:16. Usually the New Testament has "the
Father" (*ho pater*); the nominative article is used to indicate the
Semitic form behind it. *Ho pater* is added to *Abba* by Paul and
Mark to explain a word with which their Gentile audiences
might not be familiar. The usage was a metonym for "God,"
the substitution of one name for another. "Father" was used
because Jews didn't say YHWH and because it carried the
connotation of intimate, personal relatedness.[2] In the Gentile
church "*Abba*" equaled "God."

In inviting His disciples to call God "Father," Jesus was
inviting them into a relationship of intimacy with God,
inviting them into God's family. "Our Father" is in invitation

to intimacy, an introduction into a relationship in which we know and are known. We are invited to join a healthy family with a wonderful parent and many, equal siblings, all of whom are promised an inheritance, language Paul uses frequently and which must have provided great solace to dispossessed early believers. (See, for example, Galatians 3:26–4:7.) God is our Parent; we are all God's children, which means we are siblings to each other. The implication is both that we accept the conditions of filial obedience (we obey God) and the responsibility of love and care for all the other children in the family. Calling God "Father" is already a form of intercession because it implicates us in the welfare of other children in the family. Elizabeth Schüssler Fiorenza calls this "a critical subversion of all structures of domination."[3]

The God with whom we are invited by Jesus to be in relationship is faithful, trustworthy. We can grow in relationship to God because we can have a basic confidence in the other party in the relationship. And this God is not, according to several biblical accounts, static or immoveable. God responds to vocal prayers. God apparently changes God's course of action in response to human entreaty. Perhaps the most famous example is Abraham's bargaining with God in Genesis 18:22–33. The biblical record makes it very hard for me to accept theological systems that assert Divine implacability.

"Praying with words," then, assumes that one is "speaking to God" in some way that is relational. If that is the case, there are three immediate obstacles to this way of praying. The first and most dangerous is an inadequate understanding of God. Nobody can fully know God. But we can work at doing so and grow in our knowledge. Persons who want to pray need to spend a fair amount of time coming to know the God of creation (cf. Romans 1:20), of Scripture and of Jesus Christ. We must be careful not to make God in our own image, the idol of our own deepest needs and fantasies. In fact, Jesus on the cross smashes every idol of what God "ought" to look like and do. As Ann and Barry Ulanov say so eloquently, "We come to God at first through the way we need God to be. Only slowly and with much experience of prayer can we allow God to come to us."[4] We need to become aware of our images of God in prayer, images like "Father" or "Judge," notice them, welcome them, change them, and realize they are not "the last word," but a very partial word indeed.

The second obstacle to praying with words, or to any kind of prayer, is to think we have to be in a "spiritual" frame of mind to pray. While the emotive or affective element of prayer is important and must be present for the whole person to be engaged, it is a mistake to wait for some sort of feeling before one prays. The will to pray precedes any feeling, and is itself an invitation from God. Relatedly, honesty in vocal prayer is crucial. It's no good doing a "pious act" before God if, in fact, one is angry or depressed or estranged. Relationships are built on honesty, not playacting. As Robert Wicks quips, "Hiding things from God goes hand in hand with hiding things from ourselves."[5] And, in any case, God knows the reality of our inner lives. The more candid we are in our converse with God, the deeper will be our life of prayer. God is big enough and loving enough to absorb our angers, hurts, and partiality. Job is a great example of honesty in prayer. So is Mark's Jesus, who on the cross who cries out in abandonment.

Finally, one's sense of the presence or absence of God is not very important to the efficacy of prayer. It is a great consolation when I am able to feel God's presence. It brings joy and delight to the one who loves God and who prays. It is a special trial if, after experiencing God's presence, it seems withdrawn. But, ultimately, that absence is not crucial to the continuance of the life of prayer and may, in fact, be very important to its growth, as St. John of the Cross so clearly understood and eloquently explained.[6] As the anonymous writer of "The Letter on Prayer" in *The Cell of Self-Knowledge* explains, "pure love of God consists in loving him for himself and not for his favors."[7] A great deal of prayer is practice, the finger exercises and scales, not the Chopin Nocturnes or the Beethoven piano concerti. Even when we don't feel like praying, and especially when God seems absent, it is important to act volitionally, to choose to continue to pray, to practice, to carry on with our habitual ways of praying. Christians continue with prayer in dry periods knowing that Scripture makes particular promises to them in these times. Hebrews says that Christ "always lives to make intercession for them." (7:25) Jesus has promised the assistance of the Holy Spirit (John 14:26). Paul teaches that the Spirit is of particular assistance in the difficult aspects of prayer. He writes, "...the Spirit helps us in our weakness; for we do not know how to pray as we ought, but that very Spirit intercedes with sighs too deep for words ... the Spirit intercedes for the saints [that is, believers] according to the will of God." (Romans 8:26–27)

Types and Modes of Vocal Prayer

In his book on models of Christian prayer, *The Tree of Life*, Steven Chase makes a helpful distinction between corporate and personal prayer. He notes that "common prayer is any prayer involving more than one person, while personal prayer is the prayer of an individual."[8] Although one can find many of the following types of prayer in common and liturgical prayer, this is a discussion of these types in personal prayer. Note, please, I did not say "solitary" prayer. Because there are no first person singular pronouns in the Lord's Prayer, I think all Christian prayer must be, in some sense, communal or common. Christians pray in and with the "great cloud of witnesses," and when we can't pray, they pray in our stead. Praying with words includes forms of prayer that are primarily "saying things." These prayers can be spontaneous and incidental, made up on the spur of the moment in a particular experience. Personal prayers can be "prefabricated," as in the Liturgy or the Hours, the Anglican *Book of Common Prayer*, the traditional pattern of the rosary, and the use of liturgical canticles, litanies and hymns. I will not say very much in this book about these traditional prayer forms, although I heartily recommend them, especially when one's own, spontaneous prayer seems to be drying up. Praying with words can also include praying the Bible itself about which we will say more in chapter 3.

The following is a list of nine types or modes of praying with words. Several of them occur in Philippians 4:6 ("...in everything by prayer and supplication with thanksgiving let your requests be made known to God.") and 1 Timothy 2:1 ("First of all, then, I urge that supplications prayers, intercessions, and thanksgivings be made for everyone..."), indicating that the scriptural tradition recognizes different kinds of verbal prayer. Most, but not all, of the things we say to God in the relationship that is prayer fall into one of these categories.

1. Invocation
In a way, prayers of invocation are the Christian equivalent of the Shinto practice of clapping the hands or ringing the bell at the entrance to the shrine to get the attention of the *kami*. The word "invocation" comes from the Latin roots *in* (on) and *vocare* (to call). To invoke is to call upon. Prayers of invocation (like those at the beginning of many Protestant worship services) call upon God to be present. Of course, as we have noted, God is, in fact, already radically present. So the comparison with the Shinto practice doesn't quite hold. For Christians, invocation is a confession of desire, our desire to be in God's presence. Prayers of invocation really remind *us* to attend to that presence; they serve to usher us into God's presence. And that requires some preparation.

2. Confession and penitence
In the southern mountains where I grew up, indoor plumbing and running water was for a long time the exception rather than the rule. Washing up was easy enough, but full baths

were a production that involved hauling and heating water. The traditional custom was for the family to have a full bath on Saturday night in preparation for worship on Sunday morning. The lustral baths of the Greco-Romans and the *mikvoth* of the Jewish tradition are but two other examples showing that human beings seem always to have had a deep sense of the need to "clean up" for God.

Prayers of confession and penitence (while not strictly equivalent) are a way of "cleaning up" before attendance upon God. Confession (Latin *com + fateri*) is to acknowledge together, to admit one has made mistakes, to admit sin, to express sorrow for wrongdoing, and in penitence to express willingness to atone and amend. Confession is an admission of active wrongdoing or neglecting to do what should have been done or, even before they become actions, of having attitudes that are displeasing to God. The motivation for prayers of confession is not so much that God is "up there" ticking off our sins in a big book, but that we love God. Prayer is relational. If we love somebody, we strive to do what pleases him or her and to avoid what pains the beloved. If we err and offend the beloved, we ask for forgiveness and promise not to do that thing again. Confession is intended to restore the relationship, which, as I noted earlier, is in the hands of the wronged party. In prayer, we confess our sins to God and express our sorrow for having committed them (penitence) first and foremost because we love God. This is how we "clean up" to come more fully before God.

3. *Adoration*

Confession and penitence prepares us to enter into God's presence and to speak to God. Adoration is from the Latin *ad* (to) and *orare* (to speak). But the prayer of adoration has more in common with the popular usage of "adore" than with its etymology. To adore is to worship or love greatly. Prayers of adoration are prayers that worship God, not for what God has done, but for Who God Is. As Richard Foster so wisely and succinctly explains, "When our reply to God is most direct of all, it is called *adoration*. Adoration is the spontaneous yearning of the heart to worship, honor, magnify, and bless God."[9] (Italics Foster's.) Vocal prayers of adoration lift the mind and heart to God to enjoy God's presence. Of the forms of vocal, personal prayer it may most easily move into deep, wordless prayer. It is the lover gazing on the beloved. *Adoro te* is the cry of one who loves deeply.

It is also the cry of one who loves life. In his *Letters to Malcolm, Chiefly on Prayer* C.S. Lewis remarks that "*pleasures* are shafts of the glory [God's glory] as it strikes our sensibility." "...pure and spontaneous pleasures are 'patches of Godlight' in the woods of our experience."[10] (Italics Lewis'.) Lewis records that he tries "to make every pleasure into a channel of adoration."[11] Such a practice indicates how very close are adoration, praise and thanksgiving.

4. Praise

Praise is related to adoration because, ideally, we praise God for being God. The Latin root of praise is *pretium*, "worth." God is "worthy" to be praised. Praise expresses approval of something or someone, commends worth. In common parlance, to praise is to express the value or merit of something. Prayers of praise laud the glory of God who doesn't really need our praise. Scripture frequently asserts that God prefers obedience to sacrifices and praise. (See, for example, Isaiah 1:10–17; Psalm 40:6–8.) In the life of prayer, praise is good for the one *who* praises more than the One Who *is* praised. Praise re-establishes our place in the scheme of things, reminds us we are creatures responding to our Creator, reminds us we are contingent, reminds us that God is God. And so praise moves naturally to thanksgiving.

5. Thanksgiving

Prayers of thanksgiving are expressions of gratitude, and many spiritual teachers think that gratitude is the basic attitude of the spiritual life. Meister Eckhart is reported to have said that if the only prayer we ever say is "thank you," it is enough. More recently, Br. David Steindl-Rast, O.S.B. has written a spiritual classic, *Gratefulness: The Heart of Prayer*. The title says it all. Br. David believes that gratitude is the only proper response to "the gratuitousness of absolutely everything. The universe is gratis. It cannot be earned, nor need it be earned. From this simple fact of experience springs grateful living, grace-filled living."[12] Br. David believes "everything is gratuitous, everything is gift. The degree to which we are awake to this truth is the measure of our gratefulness. And gratefulness is the measure of our aliveness."[13]

Normally we thank God for the blessings of life. Saints thank God for everything in life because everything, the apparently good and the apparently bad, can draw us closer to God. As the eighteenth-century Jesuit spiritual master Jean-Pierre de Caussade, S.J. noted, "What God arranges for us to experience at each moment is the best and holiest thing that could happen to us."[14] Therefore, we should thank God for it. As Paul wrote to the Thessalonians, "give thanks in *all* circumstances; for this is the will of God in Christ Jesus for you." (1 Thessalonians 5:18, italics mine.) It is only in gratitude for what God has already done for us that we dare to ask God for more.

Adoration, praise and thanksgiving are intimately related but not synonymous. Stanley Grenz makes these helpful clarifications: "Adoration or praise centers on the nature and character of God, whereas thanksgiving is the expression of gratitude for what God does on behalf of the church and the world. Thanksgiving arises from the reception of God's gifts; adoration focuses on the Giver."[15]

6. Intercession
Intercessory prayer, which is also called "petitionary prayer" or "supplication," is perhaps the form of vocal prayer that is most

familiar to us. Simply put, it is praying for others. To intercede is literally to go between (*inter* + *cedere*) or bridge a human
or worldly situation and God. Etymologically the word means
intervening for the purpose of making agreement, something
along the lines of "Blessed are the peacemakers." (Matthew
5:9) Prayers of intercession are prayers that make requests to
God on behalf of others. In intercession we put the needs of
others before God, and this is trickier than it sounds because it
means we have made a clear distinction between their need and
our desires. My friend Sr. Mary Ellen Rufft, C.D.P. suggests
we need to add "The Silver Rule" to "The Golden Rule." It
is "Do unto others as you think they would most like to be
done unto."[16] Prayers of intercession are for what is best for
the one prayed *for*, not what the one who prays wants. Personally, I don't always know what is best for those for whom I
pray, so I frequently provide the noun and leave the verb to
God.

Intercessory prayer is one of the most effective ways that we
can love others. Thomas Merton speaks movingly of the need
"to express my love by praying for my friends; it's like
embracing them. If you love another person, it's God's love
being realized. One and the same love is reaching your friend
through you, and you through your friend."[17] In *Thoughts in
Solitude* Merton says, "Prayer uses words to reverence beings in
God."[18] That is one of the best possible definitions of intercessory prayer, and perhaps also of praise, thanksgiving,
adoration and petition.

Prayers of intercession normally arise from a deep sense of
dissatisfaction with the way things are. Sickness, brokenness,
war, starvation, homelessness, abuse, absence, delay, partiality,
death—the sufferings of life are not God's will for us. So, very
fundamentally, when we intercede (or petition) we are asking
that people and the world be brought back into God's will for
them. Thus Stanley Grenz subtitles his very fine book on
prayer "the cry for the Kingdom." In intercession, whatever we
are asking it is, on some level, that "Thy Kingdom come"

because this is not the existence God desired for creation and the coming of God's Kingdom means beatitude for the whole creation.

7. *Petition*

Petition, from the Latin *petere*, means simply "to ask," in this case to ask for ourselves. It is an earnest request or entreaty for our own needs. I have encountered a remarkable number of Christians who either think they should not ask God for things for themselves, or feel guilty if they do so. This is a false humility; it can be pride masquerading as humility. Am I hesitant to ask God on my own behalf because it involves facing up to the fact that I *have* needs? Petition is also a form of confession that I am not self-sufficient; it requires me to admit my needs and imperfections. It is extremely difficult for most of us to say simply "I need" or "help me." We are thinking about prayer as a relationship. Generally speaking when we are in need we only ask our best friends for help, because to ask for help is a confession of partiality, incompleteness, sometimes helplessness. I only want my really good friends to see me this way, because they also know me as loveable, competent, etc. I don't normally ask strangers for help because they might think of me as weak or helpless. In this I am far from Jesus, who asked a Samaritan woman for a drink of water and, thereby, initiated a crucial conversation. (John 4:1–42)

Prayers of petition help us to grow in humility. The French Benedictine Henri Le Saux (known as Abhishiktananda), said simply, "The prayer of petition is essentially the recognition and acceptance of our weakness and nothingness..."[19] Petition, like other types of vocal prayer, re-establishes me in right relationship to God. I *am* needy. I *do* require help. Divine help. And, in any case, in many places Scripture invites us to pray for ourselves. As Philippians 4:6 attests, Paul is particularly clear on this matter. So is the book of James which records, "If any of you is lacking in wisdom, ask God, who gives to all

generously and ungrudgingly, and it will be given to you."
(James 1:5)

It probably goes without saying, but both petition and intercession are always in the light of "Thy will be done" or "if it be thy will." To maintain honesty in relationship, we ask for what we really desire. To maintain right relationship with God, we acknowledge that our information and wisdom is limited, that God's will is ultimately the best that can be asked in any situation. I may not know what that is, so I ask for what I honestly want or *think* is best/correct, but leave the matter of God's response entirely up to God. I will not try to tell you that this is easy, but I will suggest that you not attempt to "boss God."

8. *Oblation*

In a healthy relationship when one has received a great deal from another it is natural to want to reciprocate, to give something back. Prayers of oblation (Latin *oblatus*, to offer) are prayers of offering to God. The point is not that God needs or requires what I offer; the point is that I need to give. As Christians in union with Christ, our prayers of oblation offer ourselves, our lives, our possessions, our labor to God to be used for God's purposes. This is why in many traditional Christian liturgies at the point of receiving "the collection" or "the offering," one hears the phrase "accept our alms and oblations." As in so many forms of verbal prayer, oblation comes from me, is an offering of myself, but is not *about* me so much as about God's work in the world.

A simple prayer of oblation is: "What I am, you have made. What I have, you have given. I now give it all back to you to be used for the purposes for which you created." The nineteenth-century hymn by Frances R. Havergal, "Take My Life" which begins "Take my life, and let it be consecrated, Lord to Thee," is an almost perfect example of a prayer of oblation.

9. Lamentation[20]

I reserved lamentation as a form of prayer for last because it is a difficult form and reminds us that the life of prayer includes very dark aspects. Prayer can be very difficult, very hard work. To lament is to express grief, sorrow, or regret, to mourn aloud, to cry out, to wail, to moan. Lamentation is prayer's equivalent of King Lear on the heath in the storm screaming into the wind. If intercession and petition are confessions that life is not perfect, that the world is not what it should be, lamentation is the most dramatic expression of that hard reality. Sometimes, as Kathleen Norris notes, "the power to name, to describe, and to lament is the only power we have."[21]

How could anyone think that a religion with a Roman cross at its heart would always be a matter of sweetness and light and happiness and success and health and cheerfulness and all the pernicious myths of the "good life" which some modern "cultural Christianity" peddles? Biblical religion does not shy away from the hard realities of life, from suffering, from darkness. The Hebrew Bible includes a whole book of lamentation, the Lamentations of Jeremiah. Job laments, and God responds. Psalm 88 is an expression of unremitting darkness and solitude, which closes in some translations with "darkness is my only friend." Psalm 130 cries to God "out of the depths." (And see Psalm 38, 39 and 44.) Rare is the person who has entered into a serious and extended prayer relationship who is without seasons of *De profundis* and Gardens of Gethsemane. Complaint, mourning and grief are difficult, but acceptable forms of personal vocal prayer that require profound courage and are often a mark of spiritual strength, or the first steps toward it.

Some Patterns for Vocal Prayer and Some Practical Suggestions

We have examined nine types of personal, vocal prayer. My hope is that, if your primary method of vocal prayer was intercession/supplication, presenting various types of vocal prayer might widen your repertory. Having presented nine ways to pray with words, I now turn to some methods you might use to organize or shape your time of voiced (aloud or silent) prayer. In order not to fall into intercession alone it is useful to have a habitual pattern or structure for your prayers in this mode.

The first and most obvious thing to say is that Jesus taught such a structure, one which included various of these types of prayer, in the "perfect prayer," the Lord's Prayer. (Matthew 5:5–15; Luke 11:1–4) Many scholars, in fact, think it was intended not so much as a rote prayer to be memorized and repeated and used in public worship, but as a structure on which to hang prayer, a pattern for how to pray. Here is a simple schema of the structure of the Lord's Prayer:

Invocation: Our Father in heaven
Intercession/Petition focused on the glory of God (You/Your):

        1. Hallowed be Your name. (adoration)
        2. Your Kingdom come. (confession)
        3. Your will be done on earth as it is in heaven.

Intercession/Petition focused on human need (our/us):

        4. Give us this day our daily bread.
        5. Forgive us our debts (trespasses) as we forgive our debtors.
        6. Do not bring us to the time of trial, but rescue us from the Evil One.

Adoration/Praise: For yours is the Kingdom and the power and the glory forever. Amen.

In simple terms, the schema of prayer is Invocation, Adoration, Intercession/petition (which are synonymous in this prayer since it is prayed for "us"), Adoration/Praise. The first half of the Lord's Prayer (1–3) focuses on God, that God's name be sanctified, God's rule established, God's will done. Petitions one and three are in third person aorist imperative passive, a Greek verb form which suggests an act of reverence, a surrogate for use of the Divine Name. This is called a "Divine Passive," a way of alluding to God without daring to speak God's name. It reflects Jesus' Jewishness. The prayer opens with its focus squarely on God. The second set of petitions (4–6) attends to human need. Only after prayer that adores God and submits to God's will is it appropriate to turn to our own needs. The pattern of the prayer applies the principle in 6:33 "...seek first [God's] Kingdom and [God's] righteousness." Petitions 4–6 are first person plural and address needs common to the human family: sustenance, forgiveness, protection. The verbs are in active voice because, like the poor whom Jesus says are always with us (Mark 14:7), these needs are always present. The doxology at the end (Greek *doxa* translates "glory") returns the prayer to a focus on God.

As an outline for a period of personal, vocal prayer, then, the Lord's Prayer begins with an invocation ("Our Father") as a way of drawing us into God's presence, establishing relationship, reminding ourselves we are part of a family. It continues with adoration and praise ("Hallowed be thy name.") "Thy Kingdom come; Thy will be done" is a confession, in that it acknowledges that the first isn't here and the second isn't done. "Give us our daily bread" is intercession and petition, a prayer for the necessities of life for all human beings. "Forgive us..." is another opportunity for confession. "Lead us not into temptation" is both intercession/petition and a call for self-examination. And doxology closes the prayer with praise and adoration.

Another way to organize personal, vocal prayers is by the use of an acrostic like ACID, ACTS or FACTS. While I'm not sure the connotations of "acid" are particularly appropriate for prayer, the acrostic Adoration, Confession, Intercession, Dedication (what we called oblation) is a theologically appropriate pattern for praying. We begin with the majesty of God and adore. In the light of God's nature, we see ourselves as we are and are led to confession. Having cleared our hearts by confession, we are "clean" to ask God for the things we and others and the world need. I was once told it's no use asking God for things we aren't willing to work to bring about, and in light of that bit of wisdom, this prayer pattern appropriately closes with dedication/oblation, a self offering, a giving of ourselves to the purposes of God, offering ourselves as "secondary causes" to effect what we have interceded for.

A second well-known acrostic pattern for vocal prayer is ACTS: Adoration, Confession, Thanksgiving and Supplication.[22] I am going to spend a little time on this simple and familiar pattern, but I prefer to amend it and call it the "FACTS" of prayer, adding the frequently omitted aspect of preparatory *Focus* to Adoration, Confession, Thanksgiving, Supplication. My late husband spent many years as an educational missionary in the Middle East. He was a rather formal sort of person who cared about his appearance, the sort of person who, had pajamas been sold with neck ties, would have bought that kind. He was in one of the Gulf Kingdoms to solicit funds for higher education for Arab students and came down to the lobby of the hotel in a sports coat and tie. He was gently told by his host to go back and change into a suit because "you are going to visit a king." As old-fashioned as it may seem to say it, when we initiate a period of vocal prayer we, too, are "going to visit a king," and it behoves us to "dress properly," to make proper preparation.

A step that is frequently skipped in prayer is focus, preparing to pray, making some gentle delineation between "ordinary" and "prayerful," settling down to and into prayer. It is true that, ideally, all of life is prayer. But within a prayerful life there are also times given to prayer, also the specific activity of personal, vocal prayer. The little rituals that can be developed around beginning to prayer such as settling in a particular chair, listening to some calming music, lighting a candle, reading some poetry or Scripture, help us to gather ourselves up from the scattered variety of the many tasks and concerns of life, help us to be "collected." In *Prayer in Practice* Romano Guardini writes:

> Prayer must begin with ... collectedness ... . Everything depends on this state of collectedness. No effort to obtain it is ever wasted. And even if the whole duration of our prayer should be applied to this end only, the time thus used would have been well employed. For collectedness itself is prayer ...if at first we achieve no more than the understanding of how much we lack inner unity, something will have been gained, for ... we would have made contact with that center which knows no distraction."[23]

Perhaps the simplest way to be "collected," to focus for prayer, is to attend to the body, to settle the body. Because we are not like the spirit beings, the Eldil, in C.S. Lewis' space trilogy novels, because we are incarnate beings, the body is important to our life of prayer. Sitting down in a comfortable but erect and alert position and breathing deeply and gently is one of the oldest and most widely used methods of prayer. (I will say more about it later in chapters 6 and 9.) Breath itself is the bridge from flesh to spirit. God animated *adam* by breathing into his earthy form. (Genesis 2:7) Jesus Christ raised people from the dead and bestowed the Spirit upon them by breathing on them. The Sufi traditions of Islam believe that Allah placed a Divine spark within each of us and that the slow, conscious intake of air fans our Divine flame, and exhaling gives the light and warmth of Divinity back to a dark, cold world. Many Buddhist meditation practices are built around focus on breathing. To breathe is to live. To breathe with attention is to become focused. (And there is a lot of medical evidence that it has very healthy effects on the body.)

After settling oneself for prayer, focusing (F), one ACTS, adores, confesses, thanks, supplicates. (Parenthetically, wouldn't it be altogether better if, not just in prayer, but in all of life, we focused before we acted?) To begin vocal prayer with adoration is to begin in the "Hallowed be thy name" mode of the Lord's Prayer. Having settled into ourselves, focused our bodies and minds, we shift the focus to and spend time with God. We enter the mode of the lover in the presence of the beloved. This is good for the one who prays, even if God doesn't need it. I think, however, that it must delight God in the way that being loved delights the human heart. Enjoying God's presence, with or without words, can lead directly to very deep prayerfulness.

Confession is the "Forgive us our sins" aspect of the Lord's Prayer. Being in the presence of the beloved naturally makes me want to be my best self, and often shows me how distant I am from that self. Adoration leads naturally to confession, to acknowledging my sin. In Hebrew scripture, confession was a pre-requisite for receiving God's blessings. (See, for example, Psalm 66:18.) Metropolitan Anthony has written that "What we must start with, if we wish to pray, is the certainty that we are sinners in need of salvation, that we are cut off from God and that we cannot live without Him and that all we can offer God is our desperate longing to be made such that God will receive us, receive us in repentance, receive us with mercy and with love."[24] The promise of the New Testament is that God does receive us in this way, has already done so in Jesus Christ.

Confession is a matter of house cleaning, really, of getting rid of the dirt and clutter. It is a setting aside of what stands between us and God, removing all the stuff we have hidden behind closed doors—and then hidden behind ourselves! It is preparing a space for God to occupy. For many of us, confession is the first real turning toward authentic prayer because it is the first clear recognition of ourselves as we really are. Many of the great spiritual traditions of Christianity begin with confession and self-examination. This, for example, is where the Spiritual Exercises of St. Ignatius of Loyola begin. The "consciousness examine" of the Exercises is one of the most useful prayer tools available. As Stanley Grenz notes, "Adoration and confession form a natural progression. As one sees God in God's glory, one cannot help but see one's own shortcomings and failures."[25] This was certainly Isaiah's experience as recorded in Isaiah 6:1–6.

All who sincerely confess and repent *are* forgiven. St. John writes "If we confess our sins [God] who is faithful and just will forgive us our sins and cleanse us from all unrighteousness." (1 John 1:9) Having "cleared the decks" by confession, having received God's mercy and forgiveness, one's heart is filled with gratitude. Thanksgiving naturally follows. Adoration and praise are because of God's nature, God's essence. Thanksgiving is an expression of gratitude for what God has done. Paul suggests to the Thessalonian church that their basic "job" or "work" is thanksgiving: "give thanks in all circumstances; for this is the will of God in Christ Jesus for you." (1 Thessalonians 5:18) Thanksgiving is the verbal expression of gratitude for ongoing and specific blessings, both material and spiritual. Thanksgiving is the verbal expression of the life orientation of gratitude. As Br. David notes "What brings fulfillment is gratefulness, the simple response of our heart to this given life in all its fullness."[26]

Supplication is the "give us our daily bread; lead us not into temptation" aspect of the Lord's Prayer. The "S" of FACTS includes what in our nine types of prayer we called intercession and supplication. In the light of all that God has already done for us, in gratitude for all of it, we bring our concerns and requests to God, asking for our needs and the needs of others, but always in humility. We may not know what is best, and so all our intercessions and supplications are in the context of "Thy will be done." We provide the nouns and leave the disposition of the verbs to God.

Inevitably the question arises, "what should we pray for?" or "are there limits to what it is appropriate to ask God for?" The book of James tantalizingly records, "You do not have, because you do not ask. You ask and you do not receive, because you

ask wrongly, in order to spend what you get on your pleasures." (James 4:2c–3) The verses suggest that intercessory and
petitionary prayer require discernment. Generally my experience is that we cast the net of prayer too narrowly. The more
we understand the greatness and grandeur of God, the larger
our prayer requests become. But what about the trivial things?
I have a friend in a major European city who prays for parking
spaces when she has to be in the city center, and, while this
makes me nervous, I observe she often gets them. I heard a
story about a person who began a diet, but, unfortunately,
passed a bakery on the way to work. He prayed, "Lord if you
want me to have a sticky bun, make a parking place for me in
front of the bakery." And God answered the prayer. The
parking place appeared—on his tenth trip around the block.

Granted, these are apparently silly examples. While I
wonder if the Lord of the Universe really cares where I park my
car, I also know that Jesus, Himself, said that even the hairs of
our heads are numbered (Luke 12:17) and that God cares about
birds of the air and lilies of the field. (Matthew 6:25–33)
These are images of the intimate attention of God to creatures.
There must be some proper balance between the "big prayers"
for world peace and justice and healing for terribly ill people,
and apparently trivial prayers for parking spaces. I suspect it is
found in the principle in Matthew 6:33: "strive *first* for the
Kingdom of God and its righteousness, and all these things
will be given to you as well." (Italics mine.) My concerns
about what to pray for are addressed in chapter 3 of Stanley
Grenz's book *Prayer*. The chapter is entitled "The Workings of
Supplication." Grenz argues persuasively that Christian petitionary prayer is to be directed toward the coming Kingdom.
It understands that what is is not what is meant to be. God
does not desire war, suffering, hunger, poverty, disease. Petitionary prayer is an expression of "holy discontent with the
present."[27] It is oriented toward God Who can make things
different and Who has promised to do so. "Petitionary prayer
... requests the coming of the future into the present."[28]

If we err in petitionary/supplicatory prayer it is probably, as we noted earlier, because of a lack of understanding of God; it is a theological problem. Praying for bicycles or Barbie dolls or parking spaces reflects a selfish focus, a sense that God is a cosmic bell hop or waitress. It wrongly views prayer as a fast food restaurant where you drive in, place your order and get it at the pick-up window. God does not exist to "fill my order." Similarly, bargaining with God in prayer ("God, if you do X, I'll do Y") misunderstands the God Who has the right to call the shots. And "Fox Hole prayers," while undeniably genuine, get the order wrong. My father, a mining engineer, told the story of some miners who were trapped underground. They did everything they had been taught to do in safety training, then prayed for deliverance. Happily, they were rescued. But the order of their activity is telling, and, I suspect, paradigmatic for faithful people.

For many people the really big question is "how does intercessory prayer work?" I'm afraid I don't know and can't tell you. Grenz suggests that petitionary prayer acknowledges human need and therefore allows "the release of God's resources."[29] Some years ago I was privileged to attend a series of lectures, "Great Prayers of the Old Testament," given by one of God's great saints, Donald Gowan, professor of Old Testament at Pittsburgh Theological Seminary for many years. Naturally, someone asked the saintly man how prayer works. After suggesting that intercession is a way we bear one another's burdens, and share God's love for others, and make ourselves available as "secondary causes" in what we pray for, he said that he didn't know how it worked, but that he prayed because Scripture invited, even commanded, prayer. He prayed as an act of obedience.

Rowan Williams' book, *A Ray of Darkness*, includes a sermon entitled "Intercessory Prayer" based on Genesis 18:23–33 and Ephesians 6:10–24 and contains the following very wise words about intercession:

...our intercession is a sharing in Christ's terribly costly struggle to hold together God and the world, love and suffering, light and darkness. ... Intercession is part of this, planting the flag in the remotest and bleakest places, saying of this or that situation, "Lord, I know even *this* cannot defeat you or send you away." Intercession does not and must not shrink to a utilitarian thing ... . We do it because our faith absolutely demands this "holding together" operation. We do it even when we can't see what imaginable hope there might be, when we have no idea at all what might happen or how exactly things might get better, no idea, even that we can *do* about the situation. It is a cry of naked faith: in some inconceivable way, God is here too.[30]

Many of you who are reading this book are already obedient to the life of prayer, already "holding it together." You may have long intercession lists about intractable situations. For you, a practical issue is how to keep track of those for whom you are bound to pray and for whom you want to pray. Here are some simple, practical suggestions. First, keep a small prayer calendar, literally a calendar, perhaps one of those little ones businesses give out free at Christmas. When someone asks you to pray for something specific, say a surgery or a trip or a meeting, write down the person's name and the request on that day. Then, each morning, consult the calendar and pray as requested. Incidentally, I try to remember to pray my own date book/calendar each morning, to pray for the people and meetings and assignments I have that day. Second, if your church bulletin or newsletter prints a prayer list, tuck it in with your prayer calendar or Bible and use it.

I don't try to pray for everybody for whom I want and need to pray every day unless, of course, someone has asked me to do so or I judge a situation to be critical. (Okay. You're right. Who am I to judge?) I keep a small notebook with pages labeled "daily," "current," "self," and one for each day of the week. "Daily" are the people and situations for whom and to which I feel called to attend in prayer each day. "Current" are present situations. These change as the world and people's situations change. "Self" are the things I need for myself (so this is a supplication list). Then I divide the people for whom I pray among six days of the week, keeping Sunday for Thanksgiving only. To use old-fashioned language, I feel a special "burden" for certain things. So, Monday I pray for education; Tuesday, missions; Wednesday for the blessed (and not so blessed) dead; Thursday for "conversions" or spiritual awakening for specific people; Friday for postulants, clergy, monastics, religious; and Saturday for various aspects of world affairs or current events (I know people who "pray the morning paper," using the headlines to direct their intercessions. I know of a group of women who meet weekly to pray this way.)

Let me conclude this discussion of structuring personal, vocal or "said" prayers with three categories from the Buddhist tradition that have been helpful to me: preparation, motivation and dedication. Buddhism teaches that one doesn't just start praying, but that one prepares the mind and body for it. Buddhism is replete with preparation practices. Second, like Jesus in the Sermon on the Mount, Buddhism suggests that motivation, the reason we do what we do is important. It raises the question, ultimately, of whether I am praying for myself, because of God, or for others? Honestly examining my own motives and reasons for praying, perhaps doing so with a spiritual friend or director, helps me grow spiritually. Finally, there is in Buddhism the very beautiful practice of "dedication of merit" in which any good that comes from one's actions is "assigned" to someone or something. Translated and put crudely in this context, "who gets the merit for my prayers? Me? God? Others?" Are my prayers to give God and Jesus Christ glory? Are they for the wellbeing of others and the world or to make me feel good and pious and holy? These are hard, but important questions. Practically, dedication of merit might mean beginning a time of prayer, "Lord, if anything in these prayers pleases you, please give your response of blessing to X." "Preparation, motivation, dedication" is a good pattern for Christian prayer.

Praying the Psalms

If, as John Calvin asserts "prayer is the chief exercise of faith" (*Institutes* 3.20.1), the Psalms have been one of the chief "exercises" of Christian prayer. The great Roman Catholic biblical scholar Roland Murphy noted that prayer "is not simply asking for things: it is the varied expression of the human condition in the presence of God."[31] In my view no single collection of prayers better expresses the varied aspects of the human condition than the Psalter, the "hymn book" of Second Temple Judaism. All of the forms of prayer I introduced above appear in splendid profusion in the Psalms, which exhibit the full range of human emotions and often say what I, at any rate, can't quite articulate. Thomas Merton writes in his little monograph "Praying the Psalms," "There is no aspect of the interior life, no kind of religious experience, no spiritual need ... that is not depicted and lived out in the Psalms."[32] And, I would add, "including a level of violence which is very shocking."

Kathleen Norris quipped that "...the Psalms are blessedly untidy," and that in them even the worst human emotions are brought into the open and put before God.[33] That is their glory and challenge. In the Psalms we find beautiful expressions of praise and gratitude, expressions of restfulness and deep consolation, and eruptions of terrible violence and of the deepest, unrelieved depression. The Psalms are as messy as life tends to be. In particular, the Psalms force me to come face to face with the bundle of contradictions that I am. They insist that I own my darkest desires as well as my most enlightened impulses. The Psalms are the record of profoundly honest, and thus, intimate relationship with God. Studying them and praying them teaches us a great deal about prayer.

One approach to praying the Psalms is to mine them for patterns of prayer. The method of biblical study known as form criticism analyzes and interprets biblical passages through analysis of their literary types. Form criticism has isolated many types of psalms, but the two most frequently occurring are the hymn and the lament. The hymnic psalms have this general pattern: a summons to praise (a sort of invocation in second person plural imperative like Hallelu-Yah, "You! Praise God!"), a listing of the motives for praise (a series of statements about God's actions or attributes), and a conclusion. (See, for example Psalm 8 or 148.) The hymn psalm can provide a pattern for prayers of adoration, praise and thanksgiving. The psalm of lament, on the other hand, is the largest single category of psalm in the biblical book. Laments, too, follow a general pattern which include several of the following elements, although not necessarily in this order: invocation to God (a statement of appeal to establish contact with God); a description of the distress; a confession of trust in God (perhaps the most spiritually important part of the psalm); a petition for help; the reasons why God should help the speaker (this may sound odd to modern ears, but is common in the Psalms); an expression of confidence and an expression of thanks. (See, for example, Psalms 6, 32, 38, 102, 130, 143.) Of psalms of lament Walter Brueggemann writes, they "are powerful expressions of the experience of dis-orientation. They express the pain, grief, dismay, and anger that life is not good. (They also refuse to settle for things as they are, and so they assert hope.)"[34]

You can use the framework of the various types of psalms on which to hang your own prayers. Perhaps more simply, you can just pray the Psalms as they are written. Often devotional books will list a psalm and a reading for the day. Or, you can open the Psalter and choose a psalm randomly. From its origins, the Psalter has been the basis of monastic prayer. In fact before postulants were accepted for monastic formation, they were required to memorize a number of psalms. In many monastic communities, the whole Psalter is prayed or chanted each week. You could adapt this ancient monastic practice of working your way through the entire Psalter in a variety of ways. If you follow a daily office book, you will get through most of the Psalter regularly. For years, I have prayed through the Psalter each month following the divisions in the *Book of Common Prayer* of the Anglican/Episcopal tradition, which assigns a few psalms each morning and each evening. Or you can pray a "perpetual Psalter" by starting with Psalm 1 and making your way through to Psalm 150, reading as much as seems appropriate to a period of prayer, and then starting over when you reach the end of the book. In praying the Psalms familiarity does not breed contempt, but appreciation. I find myself looking forward to certain days of the month because I know particular psalms that speak deeply to me are coming on those days.

The Psalter can be said, read, or chanted. A number of books help us do this.[35] Gregorian chant arose in part as a way to pray the psalms in the monastic choir. The tradition of psalm singing was kept alive in the German Reformation and especially in the Scots tradition of metrical psalm singing (which so influenced the shape note singing of the American south). Many modern hymnbooks contain a large selection of these psalm settings. The Anglican/Episcopal tradition preserved in parish worship the monastic tradition of chanting the psalms. Priest Cynthia Bourgeault, Ph.D. has prepared a wonderful audio series teaching not only about psalmody, but also how to chant/sing the Psalms.[36] You may also be able to learn how to chant/sing psalms at a local Episcopal or Anglican church. I find chanting the Psalms are a particularly good way to engage the body in prayer.

What I love most about the Psalms is that you don't have to "dress up" to pray them. When I was a child, we had to dress up to go to church and pray. Uncomfortable, scratchy underclothes and dresses. Hats. It could put a kid off church altogether. The Psalms require no costume; they take us exactly as we are. Nothing human is foreign to them. They accept us in our every day, work clothes, and thus invite us to greater honesty in prayer. And, as I have noted, this honesty is crucial to prayer. Although a basic metaphor in Pauline letters to the Colossians and Ephesians is that of changing clothes, God does not require fancy dress in prayer. Who we are and what we normally attire ourselves in is what God longs for (and often later shows us we must change!). The voice of the Psalms invites me to be as honest in my prayer as the Psalmist is. And let's face it, as "British Benedictine Sebastian Moore has said, ... 'God behaves in the psalms in ways he is not allowed to behave in systematic theology...'".[37]

Praying the Psalter is a great asset in developing the habit of voiced prayer. Through doing so we give voice to all the deepest (and most raw) impulses of the human heart. Praying the Psalms unites us to the ancient traditions of Israel and of the church, and in this, they save us from the tyranny of individualism when we pray. And when we cannot find the words with which to pray, the Psalmist often provides them for us. But C.S. Lewis suggested that "The most valuable thing the Psalms do for me is to express the same delight in God which made David dance."[38] Perhaps the most enduring motivation for prayer is this "delight in God" which we can learn from the Psalmist. Writing in the sixteenth century for fellow monastics, Blessed Paul Giustiniani said:

> How sweet it is to read the Psalms! It is not tiresome, but most delightful. What could I do that would please me more? In the Psalms I praise and glorify my Creator; I invoke, honor, and entreat Him; in the Psalms I thank Him and bless Him; in the Psalms I confess my sins and implore mercy; in the Psalms I consider the vanity of the world and the falsity of all things; in the Psalms I see myself mirrored and I understand the frailty of life.... [39]

That just about covers it!

Conclusion

I close this chapter on voiced prayer with three practical lessons about personal, vocal prayer I have learned from three
persons I heard praying, because I think these life lessons are so
powerful. The first lesson in voiced prayer I "overheard" is
about invocation and adoration. As a seminary professor, I was
fortunate to audit a colleague's course on Afro-centric biblical
interpretation with some of my students. At the beginning of
the class, the professor called randomly on a student to pray.
When so "elected," one student repeatedly referred to the
Divinity as "Master." In the context of the class discussions of
slavery and its impact on African Americans I was completely
undone. This woman knew what "Master" could mean . . . that
if you are owned, everything depends upon the nature of the
master. It was a powerful reminder to me of who is in charge
in the life of prayer, of the confessional power of invocation.

The second lesson is about Thanksgiving. I was seated at a
big, beautiful, festive Thanksgiving table with a biological
family and those of us who through their love and generosity
had been "grafted in" over the years. It had been a difficult
time for the family. One of the children struggled with
addictions, drugs and ultimately prison. The father of the
family prepared to say grace when the youngest child asked for
and was given permission to do so. She prayed simply, "Thank
you for *all* you've given us. Amen." There was a stunned
silence of recognition of the depth and wisdom of that prayer.
The *all* included not only the lovely things to eat on the table
and the loving circle of friends and family gathered, but the
struggle and suffering and difficulties. The "all" was the word
of redemption.

The third lesson is about intercessory prayer. I was having
supper with unconventional friends. The husband was a
musician with the uncertain work life and odd schedule of
hours that went along with it. He first thanked God for the
food and friends and then said, "Be with those who really need

you tonight. Amen." I imagine that in his gigs in bars and theaters he had seen a lot of needy people, a lot of people for whom night was a time of loneliness and temptation and danger. He didn't know who they were, but he knew they were out there and knew their need and the Source of protection for them, and, on their behalf, he asked for it.

We learn vocal, personal prayer by praying—and by listening to other people's prayers. We begin where we are, with our desire to pray, with a sense that there is a great deal to be asked of God, But we don't stay there. We come to know that vocal prayer invokes the nature of God and our own creatureliness, the needs of all God's creatures and world, gratitude for what God has done, is doing and will do for us all. And sometimes it involves cries in the night, inarticulate groaning, sweating blood and the giving up of our selves, our lives for God's purposes. In my view, all prayer moves toward adoration, and adoration moves toward the holy and inhabited silence into which the journey of prayer continues.

For Further Reading and Exploration

Steven Chase, *The Tree of Life: Models of Christian Prayer* (Grand Rapids MI: Baker Book House, 2005).

Floyd V. Filson, "Petition and Intercession," *Interpretation* 8 (1954) 21–34.

Richard J. Foster, *Prayer: Finding the Heart's True Home* (San Francisco: HarperSanFrancisco, 1992).

Stanley J. Grenz, *Prayer: The Cry for the Kingdom* (Peabody, MA: Hendrickson, 1988).

Margaret Guenther, *The Practice of Prayer* (Cambridge: Cowley Publications, 1998).

Otto A. Piper, "Praise of God and Thanksgiving," *Interpretation* 8 (1954) 3–20.

Chapter 3

Praying the Word:
Lectio Divina

*...the word of God is living and active,
sharper than any two-edged sword, piercing
until it divides soul from spirit, joints from
marrow; it is able to judge the thoughts and
intentions of the heart. (Hebrews 4:12)*

Introduction

At the outset of this book I noted that the traditional categories of prayer are *oratio* (praying with words), *meditatio* (praying by using the mind and imagination) and *contemplatio* (the prayer of rest or stillness). Actually, there are not hard and fast divisions between these categories. Some ways of praying involve both *oratio* and *meditatio*. Some forms of *meditatio* lead to *contemplatio*. In fact, one can be given *contemplatio* as a grace at any time, although there are practices that normally help one to be open to receive it. It has been my experience that all the methods of prayer are to lead us to something deeper, to use the categories of Br. David Steindl-Rast, to lead us from praying to prayerfulness.[1]

This chapter introduces a way of praying with Scripture that has its origins in early Christian monasticism. There are many other ways to pray with Scripture; one in particular, the

"Exercises" of St. Ignatius of Loyola, founder of the Jesuits, is very famous, but I will not treat it here.[2] Ignatius' exercises were composed as a handbook for a person making a retreat, traditionally one of 30 days in silence and solitude. The "exercises" lead the retreatant through an understanding of his or her own sin, and then focuses his or her prayer on events from the life of Jesus, especially His Passion and Resurrection. In fact, Ignatius' exercises are a very effective and affecting way to pray the Gospels. The reason I do not discuss Ignatius' methods here is that they are not "do it yourself," but really require that one make the retreat under the guidance of some one trained to give it, often a Jesuit priest or brother. You do not have to be a Roman Catholic to make the exercises, and you don't need to do them in the 30-day format. Ignatius' "19th Annotation" provided for an adaptation of the method for lay people in their ordinary lives. Having made the retreat over the course of a year under the direction of a Jesuit, I can attest to its power both to "break open the scriptures" and one's own soul. If you have a Jesuit community or school or a Christian Life Community (CLC) near you, you might wish to explore the possibility of doing the exercises with a trained director's guidance.

Returning to *lectio divina*, it is a traditional method of praying the Scriptures, and is a "bridge" or "cross over" method of prayer in that while it is primarily *meditatio,* it employs *oratio* (a brief, voiced prayer) and is an invitation into *contemplatio.* Fr. Luke Dysinger, O.S.B., describes *lectio divina* as "a slow, contemplative praying of the Scriptures which enables the Bible, the Word of God, to become a means of *union* with God."[3] (Italics his.) It is this union with God toward which all prayerfulness moves. The spiritual life of most Protestants focuses on the Bible and on saying prayers, usually verbal prayers of petition and supplication. Happily, devotion to Scripture characterizes the whole church. And the monastic traditions in particular built their offices of prayer around Scripture. *Lectio divina* helps us all to take our love of the Bible into a new and more affective realm of prayer. It can be a step toward wordless forms of prayer and a life-long practice. Its use is intended to be a long-term process (very little about prayer is "instant") for our transformation.

In his book *Reading the Bible Again for the First Time* Marcus Borg describes *lectio divina* as:

> ...entering a contemplative state and listening while a passage of scripture is read aloud a number of times with periods of silence between each reading ... the purpose of the practice is not to read or hear the Bible for information or content. Rather, the purpose is to listen for the Spirit of God speaking through the words of the biblical text.[4]

Borg is describing a way that *lectio* can be done in a group, and he is quite right that it *is* a matter of listening. Fundamentally, however, *lectio divina* is a personal prayer practice, and so falls within the purview of this book. The method of *lectio* I shall present below largely follows the method taught by Br. Alberic Farbolin, O.C.S.O. (then novice director of the Cistercian monastery at Conyers, Georgia) at a workshop at Emory University, January 27, 2001. I was the grateful recipient of his teaching and hope the expansion of it here is accurate and helpful.

History

In Christian tradition *lectio* dates at least to the fifth century and St. Benedict's rule, but it is almost certainly a practice that pre-dated Benedict's Western monasticism. In the fourth century, for example, Christians would go out to meet the spiritual fathers and mothers of the desert and ask them to "give us a word." That is, "give us a spiritual teaching that we can ponder and grow with and into." Often the "word" was scriptural, gleaned from the desert monastics own *lectio,* from praying Scripture which was often memorized. Having spoken and prayed with the supplicant, the Spiritual Parent discerned which bit of Scripture would be most appropriate to that moment in his or her journey.

Later, Benedict set up a rule of life in which the monk's time was divided among three activities: prayer together with the community (the liturgy/hours/choir prayers), work (usually manual labor to support the monastic community), and *lectio divina* or spiritual reading. About four hours a day were devoted to *lectio* which is a combination of reading, private prayer, meditation on Scripture and "rumination" on biblical texts. The end of the practice is to keep the monk's mind and heart filled with the Word of God so that the whole inner life (and subsequently activity) is shaped by Scripture. This is what I meant by saying this method of prayer is for transformation. Like Ezekiel eating his scroll (Ezekiel 3), we "take the word in" in order that its presence change us from within. Just as changing from a diet of junk food to fruit and vegetables requires time before the health benefits take effect, so *lectio divina* is intended to be a lifestyle choice and continuing practice. Its transformative power is great, but gradual.

If monastic life is a life of radical conversion and the monastery is a school of conversion, then *lectio* is the whole program in miniature. But *lectio divina* isn't a prayer practice that requires being enclosed in a monastery. The Christian life is supposed to be a life of continual conversion, daily being "turned around," being re-made in Christ's image. Eastern Christianity calls this "deification in Christ." Internalizing Scripture is a primary means to the end of an ongoing life of conversion.

Prayer and Holy Scripture

Historically, the Bible has been a central source of Christian inspiration and prayer. Basil Pennington has called Christians "sons and daughters of the Book."[5] And so we are. But often, especially in the Reformed traditions, our reading of the Book is almost entirely intellectual. We know *about* the Bible, but we don't take it in. This is particularly true after the Enlightenment and European critical scholarship came to dominate the study of Scripture in seminaries and universities. *Lectio* is a way of internalizing Holy Scripture so that, paradoxically, we can live out of it. We take in the text so that we can live out of it and live it out. *Lectio* is a wonderful way to liberate ourselves from the prison of the Enlightenment with regard to Bible reading, a way to experience a second *naïveté* with regard to Scripture that is crucial to its being the "living Word" and "food" for us.

Reflecting on the *Diatessaron* (an early edition of the four gospels set up as a continuous narrative), St. Ephrem (a Syrian deacon, *ca.* 306–73 who was one of Christianity's first commentators on Scripture) wrote the following, which provides a wonderful understanding of the potential of Scripture:

> Lord, who can comprehend even one of your words? We lose more of it than we grasp, like those who drink from a living spring. For God's word offers different facets according to the capacity of the listener, and the Lord has portrayed his message in many colors, so that whoever gazes upon it can see in it what suits him. Within it he has buried manifold treasures, so that each of us might grow rich in seeking them out ... And so whenever anyone discovers some part of the treasure, he should not think that he had exhausted God's word. Instead he should feel that this is all that he was able to find of the wealth continued in it. Nor should he say that the word is weak and sterile or look down on it simply because this portion was all that he happened to find. But precisely because he could not capture it all he should give thanks for its riches.[6]

St. Ephrem understood that, because we are different and have different capacities, Scripture meets each of us where we are. No matter how many treasures we may find in Scripture, more await us because Scripture points to the living God whose riches are great, varied, and inexhaustible.

Scripture is an inexhaustible source of delight and sustenance. Here is how Esther de Waal describes the character of Scripture and its interaction with us in her book *Seeking God*:

> The "cry" of Scripture is perceived as the voice, the call of God. When the call is heard it must be embraced as a personal message with its living demands addressed to each individual. God's Word is not something static, past and dead; something lying inert between the covers of a book. It is what it is called: the manifestation of a living person whom one recognizes by the tone of voice. The call is not simply something out of a distant past; it comes today and it comes to elicit a response from us and to engage us in dialogue.[7]

How can Scripture "come to us today"? How do we listen to hear Scripture in this way? One answer is the method of prayer called *lectio divina,* and one of the several ways it might be practiced follows.

A Method

Before describing how to pray *lectio,* two words of explanation are in order. First, *lectio* is not purely intellectual, but it seeks an existential appropriation of Scripture to form our lives. "It was an activity as closely related to prayer as to study: medieval monastic writers considered *lectio, meditatio, oratio* and *contemplatio* to be four successive phases of a single movement involving the mind, the heart, the will and the body."[8] For Benedict's original monks, *meditatio* required repetition of a text aloud. For our purposes, note that *lectio* brings together several ways of praying and involves the whole person, mind, heart, will, body (more on this in the next chapter). *Lectio* isn't intellectual, academic study. "*Lectio* ... does not seek information or motivation, it seeks communion and union."[9] So this way of praying Scripture disposes us toward more mystical forms of prayer which can come to us as gifts of God. It is a way we dispose ourselves to receive gifts God wants to give us. The "way" is by listening.

Lectio is about listening in a very full sense. Although she is writing more generally about mindfulness and "whole body" listening, what Esther de Waal writes is instructive. "To listen attentively to what we hear is much more than giving it passing aural attention. It means in the first instance that we have to listen whether we like it or not, whether we hear what we want to or something that is actually disagreeable or threatening. If we begin to pick and choose we are in fact turning a deaf ear to the many unexpected and perhaps unacceptable ways in which God is trying to reach us."[10]

Second, in practicing *lectio* (or any other form of prayer) our desire is crucial. As Dom Basil Pennington wrote, "The Lord will reveal himself and enter into our lives to the extent we believe this is really possible and want it. ...we open the door of our mind and heart for him to enter."[11] We must make an act of faith when we open the Scriptures to read; we must believe that God will meet us there. A parallel from the life of Jesus is those places where He couldn't do miracles because He found no faith there. (See, for example, Mark 6:4–6.) We must open ourselves to the living quality of Scripture. God does not force anyone. If we do not believe that the Bible is living, that it is God's word, it is only a book, not "holy" in any real sense of the word. The Bible is holy for us to the degree that we allow it to mediate the Divine to us. (Theologically, in this mediatory sense, Scripture moves toward sacrament.) When we open ourselves to its living quality, it comes alive. The Wisdom of Solomon promises, "...set your desire on my words;/long for them, and you *will* be instructed." (6:11, italics mine)

Lectio divina, then, is a means of prayer whereby we "hear the Word of God, meditate upon it, and respond to it in prayer, rest in it in contemplation."[12] Here is the definition of *lectio* given by Br. Alberic Farbolin: "Lectio Divina is an exercise at once intellectual and affective consisting in the private reading of Sacred Scripture, with a devotional intent, to instruct oneself in the mysteries of our faith, to prepare for prayer, elicit a conversion of morals and, ultimately, lead to union and communion with God in contemplation." Here is a way to do this: Read a biblical text (*lectio*). Listen to it and ruminate on it (*meditatio*). Respond to it deeply (*oratio*). Wait to see what God will do (*contemplatio?*).

Lectio

The word simply means "reading," and, in this context implies a certain kind of listening. One reads the Bible expecting to receive a word from God, listening for it, expecting it. Desire and open-ness are crucial. The Rule of St. Benedict opens, "Listen carefully . . . to the master's instructions, and attend to them with the ear of your heart."[13] That is what we are doing in *lectio*. We are reading with the disposition of listening for God to speak to us. To understand this process you might read again Mark 4 and attend especially to Jesus' commands to listen and to hear. In that passage, Jesus promises that the more we try to understand and get out of Scripture, the more will be given to us. But we must be clear that the purpose of the reading is encounter with the living God. The point is not to read immense quantities or figure out scriptural conundrums (of which there are plenty!), but to read with immense attentiveness. The point is not to make intellectual headway (although that can be a byproduct or side-effect of this method of prayer), but to *be* encountered and transformed.

Practically one chooses a passage of Scripture, perhaps the

day's lectionary gospel or the appointed psalm, and reads
slowly through it, several times if necessary. When the "word"
is encountered, put the Bible down. Have you had the
experience of going to the Bible and having a verse just jump
out at you? That's the experience I am trying to describe. The
moment one encounters the "word," the individual word or
phrase that arrests one, that catches the attention, stop reading
even if you haven't finished the text or read through the whole
lectionary passage. Depth, not quantity is the point. Stay with
that word or phrase, repeating it slowly to yourself either
quietly or aloud. This is the beginning of the *meditatio* stage of
lectio divina.

Meditatio

When the word is used this way *meditatio* means not "thinking
about," but thinking with the heart. It is a holistic response to
Scripture. It is mulling over or ruminating on ("chewing" is a
good metaphor) a word from Scripture. Here *meditatio* is not
what is popularly meant by "meditation," but it comes close in
that one is centering in on or focusing on a particular phrase. If
lectio is the active act of reading, *meditatio* is the more passive
waiting on the Word to form us and call us forth. I rather
suspect this is what the Blessed Virgin Mary was doing when
Luke describes her as "pondering in her heart." (Luke 2:19)
Meditatio is carrying the word received from the *lectio*, like
Mary carried the word received from God. We gently repeat
the word in order to bring it from the mind down into the
heart and there, in the center of our being, to allow it to call
forth a response from us. So I am suggesting that we are
thinking or listening with the heart.

By *meditatio* used this way, we do not mean "meditation" as
it is commonly used of a wordless form of prayer, which
involves emptying the mind in order to experience the
Absolute. A form of that kind of prayer will be introduced in
chapter 9 as "the prayer of waiting." *Meditatio* is inviting the
heart to respond. The arrival of the "word" from the reading in

our hearts awakens an inner word, one which may be totally unexpected. And this leads to a particular kind of *oratio.*

Oratio

As we have noted, the word literally means "prayer," but not, in this context, as we heretofore used it to mean words spoken to God, but the heart's response to Scripture. It is the very particular response called forth by the *meditatio.* It is the heart's deep response that arises spontaneously and usually in the language of affect or emotion. *Oratio* is the deep, almost automatic cry of the heart when it meets the God to which Scripture points. It may take many forms, but is usually a very brief word or, in the more technical language of the spiritual life, an "ejaculatory prayer." "I adore You!" (Adoration) "I'm sorry!" (Repentance) "Help me!" (Petition—in a very basic mode!) The "spoken" (aloud or internally) word is usually a very brief, but deep eruption of emotion and response. I think that what we hear in the more emotional psalms is akin to the Psalmist's *oratio.*

There is at least one other way of understanding *oratio.* Dom Basil Pennington suggests that it is a time when one discusses one's inner condition with God. It is when one honestly opens up one's heart to God and can involve any of the forms of voiced prayer. Describing Pennington's understanding, Steven Chase writes, "Whatever the thoughts or feelings expressed in conversation and prayer, our relationship with God is evolving into areas of trust, safety, and frank honesty that lead us into deeper intimacy with God."[14]

For me, the "word" of *oratio* is often a phrase from an old hymn, sometimes a phrase of music. A line of a hymn arises spontaneously and is the "word" upon which I am to ruminate. The point is to speak to God. As Benedictine Luke Dysinger notes, "Whether you use words or ideas or images or all three is not important. Interact with God as you would with one who you know loves and accepts you."[15] In *Sadhana* Anthony de Mello writes that *oratio* is made "either by speaking

spontaneously to the Lord in whose presence you are, or by
maintaining a loving silence in his presence, filled as you are
with the grace, the unction, the attitude that these words have
induced in you."[16]

The depth of this prayer is not easy to sustain. So this aspect
of *lectio* may be quite brief. Benedict's *Rule* notes that "Prayer
should ... be short and pure, unless perhaps it is prolonged
under the inspiration of divine grace."[17] So *oratio* heeds Jesus'
warning in Matthew 6 about long, wordy prayers. When you
can't relaxedly maintain the *oratio* without distraction, either
resume *lectio* or bring your period of prayer to a close. It is
possible, but not automatic (or perhaps even necessary) that
you will move into *contemplatio.* But, at the stage of *oratio,* be
very attentive to boredom. It may be a smoke screen or what
psychologists term "avoidance". What seems to be boredom
often masks hitting something very deep in our spiritual lives.
In general, boredom is a way the Adversary deflects us from
deepening our prayer and our inner life. We can be distracted
and entertain ourselves to perdition! In any case, at its most
profound *oratio* is the recognition of God's very self in our
souls. We pass through our own hearts into the heart of God.
They are the same heart. As C.S. Lewis has said, "The door in
God that opens is the door he knocks at."[18]

Contemplatio
Contemplatio is the prayer of quiet, of rest. Technically in
contemplation we are completely passive, receiving something
given which we cannot manufacture for ourselves. Most simply
put it is "waiting for God" or "resting in God." The King
James translation of Psalm 37:7, "Rest in the Lord, and wait
patiently for him," clearly describes *contemplatio.* Dom Basil
described it as "love longing for communion."[19] Fr. Dysinger
describes it as "simply enjoying the experience of being in the
presence of God ... we cease from interior spiritual *doing* and
learn simply to *be,* that is to rest in the presence of our loving
Father."[20] (Emphasis his.) *Contemplatio* is a complete and total

"yes" to the God encountered in the Word. This comes in deep silence or quietude as a result of our complete open-ness to God, but our complete open-ness does not cause it. It is pure gift. (We will have occasion to say a great deal more about contemplation later in chapters 8 and 9.)

I close by suggesting three things *lectio divina* is not. It is not primarily exegetical or intellectual Bible study. Exegesis alone is like using a dictionary to get the meaning of a love letter. What we are talking about here is not just a rational activity (although it begins there), but a holistic activity. It asks that we take the Word of Scripture and descend with it with the mind into the heart. It is "the listening of the whole person, of body as well as intellect, and it requires love as well as cerebral assent."[21] Second, it is not a short-term activity; its effect in our lives is experienced over time. These effects are most pronounced when we make *lectio* a daily practice. *Lectio* may disappoint the person expecting a quick fix. Finally, it is not purposeful in the sense of something I accomplish. It is about God's gratuity and the peace and leisure that surround it. By definition, you can't force a gift, and the full experience of *lectio* is gift. It involves waiting on the Lord (Psalm 62:1): "We must be willing to sacrifice our 'goal oriented' approach ... because *lectio divina* has no other goal than spending time with God through the medium of His word."[22]

An Exercise to Try *Lectio Divina*

As with any prayer practice suggested in this book there is a lot of latitude about how it can be done. Remember the premise: "you can't get it wrong." But here is one simple way for you to try out *lectio*.

- Find a relatively quiet place and a moment in the day when you don't have to hurry on to something else. If you take *lectio* as a primary practice, many teachers recommend you practice it for two periods of 20 minutes to half an hour a day. Realistically, once a day or several times a week is what most of us can manage.

- Take your Bible with reverence and ask the Holy Spirit to direct your *lectio*.[23] This is a crucial step. It is the self-opening, the expression of desire to meet God in the Word. In *Seeking God* Esther de Waal provides a beautiful prayer for beginning *lectio*. "Lord God, patient and steadfast, you wait for us until we open to you. We wait for your word, help us to hear your voice. Speak and bring your Son to us, Jesus the word of your peace. We wait for your word, Lord God, patient and steadfast."[24]

- Read Scripture for a few minutes (at least 5 to 10) or until you encounter your "word," God speaking to you in the text. You might want to try *lectio* first with one of these Scriptures as they seem to be very powerful and available points of entry for this sort of prayer: Exodus 17:1–17, Psalm 27, Ezekiel 37:1–14, Mark 4:35–41, Mark 6:47–51. If you make *lectio* a daily practice you may want to follow your church's daily lectionary, or the daily Mass text if you are a Roman Catholic rather than a random selection of texts. Then you will be praying with the wider church. There is some value in knowing what text you will pray when you settle to *lectio* rather than scrabbling for one each time you try to settle down.

- Having encountered your "word," begin to repeat it. After repeating it gently for a time, notice your response to God and pray that. This is what I called *oratio* above. Often this response is "affective." It is about feeling or emotion understood as the response of the heart, the whole person. What does your word prompt you to say to God? Don't hurry this stage of the prayer. It may be the prelude to *contemplatio*.

- Wait quietly for a time.

- Finally, choose a word or phrase in the text (perhaps the one "given," but perhaps another), thank God for it, for speaking to you, and then take your word into the day with you. Repeat it quietly to yourself or think about it (ruminate on it) over the course of the day. Let it inform your decisions and actions for the day. Be alert to how it will affect your responses to the situation of your day.

To try *lectio*, sit quietly for a few moments. Offer a prayer of invocation. Read a text of Scripture several times slowly. Sit with it for 5 or 10 minutes listening. When/if a "word" or phrase emerges for you, repeat it quietly and gently, paying attention to your response. That response is your *oratio*. The most helpful question may be "what did you find of God or the *experience* of God in the text?" This may lead naturally to "feeling words" because *lectio* is not information gained or thoughts *about* the text, but the experience of God mediated *by* the text. The great tendency and temptation is to talk of or notice cognitive insights *about* the passage rather than your participation *in* it. Be very wary of this.

Lectio divina may not be the form of prayer for you. But you might well find that it can deepen your relationship with Scripture and open you to a more profound encounter with the living God to Whom it points.

For Further Reading and Exploration

Enzo Bianchi, *Praying the Word* (Kalamazoo, MI: Cistercian Publications, 1992).

Luke Dysinger, O.S.B., "Accepting the Embrace of God: The Ancient Art of *Lectio Divina*," *Valyermo Benediction* 1/1 (Spring, 1990) 33–42.

Thelma Hall, R.C. *Too Deep for Words: Rediscovering Lectio Divina* (Mahwah, NJ: Paulist Press, 1988).

Anthony de Mello, S.J. *Sadhana: A Way to God* (Anand, India:

Gujarat Shaitya Prakash, 1978) especially "Exercise 33: The Benedictine Method."

M. Basil Pennington, o.c.s.o., *A Place Apart* (New York: Doubleday, 1983).

M. Basil Pennington, o.c.s.o., *Lectio Divina* (New York: Crossroad, 1998).

Chapter 4

Prayer: Toward an Anthropology

*I praise you, for I am fearfully and wonder-
fully made. (Psalm 139:14)*

*My heart and my flesh rejoice in the living
God... (Psalm 83:3, LXX)*

Introduction

In our examination of Christian prayer we have begun to use
terms that suggest various aspects of the human person. In the
chapter on *lectio divina,* for example, we spoke of "descending
with the mind into the heart." In the next chapter on the Jesus
Prayer a great deal will be said about the heart. So perhaps it is
time to consider human beings and their make up, by which I
do not mean cosmetics. But cosmetics may be one reason why
we need to examine this matter. We live in an "exteriorized"
culture. What I mean is that the life emphasis of popular
culture is on what is "outside," what we wear; how we look;
where we live; what we own. You get the idea. People who
blindly accept servitude to what advertising tells us about
"needed" externals often have not traveled extensively in
or perhaps even visited the interior world. Indeed, we are
massively entertained and distracted by all manner of

technological gadgets in order to *prevent* our exploration of the depths and mystery of our being. Advertising doesn't want us to go there because going there very quickly exposes the lie of exteriorization. When we grasp the lie, we withdraw from blind consumption. Prayer may be bad for business.

But at some point in the journey, Christian prayer calls us to visit the interior world. I once tried to express the point in a poem called "A Burning Deep Within."

> A burning deep within—
> like a mysterious light
> glimpsed far deeper in the woods
> than you have dared to walk.
> A beckoning, "come home:"
> home to your uniqueness;
> home to the home
> this world cannot offer;
> home to the place you belong,
> that which you love.
>
> To go there you must
> develop *apatheia*,
> the discipline of detachment
> from all this is trivial,
> that fragments or scatters,
> develop a unifying heart
> that gathers like a glass
> refracting rays of light
> from the source
> of the burning deep within.

We will visit some of these ideas later, but you get the point that at least part of the life of prayer must be "inter-iorized" life.

In the seventeenth century Pascal wrote, "The Christian religion alone is adapted to all, being composed of externals and internals. It raises the common people to the internal, and humbles the proud to the external..."[1] We will have reason to say more about the interior world in later chapters. Now, it seems time to provide some information so that you can develop your own anthropology, an understanding of human beings that includes the exterior and the interior. Let me warn you that what follows is an exercise in biblical theology. If it seems heavy going to you, you might want to move on to other more practical chapters, although the grounding for the practices introduced in those chapters may reside in this one.

In Greek *aner* is translated "man," and *gyne* is translated "woman," but *anthropos* is "human being," the personhood of the whole human race, male *and* female. What is the nature of person? Jesuit philosopher W. Norris Clarke spent a great deal of his career answering this question. In an article in 1996 he describes the human person "as a 'frontier being,' living on the edge, on the frontier, between matter and spirit, time and eternity, who has to live with the tension caused by the diverse pulls of these two apparently conflicting dimensions..."[2] Additionally the human person is a "microcosm ... which unites in itself all the levels of the universe from the depths of matter to the transcendence of spirit, capable of union with God ... and so mirroring the unity of the cosmos itself."[3] Clarke understands the human person as uniting the material and spiritual worlds, as a mediator between the two and able to offer both back to God with gratitude and love.[4]

In the classic work *The Spiritual Life* Evelyn Underhill suggested something very similar, that humans live an amphibious life, a life of sense (flesh) and spirit.[5] Genesis 1 and 2, the story of our origins that we visited first in chapter 1 of this book, confirms these views. Being made in the image of God means person is male *and* female, of earth and of heaven. We were made of "dust" and "breathed into" by God, so we are creatures of matter and spirit, "outside" and "inside." But the two are not separate. We are not matter *and* spirit; these are two aspects of the same being. The philosophical question would be: "Are people of one substance or nature or two? Is there anthropological monism (a single nature) or dualism (a two-part nature)?" The biblical answer always embraces some form of monism. We are one person who is both corporeal and incorporeal. We are a body, a *soma*, the word Paul uses for "a human being in all his or her wholeness."[6] (See, for example, Romans 8:23 or 12:1.) Many scholars think that New Testament anthropology derives more from the Hebrew view of person as a unity of body and spirit than from the Greek, which tended to view the body as the "prison house of the soul." In a survey of Christian theological perspectives on the human body James Keenan, S.J. noted the consensus "nowadays, just as medieval writers [held], that the condition for ensoulment is the presence of a true human body."[7]

In launching into Christian anthropology, we are entering a field in which much has been written. What follows is but one view of many, and it would be well worth your time to read further from the suggested works at the end of this chapter and from material cited in the notes to gain a wider perspective. My thoughts here are to stimulate your thinking. My view of Christian anthropology is certainly not the only one. I am going to deal with the following New Testament terms that describe aspects of personhood: body, flesh, soul/spirit, mind and heart. I suggest an anthropology for Christian prayer in which "body" means "whole person." The body consists of flesh and of spirit/soul and mind and heart. "Body" is the totality of person which is made up of a corporeal nature (flesh) and an incorporeal nature (soul/spirit, mind) which are unified in the heart. A Venn diagram of "body" (all that is within the outer lines) would look like something like this:

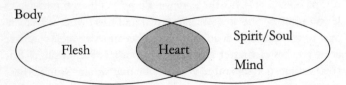

Body

Flesh   Heart   Spirit/Soul

                              Mind

Often in Christianity if we speak of person in any analytical way at all we start with the incorporeal, the soul/spirit/mind part, and then malign matter (flesh), and ignore heart. That, I would suggest, is more Greek than it is biblical. It might be an effective approach to moral teaching (although in the long run, I doubt it), but it's not very helpful as an approach to the spiritual life. In the world in which we live, one in which "exterior" and "matter" predominate, it may well be that we need to go back and begin with matter in the Christian life precisely so that we understand the holiness of life in the whole of the body. As Anne Lamott wrote in *Traveling Mercies*, "...sometimes you start with the outside and you get it right. You tend to your spirit through the body."[8] (By "body" in this quotation Lamott means what I will call "flesh" below.)

God made us bodies. So the Psalmist eloquently understood.

> ...it was you who formed my inward parts;
> you knit me together in my mother's womb.
> I praise you for I am fearfully and wonderfully made.
> My frame was not hidden from you,
> when I was being made in secret,
> intricately woven in the depths of the earth.
> (Psalm 139:13–15)

The Psalmist conceives of the human being as both "inward parts" and "outward parts," and God made both. We are created by God in this way. Examining the biblical language for aspects of the person can be both complex and clarifying.

Body (*soma*)

If you look up the word for "body" in a Greek dictionary, the first usage of *soma* is the living person as an integrated totality. It might be translated "individual." Body is the whole of our creatureliness. Our language reflects this; we are "somebody" or "anybody" or "nobody," except a person can't be "no body."

Person *is* body. Unfortunately, when we say "body" in English, we normally mean what the Greek language means by "flesh" (*sarx*). And this has led to no end of confusion. Here is one highly theological example. In Mark 14:22 (and its parallels) Jesus says "this is my body (*soma*)," that is, "my very self" I am giving you. Jesus doesn't say "this is my *sarx*, my flesh," which would be His corporeal nature alone. Similarly 1 Peter 2:24 speaks of Jesus' body that dies and rises again; all of Him, not just His physicality, died and was raised.

St. Paul was very interested in "body." I read somewhere that he used forms of the word 91 times, 51 times in 1 and 2 Corinthians alone.[9] For Paul "body" usually means "whole person," as in "your bodies are members of Christ" (1 Corinthians 6:15) or "glorify God in your body." (1 Corinthians 6:20) Such usage reflects Paul's Hebrew monism as opposed to a Hellenistic dualism.[10] Paul's famous somatic metaphor for the church as the "Body of Christ" makes clear that it is a unity of various parts. (See, for example, 1 Corinthians 10:17, 11:29 and 12 and Romans 12.) As R.Y.K Fung notes, "the church as the body of Christ is a living organic unity composed of a multiplicity of members ... each necessary to the other and to the growth of the whole...".[11]

It is in this sense that I suggest "body" be used in thinking about prayer. "Body" is the totality of a person, corporeal parts and incorporeal parts. It is the living organic unity of all the parts, all of which are necessary for spiritual growth and fleshly and spiritual health of the whole. Rudolf Bultmann noted that the only existence we have is somatic existence. "...the human does not have a *soma*, but rather is a *soma*."[12] When the scribe asks Jesus which is the first commandment, Jesus quotes Deuteronomy 6:4, "you shall love the Lord your God with all your heart, and with all your soul, and with all your mind, and with all your strength." (Mark 12:30) That is, Jesus says, "love God with your body," all of who you are: corporeal (strength or flesh), incorporeal (soul and mind), held together as in our Venn diagram by "heart."

Flesh (*sarx*)

"Flesh" is the Greek term for the corporeal part of "body." Flesh is the physical aspect of "body." It's a bit crude, but we might think of flesh as "meat." Flesh is the human being in its corporeality, so it becomes a metaphor in Scripture for the external or outward side of life, or as in 1 Corinthians 15:39, for the whole of physical existence. (Compare Galatians 4:13.) Sometimes Paul uses forms of *sarx* for life in its earthly (or earthy!) aspects as opposed to life in its heavenly (or spiritual, *pneumatic*) aspects. (See Romans 1:3–4.)

For Paul "flesh" can be morally neutral or morally negative, although, alas, the former has predominated in Christian teaching after him. It has been noted that when Paul writes "according to the flesh" plus a noun, what follows is morally neutral. When he uses "according to flesh" plus a verb, but without the article, it is morally negative.[13] Because Romans is such a weighty letter, because it has received so much attention in Christian theology (remember, theological historians, Augustine, Luther, Calvin, Barth!), and because in Romans Paul often uses "flesh" as a metaphor for fallen or rebellious human nature, the flesh has gotten a bad rap in Christian moral teaching. In fact, Paul also uses "flesh" "as the natural sphere in which earthly life is conducted (cf. Romans 1:3)." Erickson correctly reminds us that "...Paul continued to share the Jewish heritage of a high regard for creation."[14] When one reads Paul carefully, one finds that it is not "flesh" *per se* (our "meat") that is morally evil. In Galatians 3:2–3 and Romans 8 "flesh" is a sort of metaphor and seems to indicate a spiritual condition, "an independent reliance on one's own accomplishments over against a spirit of dependence on God and submission to his rule."[15]

My point is that corporeality is not *ipso facto* negative. Our flesh can't be intrinsically bad or God wouldn't have made us fleshly creatures. In fact, in the life of prayer, the flesh is our great ally. As an aspect of our flesh, our senses, can bring us to and enhance our life of prayer. (For a wonderful meditation on this, read W.H. Auden's poem "Precious Five.") Stilling the flesh is a helpful means of bringing the incorporeal side of our nature (spirit/soul and mind) to prayer. The flesh as God made it, and for the purposes for which God made it, is good. If you think of flesh as meat, its main characteristic is not that it's bad (meat can be quite delicious!), but that it rots. Don't believe me? Leave a bit of minced meat in a dish on your kitchen counter for a day or so. "The body is marked by weakness and corruptibility."[16] If you think of flesh as the impermanent part of the human being, you may be coming close to something useful. John 6:53 was so shocking to those who heard Jesus say, "Unless you eat the flesh (*sarx*) of the Son of Man..." not only because it suggested cannibalism, but it seemed ("seemed" being the operative word) Jesus had taken on some sort of corruptibility. It is also why John 1:14, the great Christmas gospel, is shocking. "The Word became flesh (*sarx*) and dwelt among us." That is, the Word became subject to impermanence, the same limitation to which we are subject. (In John 3:6 "everything human is *sarx*."[17]) But the theological point is that flesh is suitable for divine life. So in a Christian anthropology, the fleshly life of the body is divinized in addition to being "good" in its creation.

Lest you are beginning to feel a little lost in the material, let me summarize to this point: "flesh" is the corporeal or "meaty" aspect of "body," which also has incorporeal aspects which I shall treat as "soul/spirit" and "mind." "Heart" links the two aspects of the human person.

Spirit (*pneuma*) and Soul (*psyche*)

The New Testament uses these two words similarly and sometimes even interchangeably. I have a tendency to associate "spirit" with animation of the flesh, and "soul" with "body" in that *psyche* can also be used to mean the whole person as, for example, when Jesus says He gives His *psyche* as a ransom for many. (Mark 10:45) But this is a rather simplistic and not entirely accurate distinction. One must be careful with the term "spirit" (*pneuma*) in the New Testament as it is used in several ways and contexts. It can refer to an incorporeal aspect of a human being or to the Holy Spirit, the third person of the Trinity.

"Spirit" is literally moving air, a wind, "breath." In Greek mythology there was a connection between wind and the generation of life. The English word "inspiration" has the Latin root *spirare*, to breathe. Inspiration was a way the Greco-Romans thought divinities imparted their power to humans. The gods "breathed into" them. (Compare Genesis 2:7.) *Pneuma* is the Greek word used to translate the Hebrew *ru(a)h* meaning breath or wind, thus allowing Jesus to make a delicious pun in John 3:8: "The wind blows where it chooses, and you hear the sound of it, but you do not know where it comes from or where it goes. So it is with everyone who is born of the Spirit." In Hebrew scripture, spirit gives life (Genesis 7:22; Ezekiel 37:5–6), and its absence leads to death. (Psalm 104:29) *Ru(a)h* is associated with God's effective and creative power. "Continuity between the physical and the spiritual body is a work of God's creative power. Humanity is first made *of* dust but will then be made *from* heaven."[18] God breathes into *adam*, and he becomes a living person. Both St. Paul and St. John use "flesh" and "spirit" metaphorically and antithetically. In Galatians 3:2 and 5 "the antithesis of Spirit and flesh is that of divine power and human weakness."[19] John seems to use "flesh" as metaphor, respectively, for the world and the sphere of God. (See John 3:6, 6:63, and compare Romans 1:3–4.)

I think of "spirit" as the animating principle of the inner life and of "soul" as its immaterial essence. "Soul" is the vital force that is received from and finds outlet in breath/spirit. But for the Greeks *psyche* was "the epitome of the individual." It was "the impalpable essential core of a person, the agent of thought, will and emotion, the quintessence of human life."[20]

The Jews, however, did not think in terms of this "soul" as disembodied. Jews thought of humans as body and soul, one "psychophysical organism." A person "did not *have* a body but *was* an animated body, a unit of life manifesting itself in fleshly form."[21] So "soul" (*psyche*) meant the life principle of the living being. Accordingly, in the New Testament "soul" is often metonymy for the whole person. (See, for example, Mark 10:45, 1 Thessalonians 2:8, Philippians 2:30.) Paul never uses the word *psyche* negatively.

Scholars have tried in a variety of ways to delineate "spirit" and "soul" in the New Testament.[22] None that I have read completely succeed. Nor is a completely scientific set of distinctions necessary for our anthropology of prayer. The important point to be made is that just as human life, what we have been calling "body," has a corporeal manifestation of divine origin which we call "flesh," there is an incorporeal manifestation of divine origin, a continuity of divine activity in body's incorporeal manifestation. One receives the spirit from God. (It might be going too far to say "spirit" animates "soul.") If "spirit" and "soul" are general terms for inner life, a function of that inner life is "mind."

Mind (*nous*)

As an aspect of the totality of one's inner or incorporeal life, mind is an aspect of spirit or soul.[23] Thus I placed it under "spirit/soul" in the Venn diagram. It is the soul in its attitude of thought or reason. *Nous* was an important category for the Greeks. Anaxagoras used the word for the cosmic reason that orders the universe. We find that idea echoed in St. John's "*Logos*." (John 1:1) Epictetus went so far as to say God's being is *nous*. But *nous* is rare in the LXX, which uses "heart" instead. In the New Testament, with two or three exceptions, the term "mind" occurs mostly in Paul who contrasts intellectual life to physical existence. (See Romans 7:23.) "Mind" is the faculty of intellectual perception, a power which can help one arrive at moral judgements. "Mind" can be a way of characterizing one's general attitude or way of thinking, as in one's mental state. In the southern mountains from which I come people say, "I have a mind to do such and such." Exactly.

Those of us who live post-Enlightenment and post-Descartes are shaped by the massive attention given to "mind" and its faculty, "reason." If we can think (!) of the spirit/soul as being composed of imagination, reason, affect, and will, it is pretty clear reason is the quality that our culture has most valued. Our inner life, personally and corporately (Latin root, *corpus*, body!), is frequently out of balance in the direction of reason, and the state of the western/northern world and its dominant lifestyle is proof of this fact. We are, alas, like those about whom God spoke to the prophet Isaiah. We listen and look and do not understand that the mind can be dull and uncomprehending of God's truths. (Isaiah 6:9–10) A great deal of the work of the spiritual life is not best done with mind. Mind is a great servant in the life of prayer, but a killing master. Philip Newell has wisely noted that "in our pursuit of the knowledge of God our mind is to be like a door that opens onto what is boundless rather than a wall that attempts to hold the mystery in."[24] Perhaps for this reason (!), the biblical record is not very interested in "mind," but it is very interested in "heart." In the LXX the organ of *noein*, of rational reflection and understanding, is the heart.

Heart (*kardia*)

To understand what "heart" means in a biblical anthropology we must face a hurdle not unlike the one we met in our use of "body." "Body" does not mean the carnal self. My term for that would be "flesh." Likewise the "heart" is not as is now popularly thought, the organ of feeling, but of thought, reason and will. Thus the writer of Hebrews speaks of the "thoughts and intentions of the *heart*." (4:10, italics mine.) At the center of "body" is "heart," the interstices of flesh and spirit/soul.

(Recall our Venn diagram.) It is a physical organ of the flesh and also the intellectual and moral center of the spirit/soul. When the Psalmist writes "my heart and my flesh rejoice in the living God" (84:2), he means that his life-center, where he thinks, wills and feel, and his physical self rejoice. He prays with his body. (More on this in chapter 6.) To the degree that we limit "heart" to feeling or even more narrowly to romance, we are a heart-broken people.

Although rare in secular writing of the period, Professor Jacob reports that "heart" is "the most common anthropological term (850 instances) in Hebrew scripture ... it denotes the totality in its inner worth."[25] *Kardia* was a common word in the LXX, which understood it as the center and source of physical life and of spiritual and mental life as well. "Heart" was the locus of the whole of a person's inner life, thinking, volition and feeling, and as such was the "dwelling place" of heavenly powers and beings. "One believes with the heart." (Romans 10:10) This is the Pauline understanding. (See, for example, Romans 5:5; 2 Corinthians 1:22; Galatians 4:6; Ephesians 3:17.) J.D.G. Dunn has called the heart "the integrating center of man."[26] St. John Chrysostom noted "'find the door of your heart, you will discover it is the door of the kingdom of God."[27]

In biblical writing the heart "is the chief seat of the intelligence—thinking is practical rather than speculative, and thoughts readily pass into actions."[28] This is why Jesus' teaching focuses on the heart; it is the origin of action. "For it is from within, from the human heart, that evil intentions come," Mark's Jesus says and follows with a long list of vices. (Mark 7:21) Luke reports Jesus as saying, "The good person out of the good treasure of the heart produces good, and the evil person out of the evil treasure produces evil; for it is out of the abundance of the heart that the mouth speaks." (Luke 6:45) The summary of Jesus' teaching in Matthew's gospel begins with blessings one of which is "blessed are the pure in heart, for they will see God." (Matthew 5:8) Indeed, they will "see God" *in* their hearts, for it is here that God "dwells." (More on this point will follow in the next chapter.) It is little wonder that Mary, the Mother of Jesus, was a "heart person." (See Luke 2:19, 51.)

Kallistos Ware, in an article entitled "How Do We Enter the Heart?" provides this beautiful summary:

> In the Old and New Testaments there is no head/heart dichotomy. In Hebrew anthropology ... the heart is the organ with which we think. For Biblical authors, the heart does not signify the feelings and emotions; for these are located lower down, in the guts and the entrails. The heart designates ... the inwardness of our human personhood in its full spiritual depth ... the heart is the primary center of the total person, the ground of our being, the root and source of all our inner truth. It is in this way a symbol of the unity and wholeness of our personhood in God.[29]

Little wonder in the chapter "Heart and Mind" in *Gratefulness: The Heart of Prayer*, Br. David Steindl-Rast calls the heart "the taproot of the whole person." No wonder the Eucharistic liturgy begins with the command *sursum corda*, "Lift up your hearts!" Br. David continues, "...the heart stands for that core of being where, long before alienation, primordial togetherness held sway." "...the heart...is our meeting place with God in prayer. Prayer, in turn, is the very heart of religion."[30]

Some Implications

"So what?" is a fair question at this point. Why all this ancient anthropology when what you want to do is pray? Well, it's to begin to get at the conundrum, "who is the you who prays?" We start where we are and bring who we are to prayer. To follow the classical imperative, to "know thyself," is to be able to pray with more awareness, although I, personally, think perhaps a string of imperatives suggesting a Christian process might be: "know thyself! own thyself! forget thyself! give thyself away!"

I hope you now have a better understanding of some of the things I was trying to communicate in chapter 1. God breathed into mud to make a human being who is mud and divine breath. The human being is flesh and spirit, a body with "outer stuff" and "inner stuff." The "inner stuff" includes spirit/soul and mind which, in a well-ordered body, is subservient to it. Central to flesh and spirit is heart, to which mind is also subservient. The whole body prays and is taken up into prayer. Authentic prayer engages all of us, must engage all of us if we are to encounter the living God.

Most of us come to know the life of the spirit by means of the flesh because we are body. I think this is what the Johannine writer had in mind when he opened his first letter, "We declare to you what was from the beginning, what we have *heard*, what we have *seen* with our eyes, what we have *looked at* and *touched with our hands*, concerning the word of life—this was revealed, and we have *seen* it and testify to it . . . we declare to you what we have *seen and heard*. . ." (1 John 1:1–4, italics mine) As Anne Lamott, with whom we opened this chapter, said, sometimes we start with the outside and get it right. But this presumes that the "outside" is valued and honored. Unfortunately Christianity has had a tendency to denigrate the "flesh" part of "body" rather than to understand it as an incredible gift to be celebrated for itself and for its contributions to spiritual life. Thomas Merton reminds us that "The spiritual life is first of all a *life*." "If we want to be spiritual, then," Merton says, "let us first of all live our lives."[31] We live our lives in the flesh.

What we do in and with the fleshly aspect of our whole body matters because "Christian tradition has always regarded the body as constitutive of human identity."[32] If we are to pray well, we must be fully alive, and aliveness is *physical*, wonderfully, wonderfully carnal. I am sad to report that I see in Christian circles precious little evidence of a fleshly joy in living. I see a lot of *flesh*, but I worry that it is a way people are cushioning themselves from life, hiding from life. Indeed, too much flesh may be a matter of inattention to fleshly life, to its real hungers and how they are satisfied. Flesh is a very spiritual matter. How much we eat, and what we eat is spiritual because we are body. Who we are sexually and with whom we share that treasure is a spiritual matter because we are body. Whether or not we exercise, how we deal with sickness, accident, hereditary illness is spiritual because we are body.

Another important aspect of "body" is that it has physical, spiritual *and* energetic centers. I have been speaking of "body" largely from the Western and biblical traditions. But the human family has also understood body in terms of centers of energy that affect both physical organs and spiritual processes. For example, while Western medicine tends to view disease as a matter of pathogens, Eastern medicine often speaks in terms of energy imbalances. The ancient traditions of the East have both traced the energy meridians (pathways) of the body and located its primary energy centers. The addition of "holistic centers" to major research hospitals is an indication of the seriousness with which these approaches are being taken. Massage, acupuncture, healing touch and energy work open up not only new approaches to healing, but new aspects of person and prayer which I find inviting and promising as we continue to grow together as the human *anthropos*.[33] Christian yoga is but one way we see the embrace of the wisdom of the East and traditional Christianity.[34]

And all this is related to prayer because prayer engages all of us. Unfortunately, if prayer is taught at all, it is taught primarily as a "dis-embodied" or "spiritual" discipline. No wonder people "can't pray," or that the tender shoot of prayer dries up! If prayer is taught as "mind only" or "spirit only," what about flesh? Prayer with only the mind or only the spirit is amputated prayer from the outset. So, yes, I am delighted by chanting, singing, breath prayer, by bowing, genuflecting and prostrations, by walking meditation and yoga because they keep us in, or bring us back to the flesh, to our embodiedness, our incarnation. And incarnation is of fundamental theological importance in Christianity; it *is* Christianity.

John writes that "the Word became flesh," that is *sarx*, impermanent "meat" just like we are. (John 1:14) If *logos* becomes *sarx*, then flesh must be pretty good stuff, worth valuing, worth attending to. Fr. Thomas Ryan, a teacher of yoga for Christians whose writing I have found very helpful, has noted, "Where we are and what we are is now the intimate habitat of God." He continues:

> In the Incarnation, Jesus in his flesh took the world as part of himself. The world quite literally became the body of God. Since God is identified with and dis-covered within this bodiliness, this fleshiness, this materiality, this sensuality, we have no right to dismiss the world as some second-rate practice field for the real life in heaven. The Incarnation states that there is no practice and nothing is second-rate. Life in this world is the life of God.[35]

Word had to become flesh. Disembodied reason is not, contrary to Greek thought, the highest good. (Nor is sybaritic paganism.) According to Jesus, God is spirit, *pneuma* (and, yes, *logos*, the principle of reason in the universe), not primarily *nous* alone. Those who worship God must worship God as God is. (John 4:24) But we can't worship what we don't know, and, as incorporeal spirit or as mind alone, God is pretty unknowable. I have explained that I think prayer is relational. I confessed that I have trouble being in relationship with an abstraction like Truth or Justice or Beauty. The Incarnation was necessary for everybody. It is the trajectory by which Jesus embodies *pneuma* and moves *sarx* to *soma*. Incarnation is the reconciliation and unification of how God made us. We came into being when God breathed into our flesh. Perhaps every breath should be a sacrament, as it is again and again receiving God's animation of our "stuff." Breath connects flesh and spirit/soul. Breath can take us to our heart center.

So I close this chapter by suggesting that breath itself can be understood as a form of prayer. In the yogic tradition and in Buddhism, learning to breathe properly and attentively is a fundamental practice in developing a life of prayer.[36] Pay attention for a moment to how you breathe.[37] Do you take long, deep, slow breaths that trust God's constant provision of air? Is your breath shallow and fast, the way people who are fearful breathe? Gently exhale as fully as you can. Now take a slow, deep, breath. Hold it for a moment, then exhale gently and fully. How do you feel? Stilling and relaxing the body by means of deep breathing is a wonderful preparation for other methods of prayer. In fact, breathing is an image of the spiritual life: we receive (inhale) and give back (exhale); we exhale, and the flesh contracts as we submit; we inhale, and the flesh expands as we receive. Take your life gratefully from God as you inhale. Give it back unstintingly as you exhale. Be the somebody you are.

For Further Reading and Exploration

Paul Brand and Philip Yancey, *Fearfully and Wonderfully Made: A Surgeon Looks at the Human and Spiritual Body* (Grand Rapids, MI: Zondervan, 1980).

Robert Jewett, *Paul's Anthropological Terms* (Leiden: Brill, 1971).

Jerome Murphy-O'Connor, O.P., *Becoming Human Together: The Pastoral Anthropology of St. Paul* (Wilmington, DE: Michael Glazier, Inc., 1982/84).

John A.T. Robinson, *The Body: A Study in Pauline Theology* (Philadelphia: Westminster Press, 1952).

Chapter 5

Praying the Name: The Jesus Prayer

... hallowed be your Name...
(Matthew 6:9)

... do everything in the name of the Lord
Jesus...(Colossians 3:17)

Lord Jesus Christ {Son of God} have mercy on
me {a sinner}. (The Jesus Prayer)

Introduction

At the outset of this book, I suggested (in the words of Jean Danielou) that prayer is a "mode of being." Presently we shall think about that "mode of being" as a "quality of attention." Heretofore we have looked at some ways of praying with words and a way of praying the Word, Scripture (although the method transfers to any spiritual writing). Then, in the last chapter, we stopped to ask the question "who is the person who prays?" and suggested some biblical terms that might be used in constructing a Christian anthropology. Whatever and whoever "person" is, in the life of prayer his or her center is the "heart." Indeed, in *Springs of Water in a Dry Land* Mary Jo Weaver defines prayer as "a deeply personal response to the desires of the heart in relation to the divine being."[1] The Jesus Prayer is one of the oldest methods that the Christian tradition has to offer of going deeply into the heart in prayer.

The biblical record is full of stories of how people "go out" somewhere to meet God (or they go out not expecting anything, and God comes to them!): Jacob at the fork of the Jabbok River, Moses to Horeb in Midian, Elijah to the mountains in the wilderness, Isaiah to the Temple, Paul to the Arabian desert and in the dungeons of the Roman Empire. The paradigmatic example for Christians are the references to Jesus "withdrawing" to pray. (See Mark 1:35–39, 6:46 and most dramatically 14:32–42.) Parenthetically the Greek word for withdraw, *anachoreo*, literally means something like "go away to come back." Mark's Jesus invites the disciples to "do likewise:" "Come away to a deserted place all by yourselves and rest a while." (Mark 6:31) In Scripture, going to a wilderness place to pray is both a literal, geographic designation, and a metaphor for withdrawal to a place of silence and solitude, a place where God's voice is not choked out by the normal noise and hubbub of life.

Where do we "go," literally and metaphorically, to meet God? Thomas Merton writes:

> There exists some point at which I can meet God in a real and experimental contact with His infinite actuality. This is the "place" of God, His sanctuary—it is the point where my contingent being depends upon His love. Within myself is a metaphorical apex of existence at which I am held in being by my Creator. God utters me like a word containing a partial thought of Himself.[2]

The "apex of existence" within, where God resides and is found, is in the heart. The Jesus Prayer is also called "the prayer of the heart." It is one of the oldest, most beautiful and richest ways of praying in the Christian tradition. I tend to think of it as a transitional prayer; it is a bridge, a spoken prayer that is a means to the contemplative state, a word prayer that is intended to lead us to wordless prayer.

In his book on Eastern Christian Spirituality, *Way of the Ascetics*, Tito Colliander says "when you pray, you yourself must be silent ... let the prayer speak."[3] The Jesus Prayer is intended to help us "pray constantly." (1 Thessalonians 5:17) It is a way of "igniting" (for lack of a better term) a prayer that prays itself deep within us all the time. Those of you who know the Islamic tradition will immediately think of the *dhikr*, which arose in the same part of the world as the Jesus Prayer and has many similarities to it. Colliander's is a very direct way of saying that real prayer is a state of being, not any particular words which we might say. Writing of prayer in Orthodox Christianity, the branch of the family that gave and preserved for us the Jesus Prayer, Anthony Coniaris says, "the whole purpose of the spiritual life is to descend with the mind into the heart through inner prayer and to discover there the kingdom of God .... The heart is the Lord's reception room. Meet Him there. 'The kingdom of God is within you,' said Jesus."[4]

History

The Jesus Prayer is associated with a tradition of inner, mystical prayer made famous by the monks of Mount Athos but which is much older than that in Christian tradition. It is associated with hesychasm. The word *hesychia* means "quiet," "solitude" or "inner stillness." "Quiet serenity" might be a good modern translation. The word is used first in connection with the desert fathers and mothers of the fourth century. "A hesychast is one who in silence devotes himself to inner recollection and private prayer."[5] St. John Climacus (d. 650 AD), writing in *The Ladder of Paradise*, says, "The Hesychast is he who strives to confine the Incorporeal into his bodily house ... Let the remembrance of Jesus be present with each breath; then you//will know the value of solitude."[6]

The historical background of hesychasm as a movement is the failed attempt at reunion of the Eastern and Western churches under Emperor Michael VIII (1259–82). Its founder was said by some to be Arsenius the Great (d. *ca.* 449 AD), and its theology comes from St. Symeon the New Theologian (949–1022). The revival of the practice is associated with a monk of Mount Athos, Gregory Palamas (1296–1359). Gregory taught that "the entire creation is permeated with divine energy which illuminates the universe and establishes the most intimate personal relations between man and the Creator."[7] Gregory builds on the thought of St. Basil, who said we could know God from God's energies, but not God in God's essence. Gregory taught that since God is Light, the experience of God's energies takes the form of light. Thus for Orthodox Christianity the story of Jesus' Transfiguration becomes paradigmatic for all Christian prayer. The ancient forms of prayer that centered on the repetition of the name of Jesus assisted Christians in coming to experience God's energies in the heart. The Jesus Prayer came to be known as "the prayer of the heart," which it was hoped would literally lead one to enlightenment, to experiencing God's light. As Bishop Kallistos Ware put it, "The Jesus Prayer causes the brightness of the Transfiguration to penetrate into every corner of our life."[8]

These are, of course, powerful and extraordinary claims. And it was the claim to experience directly God's divine light that touched off the hesychast controversy, which, fortunately, we don't have to worry about in this context except to say that the controversy was one of the reasons for the dying out of many aspects of contemplative prayer in the Western Church. The suppression of the monasteries at the Reformation and the prosecution by the Inquisition of forms of prayer that predisposed people to mystical experience very nearly killed contemplative prayer altogether in the West and are sad chapters in church history. The good news is that it is impossible to stamp out forms of spirituality that are pleasing to God. *Vocatus atque non vocatus, Deus aderit.* ("Invoked or not invoked, God is present.")

The Prayer and Holy Scripture

Hesychasm and the Jesus Prayer are firmly rooted in biblical tradition. The most apparent biblical warrant for the Jesus Prayer is found in St. Paul's earliest letter as he commands the Thessalonian Christians to "pray ceaselessly." (1 Thessalonians 5:17) The theological grounding of the practice rests in the early church's focus on the power and holiness of the name of Jesus.[9] Names in ancient religious understanding were more than labels for identification; they contained the essence and reality of the one named. This is why, for example, children used to be named "Constance" or "Prudence" or "Ernest." (Now we name children for pop stars.) We have some sense of this when we remember how important the Name of God was to the ancient Hebrews/Jews. The Name itself was a unit of power and was not to be spoken carelessly, if, indeed, it was to be spoken at all. In the New Testament, the Name stands for the person, so that evoking the Name of Jesus is evoking the person and power of the Risen Jesus.

The New Testament bears witness to the importance of the Name of Jesus in many ways. Christian life began with the Name as people were baptized in or into the Name of Jesus. (The Trinitarian baptismal formula at the end of Matthew is a later development.) Acts 19:17 speaks of Christians in Ephesus praising or magnifying the Name of Jesus. Some important New Testament quotations about the Name include:

> Therefore God also highly exalted him and gave him the name that is above every name, that at the name of Jesus every knee should bend, in heaven and on earth and under the earth, and every tongue confess that Jesus Christ is Lord, to the glory of God the Father. (Philippians 2:9–11, but the text probably pre-dates

Paul's letter and is a hymn of the early church Paul
inserted for illustrative purposes here.)

...no one can say "Jesus is Lord" except by the Holy
Spirit. (1 Corinthians 12:3)

All the prophets testify about him that everyone who
believes in him receives forgiveness of sins through his
name. (Peter in Acts 10:43)

...if you ask anything of the Father in my name, he
will give it to you... (John 16:24)

Even these few quotations bear witness to how important
the Name of Jesus was to early Christians. A vestigial
reminder of the power of the Name of Jesus is evidenced by
the fact that many Protestant Christians still sing hymns that
focus on the Name of Jesus: "All Hail the Power of Jesus'
Name;" "How Sweet the Name of Jesus Sounds;" "There's
Something about that Name," and " At the Name of Jesus" are
but a few examples.

"Orthodox believe that the power of God is present in the
Name of Jesus..."[10] In a very literal way, Jesus' Name is a
carrier of divine energy. In his book *Contemplative Prayer*,
Thomas Merton explains that in the Eastern Church "the
sacramental power of the Name of Jesus is believed to bring
the Holy Spirit into the heart of the praying monk."[11] Merton
continues: "The practice of keeping the name of Jesus ever
present in the ground of one's being was, for the ancient
monks, the secret of the 'control of thoughts,' and of victory
over temptation. It accompanied all the other activities of the
monastic life imbuing them with prayer."[12]

The most expansive form of the text of the Jesus Prayer is
itself a combination of two prayers from the gospel of Luke:
that of the blind man in Jericho, "Jesus, Son of David, have
mercy on me" (Luke 18:38) and that of the publican, "God, be

merciful to me, a sinner" (Luke 18:13). The prayer is a confession of everything that is central to our understanding of
Jesus and a compendium of important New Testament
christological terms: Lord; Christ; Son of God. It is also a basic
supplicatory prayer for all of us who stand in need of God's
mercy. Its beauty is, in part, its simplicity. It simply evokes
the Name and asks for help, invocation and petition in their
lowest common denominator. We very simply reach up to
Jesus and at the same time are called home to ourselves.

A Method

Practicing the Jesus Prayer can become a means by which one
achieves focus and peace in the inner life. But like *lectio divina*,
it is not a quick fix; it requires sustained *practice*. Fr. Thomas
Ryan explains the Jesus Prayer as follows:

> "Prayer of the heart" is the active effort we make to
> keep our hearts open so that we may be enlightened by
> the Lord and filled with the realization of our true
> relation to him. The whole purpose of this prayer as a
> form of meditation is to deepen our consciousness of
> this basic relationship of creature to Creator, sinner to
> Savior.[13]

One can pray the Jesus Prayer either informally, at any time
and while doing other things (this is called the "free way"), or
can develop it as formal practice under the care of a spiritual
father or mother (this is called the "fixed use"). The Eastern
Christian writers describe both approaches. Very simply, one
repeats the prayer text, "Lord Jesus Christ, Son of God, have
mercy on me, a sinner" in rhythm with the breath (or with the
heartbeat) and at the same time concentrates the mind on the
region of the heart, "regarded as being the focal point for
the whole psycho-physiological nature of man."[14] (If you
skipped the previous chapter, you might want to go back now

and read the section on "heart/*kardia*.") According to Thomas Merton, praying it consists in "interior recollection, the abandonment of distracting thought and the humble invocation of the Lord Jesus with words from the Bible in a spirit of intense faith."[15]

The Way of a Pilgrim is a Russian classic on the spiritual life that describes an ordinary man's quest for a life of prayer. The autobiographical narrative, a great spiritual adventure story, focuses on the effect of the Jesus Prayer on the pilgrim. The pilgrim learned the method from a monk who quoted this material from St. Simeon the New Theologian to teach the prayer practice:

> Sit alone and in silence; bow your head and close your eyes; relax your breathing and with your imagination look into your heart; direct your thoughts from your head into your heart. And while inhaling say, "Lord Jesus Christ, have mercy on me," either softly with your lips or in your mind. Endeavor to fight distractions but be patient and peaceful and repeat this process frequently.[16]

Experimenting with the method, the pilgrim continues:

> My first practical step was to find the place of the heart ... I closed my eyes and imagined looking into my heart; my desire was to visualize the heart in the left breast and to listen attentively to its beating ... while looking into the heart and inhaling I said, "Lord Jesus Christ," and while exhaling, "have mercy on me."[17]

Refinements of the method include bowing the head slightly with the chin resting on the chest or saying the prayer with the arms extended in the form of a cross, a practice especially suited to penitence. Other Orthodox Christian writers suggest making the sign of the cross after each repetition or bowing from the waist and touching the ground with fingers of the right hand, or completely prostrating with each repetition. But the basic practice is to coordinate the simple prayer with the breathing, bringing the mind to the heart. Each individual has great freedom in finding the best way for him or her to say/use this method of prayer because, as an Orthodox monk writing on the prayer remarked, "the best prayer for each person is the one, which ever it may be, to which each is drawn by the Holy Spirit, by particular circumstances, and by properly appointed spiritual direction."[18] The Orthodox tradition is insistent that, if one makes "the fixed use" of the Jesus Prayer a primary practice, he or she must do so under the guidance of a spiritual director. I heartily concur.

Notice that the prayer is not only deeply biblical and Christo-centric, but holistic. It uses the "fleshly" part of the body (lips, breath, beating heart), but also the intellect (mind) and spirit as all is drawn into the heart center. The Jesus Prayer begins as a prayer of the lips, is taken into the flesh, and becomes a prayer of the whole person. By means of it one descends *with* the mind into the heart so that the prayer effects the reintegration and reunion of our fragmented nature and becomes a means of restoring our original wholeness.[19] It is a way of uniting the mind and the heart in prayer. As we noted in the previous chapter, the heart is the place of integration, and not only for Christians. The Hindu Sri Ramana Maharshi wrote:

> Deep in the cave of the heart
> is brahman, for ever alone,
> the unique I, the unique Self.
> Enter, O man,
> into this depth of thyself
> with thought turned within,
> with mind sunk in the Self,
> at peace
> fixed in the Self,
> having become thyself![20]

In his book *Conjectures of a Guilty Bystander*, Christian monk Thomas Merton spoke of this internal locus as *le point vierge*, the virgin point, a term he learned from Islamic mysticism. The tenth-century Muslim Saint and martyr, al-Hallaj, was fond of saying, "Our hearts are a virgin that God's truth alone opens" and "I saw my Lord with the Eye of the Heart."[21] The well-known Sufi poet, Rumi, wrote, "I have looked into my own heart; it is there that I have seen Him; He was nowhere else."[22] In many religious traditions, the heart is the point of coinherence of the Divine in the human.

In contemporary language, I would suggest that the Jesus Prayer is a means of overcoming alienation. Gregory Palamas taught that eventually it could lead to a vision of Divine Light/Energy. As the Orthodox theologian Bulgakov said, "shining through the heart, the light of the Name of Jesus illuminates all the universe."[23] Gregory notes:

> Do you not understand that the men who are united to God and deified, who fix their eyes in a divine manner on Him, do not see as we do? Miraculously, they see with a sense that exceeds the senses, and with a mind that exceeds the mind, for the power of the spirit penetrated their human faculties, and allows them to see things which are beyond us.[24]

The Way of a Pilgrim, in fact, describes the way in which repetition of the Jesus Prayer literally transforms the way the pilgrim sees the material world and other people.

In practice, one repeats the prayer until it begins to repeat itself within. Bishop Kallistos Ware calls this the point where "my" prayer identifies with the action of Another in me.[25] Eventually, rather as the fingers learn a piano piece by heart, what we repeat becomes part of our inner life and plays itself. The Jesus Prayer comes to pray itself in us. The writer of the Song of Songs described something of the process when he wrote, "I sleep, but my heart is awake." (5:2) The central core of personhood is always awake, and can actually be "praying ceaselessly." Again, Bishop Kallistos says we can repeat the Name until it is not something we *do*, but something we *are*.

The French Benedictine monk, Henri le Saux, lived his Christian faith in the context of Indian spirituality for twenty-five years. Under his Indian name, Abhishiktananda, he wrote a small classic work on Christian prayer simply called *Prayer*. He devotes Chapter 9 of that book to "The Prayer of the Name" (*namajapa*). His description of the stages of the Jesus Prayer is very helpful.

> In the first stage, the beginner will set the divine Name on his lips and his tongue . . . . He will repeat the name aloud, or will . . . murmur it. . . .
>
> In the next stage the lips remain closed. It is the mind, or "in the head" . . . that the prayer is made . . . The prayer has now become the mind's unbroken attention to the Name which it repeats without stopping.
>
> The highest stage is reached when the prayer, or rather the Name, is set in the heart. . . . The prayer is now firmly fixed at the very centre of our being, and from there its light and glory radiate everywhere.
>
> The Name has now come to its true place; the sign has returned to the Reality from which it proceeded.[26]

Some Practical Suggestions

- It is possible to prayer the Jesus Prayer at any time, to make "a very brief act of prayer or praise . . . an uninterrupted offering of love and adoration."[27] And it is a particularly powerful prayer at times when I am "waiting," at a stop light or in the grocery checkout line, or waiting for my ancient dial-up computer system to get on line. Praying it transforms those moments for me, and I hope it transforms me. But if one wishes to make real progress in the inner life by means of the Jesus Prayer, it is best to set aside quiet times for it, ideally daily, and to develop one's own "fixed practice." As in any form of meditation (and we will speak more of this in later chapters), one assumes a comfortable bodily position and an attitude of receptivity. Relax the flesh/body. Bring the mind back to the body, perhaps by several long slow breaths of the type described at the end of the last chapter. Then begin the repetitions of the Jesus Prayer, coordinating them with the breath.

How the coordination works will be different for each person. You might want to experiment with the following variations: "Lord Jesus Christ" (on inhale) "have mercy on me" (on exhale). Or, "Lord Jesus Christ" (on inhale); "Son of God" (pause); "have mercy on me" (on exhale).

- You can experiment with how much or how little of the full text of the prayer you wish to use. You can use the whole prayer or part of it. Experiment with the following variations: "Jesus, Mercy." Or "Lord, have mercy." Or *"Christe eleison/Kyrie eleison"* (the Latin version). If English titles tend to make you *think* too much about theological content or christology (this is not an exercise in systematic theology!) rather than to pray, the Latin may be very helpful.

Some people find it depressing or upsetting to add "a sinner" to their use of the Jesus Prayer. I respect those feelings. But the truth is, we *are* sinners. For me (and this may *not* be true for you) "be merciful to me, a sinner," makes this a circular prayer, brings me back to the beginning. I call on the Name of Jesus because I am a sinner, or perhaps, as Br. David Steindl-Rast suggested in

Gratefulness: The Heart of Prayer, "alienated" is the
better word for our condition. Personally, I use the
prayer to correct my thoughts. When I find myself
being judgmental or thinking mean things about
others, I immediately stop and say ten Jesus Prayers
by means of reparation. I also sometimes pray the
prayer in the plural: "Lord Jesus Christ, Son of God,
have mercy on *us*." When I am utterly powerless
even to know how to pray for the suffering and
disorder of the world, I find this simple prayer is a
powerful invocation and a petition for the whole
human family.

- Those of you who have some acquaintance with or
have had some training in meditation techniques
may be wondering if the Jesus Prayer is a mantra. It
is certainly related to the use of a mantra, a short
phrase that is repeated to keep the mind focused. It
is also related to what is technically called in
Christian prayer literature "aspirations," brief
exhaled prayers, and to "ejaculatory prayers" which
we spoke of earlier. It is quite possible to use the
method of the Jesus Prayer with another *text*. Some
people pray it with "O God, come to my assistance;
O Lord, make haste to help me" (Psalm 70:1) or
"Abba, Father," (Romans 8:15; Galatians 4:5) or
"Holy, Holy, Holy is the Lord God of Hosts."
(Isaiah 6:3) Obviously, there would be other possi-
bilities. But the classic Jesus Prayer focuses on the
Name of Jesus because of the power inherent in the
Name.

- In the more informal use of the Prayer one repeats it
as much as possible during the day. Use it as a means
of recollection or re-centering. When you begin to
feel anxious or upset, or when you start to "lose it,"
repeat the Jesus Prayer. It is a way to gather up the
scattered parts of our lives into a divine focus. It is a

particularly helpful prayer for people who feel unfocused or scattered. To pray implies being present where one is, here and now, and that is always re-focusing.

Theophane the Recluse suggested that to stop "jostling of your thoughts ... you must bind the mind with one thought..."[28] With regard to how to do this, in general, I find that positive and spiritual strategies work better than negative ones. Instead of fighting scattered thoughts, one can turn the mind Godward with the Jesus Prayer. I am trying to purge the metaphorical use of "fighting" and "hitting" from my vocabulary, especially my spiritual vocabulary. In the current state of the world, it no longer makes sense to me to speak of "fighting" cancer or "fighting temptation" or even "hitting" a button on the computer. I find that somehow more spiritually irenic metaphors generate more healing energy and power.

- Le Saux writes that "The only possible place where we can truly encounter God is at the very centre of our being, the source from which we have come, the point at which we proceed from God in the eternal birth of the divine Word. This is physically symbolized by the heart...".[29]

- It is useful to locate the heart center in your body. There are two very simple ways to do this. One is simply to sit very still and "feel" for the beating of your own heart. Mostly we only do this when we exercise or are winded or have a scare, but it is possible to locate and feel one's own resting heartbeat. Second, you can chant your way to your heart. Take a deep, gentle breath, and chant out the syllable "AH." Normally, when you do this, you can discern a vibration somewhere beneath the sternum (or breast bone). That's your heart center.

Incidentally, the area over the sternum is called the "point of tranquillity" in many spiritual traditions. I wonder if this is why, when we teach children to fold their hands when they pray, they almost instinctively press their thumbs against the sternum. Are they feeling the vibration of the heart we adults have forgotten?

When you slump forward with rounded shoulders you are closing and protecting your heart center. When you stand straight and erect, shoulders back (like mother told you when she was nagging you about your posture) you open your heart center. You can very quickly take someone's spiritual temperature by checking this simple cue given by posture. The flesh bends forward almost instinctively to protect the heart center when one feels endangered or vulnerable or even sad. Conversely, "openheartedness" can describe a physiological stance that reflects ones inner disposition.

- A repetition of something I mentioned above is important. All the literature in the Orthodox Christian tradition says that if one wishes to develop the formalized use of the Jesus Prayer by coordinating breath and heartbeat as a sustained practice, he or she MUST do so with a spiritual Father or Mother. When we move into the realm of deep prayer, especially when we begin to open and enter the interior life, especially for the first time, all kinds of things can come up or be released or come to consciousness. In his book on the practice of the Jesus Prayer in the Western church Rama Coomaraswamy notes that individual prayer has as part of its aim ". . .the purification of the soul: it loosens psychological knots or, in other words, dissolves subconscious coagulations and drains away many secret poisons; it externalizes before God the difficulties, failures and distortions of the soul..." Such prayer "has the virtue (strength) of re-establishing equilibrium and restoring peace, in a word, of opening us up to grace."[30]

This process is quite normal, but it can be unsettling and sometimes frightening. Having a spiritual director or spiritual parent who has walked the road ahead of you can not only keep you from running into a ditch, but can pull you out when you fall into one, or bring you home through a dark night. (More on this later in the book.) I highly recommend seeking a spiritual director. If you wish to find one in the Orthodox Christian tradition, your local Orthodox priest will be able to help you. And you are blessed, indeed, if you have an Orthodox monastery of men or women nearby. An association for spiritual directors, Spiritual Directors International (which is a multi-faith and not specifically Christian group, although many Christian directors affiliate with it), maintains a website (*www.sdiworld.com*) to help people locate directors in their religious tradition and geographical area and there are many fine books on spiritual direction available.[31]

- The final two practical suggestions are taken from *The Jesus Prayer*, a book by an Orthodox monk. They suggest how "the Name" is to be used. First, "once spoken, the name ... may be 'prolonged' for several minutes of repose, of silence, of purely interior attention..." And, second, "our aim is not a constant, literal repetition but a kind of latent and quiescent presence of the name of Jesus in our heart."[32]

Conclusion

The Jesus Prayer is one way to "pray without ceasing." (1 Thessalonians 5:17) It begins as vocal prayer which takes one deeply into the body, to the heart center. Its intent, like that of *lectio divina*, is to transform the one who prays. In Christian tradition, "Hesychasm aims at human integration through constant remembrance of God, which can be attained by 'guarding' our hearts."[33] Let me give the last word to two Christian monks who advocate use of this method of prayer. First, Theophane the Recluse says:

> I will remind you of only one thing: one must descend with the mind into the heart, and there stand before the face of the Lord, ever present, all seeing within you. The (Jesus) prayer takes a firm and steadfast hold, when a small fire begins to burn in the heart. Try not to quench this fire, and it will become established in such a way that the prayer repeats itself: and then you will have within you a small murmuring stream.[34]

Second, Br. David Steindl-Rast writes of the Jesus Prayer in *A Listening Heart:*

> It consists basically in the mantric repetition of the name of Jesus, synchronized with one's breath and heartbeat. When I repeat the name of Jesus at a given moment in time, I make that moment transparent to the Now that does not pass away. The whole biblical notion of living by the Word is summed up in the name of Jesus in whom I as a Christian adore the Word incarnate. By giving that name to every thing and to every person I encounter, by invoking it in every situation in which I find myself, I remind myself that everything is just another way of spelling out the

> inexhaustible fullness of the one eternal word of God, the Logos; I remind my heart to listen![35]

In a vision, the Risen Jesus told Ananias that Paul was "a chosen vessel of mine, to bear my name." (Acts 9:15) and this is true of all believers. Practice of the Jesus Prayer helps us to be and to do just this.

For Further Reading and Exploration
The Philokalia (literally, "love of beauty") is a collection of texts about the Jesus Prayer from the third century to the Middle Ages. St. Nicodemus of the Holy Mountain (1748–1809) made a collection of the sayings which was published in Venice in 1782. Theophane the Recluse (1815–1894) issued an expanded translation in Russian of five volumes. The work is one of the most influential in Orthodox history. A good selection texts from these works is available in E. Kadloubovsky and G.E.H. Palmer (transl.) (London: Faber & Faber, 1951/83).

Helen Bacovcin (transl.), *The Way of a Pilgrim* (New York: Doubleday/Image, 1978).

Tito Colliander, *Way of the Ascetics* (Crestwood, NY: St. Vladimir's Seminary Press, 1985).

Rama Coomaraswamy, *The Invocation of the Name of Jesus as Practiced in the Western Church* (Louisville, KY: Fons Vitae Press, 1999).

Anthony de Mello, S.J., *Sadhana* (Anand, India: Gujarat Sahitya Prakash, 1978) "Exercise 35: The Jesus Prayer."

Bernadette Dieker and Jonathan Montaldo (eds.), *Merton and Hesychasm: The Prayer of the Heart* (Louisville, KY: Fons Vitae Press, 2003).

Thomas Merton, O.C.S.O., *The Wisdom of the Desert* (New York: New Directions, 1960).

N.A., *The Jesus Prayer* (Crestwood, NY: St. Vladimir's Seminary Press, 1987).

N.A., *Orthodox Spirituality* (Crestwood, NY: St. Vladimir's Seminary Press, 1978).

Elisabeth Sehr-Sigel (transl. Fr. Steven Bigham) *The Place of the Heart: An Introduction to Orthodox Spirituality* (Torrance, CA: Oakwood Publications, 1992).

Chapter 6

Praying with the Body: Some Exercises

... at the name of Jesus every knee should bend... (Philippians 2:10)

For you were bought with a price; therefore glorify God in your body. (1 Corinthians 6:20)

...the life of Jesus may be made visible in our mortal flesh. (2 Corinthians 4:11)

In chapter 4 we spoke of the whole human person as body, and of body as composed of flesh and spirit/soul (to which "mind" is subject). James Keenan's review essay of Christian studies of the body notes that "both the Greek and Semitic traditions would hold ... that the human 'is not someone who has a body but [someone] whose existence is corporal.'"[1] He quotes Bultmann's dictum that "the human does not have a *soma*, but rather is *soma*."[2] At the interstices of flesh and spirit/soul is heart, which unites the two and is the psycho-physical and spiritual center of person. As attested by a great body of written material from our saints, the Christian tradition has been reasonably attentive to the spirit/soul or internal aspect of personhood. The earliest of the Greek spiritual writers were consummate spiritual psychologists and wise in the "ways of the flesh." But, in my view, largely because of poor translation of the Greek terms *soma* (body) and *sarx* (flesh) and subsequent misinterpretation of Pauline thought, Christianity has not understood either body or flesh accurately theologically or very well in practice. Sometimes I think *sarx* might just as well have been translated "enemy." This is a serious theological error from which a great deal of unnecessary physical, spiritual and psychological suffering has resulted.[3]

Studying the most ancient religious records of human beings suggests there is something deep within us that wants to pray with the flesh. I have written a poem called "Rak'a" about this impulse. (*Rak'a* is the rhythmic prostration in Islamic prayer.)

> "Let us bow down,
> bend the knee,
> kneel before our Maker."
>
> Ever since God showed
> the shadow of a face
> the human instinct
> has been to bow.
>
> In this we but mimic
> grass of the field,
> trees of the forest
> at the wind's will.
>
> Rhythmic response
> confirming creaturehood,
> to bow or bend or kneel
> exercises our eternity.
>
> Prostrate in prayer,
> we kiss the dust

God fingered to make us
and know it heavenly.

To bow is to begin
the giddy free fall
into the invisible hands
that hold the world,
that cradle creation
their cherished child.

If you stand stiff-
necked—beware!
There is no solid ground
beneath your clay feet.

Until early modern times, dance has been an expression of praise and intercession. Recently I have found certain kinds of classical music move me to dance a prayer. I was much comforted to find a similar impulse described in Richard Foster's book, *Prayer*. The impulse to bow or to prostrate (lay completely down on the ground, face down) is equally ancient. As I have mentioned earlier, in Eastern religions the breath itself is treated as sacred and attention to breathing is a primary preparation for and form of prayer. In some branches of the Christian family and in many other religious traditions, the life of the senses was/is fully engaged in worship. Incense, beautiful art and fabrics, materials and color, ritual meals, chant and music all speak to fleshly engagement in worship. While there were undoubtedly difficulties with aspects of worship in Medieval and early modern Roman Catholicism (and some would argue in Orthodoxy), I have a tendency to think the zealous exclusion of the sensual from Christian worship by many of the Reformers went too far in the opposite direction. So, yes, this Protestant is nostalgic for incense, icons, bowing, prostration, crossing oneself and dancing before the Lord with the fervor of King David, albeit wearing more clothing! (2 Samuel 6:1–15) But this doesn't mean I feel the need to convince you that you should be as well. The life of prayer is one of variety, and what draws me may repel you.

It is worth interjecting that a lot of how we react to the sensual, to the use of body in prayer, is as much a matter of training and taste as it is of theology. Very simply, we live in our bodies in the ways we were taught to do as children. If our bodies were cherished and treasured, and if we were taught to love and care for them, to delight in them, we tend to do so at every level as adults. If we were not so taught as children, we often ignore or suffer or are ashamed of our bodies as adults, with predictable results. We can learn to live more healthily in the flesh, but that, like so many things, is harder to learn when we are older.

A similar thing happens in the spiritual life. If one is raised as a primitive Baptist in the southern mountains of the U.S.A. and visits a Greek Orthodox church in a city, it will seem like foreign territory (and vice versa). How we are trained as Christians determines how we pray. And that is definitely a two-sided coin. It is vitally important to be trained to pray, to be encouraged to develop habits of prayer. The other side of the coin is to believe that the way *I* was trained to pray is the *only* way or even the only *correct* way. This attitude can also keep us stuck in a mode of prayer that we have long since outgrown.

Relatedly, many people seem unaware that taste and theology are not the same thing. What they find aesthetically displeasing (or unfamiliar), they sometimes judge to be wrong rather than just different. I often think that denomi-nationalism in the modern church has less to do with history and theology than it does with socio-economic status and aesthetics. Most cradle Christians are also cultural Christians, bound to the cultural patterns of the Christianity in which we were raised. If one has the opportunity to worship in many Christian communities and in many places in the world, one is blessed indeed. Nothing counteracts parochialism more effectively than that. (You will have figured out that, in this regard, I am spiritually promiscuous; I will pray with any-body.) The bottom line is that God reaches out to many, many people in many, many different ways. For every person there is an individual invitation. It is not for me to R.S.V.P. for someone else.

To return to the more practical aspects of prayer and the body: I suspect most people think they live in their bodies rather than that they *are* their bodies. (Perhaps I am confessing that this is my tendency!) But we are body, flesh and spirit. Flesh, as we have been using the term, is a *wonderful* thing. Perhaps we can begin this chapter on prayer and the body (with an emphasis on the fleshly part) with an exercise in gratitude. Stop for a moment and think of all the joys and pleasures you have received in your flesh. Take a stroll down the sensory smörsgåsbord of your body. Recall things seen, heard, tasted, felt. Don't be embarrassed to include the delights of sex or the "trivial" pleasures of a hot bath, a good haircut, a shave, the first sip of coffee in the morning. Fr. Anthony de Mello reminds us that "Every sensation I feel, no matter how light and subtle is the result of a biochemical reaction that could not exist except for God's almighty power . . . Feel God's power at work in the production of every single sensation. . ."[4]

A good deal of what we call "sensual" pleasures, the delights we receive through our five senses, are actually gratuitous, not necessary for our survival. Granted, we need to be able to feel heat and cold and pain to survive, as anyone who has worked with lepers or those with serious nerve damage can attest. It makes survival easier if you can see and hear and speak, but the amazingly fruitful life of Helen Keller and of many persons who have been blind, deaf and/or mute demonstrate that one can live a full life without some of the senses. Music, for example, is gratuitous, purely for our pleasure and without practical use. Has it ever occurred to you that color is a gift? There is no reason why we have to perceive color. We could get along by seeing shape, black, white, shades of gray, but we have been given the gift of color. Similarly, the ability to perceive taste (sweet, sour, bitter, etc.) is gratuitous. One must ingest to survive, and people who have lost the sense of taste or whose sense of taste is marred by medical treatment can do so, but largely joylessly. God has given us taste as a means of delight. I sometimes wonder if we eat too much and become overweight because we don't delight in taste, don't attend in gratitude to the pleasure of our food. There is a sinfulness about "fast food," if it means ingesting without noticing, enjoying, being thankful. Attention to the life of the senses and gratitude for the joys we receive through our senses is a kind of prayer.

Think, also, of all the amazing *internal* aspects of flesh that are chugging along all the time: respiration, the digestive process, the electrical impulses shooting along the network of your nerves. At any given moment thousands of actions and processes are going on in your flesh to keep your body alive. A quite extraordinary exhibit has been traveling to museums in the U.S.A. It is called "BODIES...The Exhibition." It is organized according to the internal systems (musculature, nervous, digestive, respiration, circulatory, reproductive, urinary) and the role each has in the body's functioning. Life "under the skin" is graphically depicted, so graphically that some have objected to the exhibit. But I would like to suggest that seeing it can be profoundly prayerful in its depiction of how "wonderfully made" the human person is.

Being fully present to the body as it is (not as some advertising agency tells me it ought to be, and not as I wish it were) is profoundly prayer-full when it arises from gratitude for being at all and for all the gifts that come with being in the flesh. A wise friend of mine often prays, "thank you for our health even if/when it isn't perfect." In the remainder of this chapter, I am going to suggest some exercises which may help you to re-connect with your flesh, or to enjoy more fully its spiritual pleasures if you have never been "unplugged" from them. I begin with bringing the "mind" back to the "body," and proceed to some suggestions for exploring breath, heart and walking meditation. I close with suggestions of some ways you might prepare your body for contemplative prayer and the forms of prayer of waiting which will follow in this book. As always, if any of this seems not to apply to you, or if you have any scruples at all about it, just skip the material. As you explore and develop in you life of prayer, it is a good principle *never* to transgress against your own conscience or to try to push yourself to try something that feels profoundly wrong to you. Paul writes about similar matters in Romans 14–15:13 and 1 Corinthians 8–10 and lifts up the two wise and simple principles: first, mutual responsibility and "up building" (Romans 14:19; cf. 14:7; 1 Corinthians 8:9, 10:24) and, second, personal liberty and conscience ("...whatever does not proceed from faith is sin." Romans 14:23).

Finally, and happily, in recent years there have been a number of really wonderful books on the body written by Christians, including a study of Pope John Paul II's thinking on "body." I have included several of the most practical and those more pertinent to prayer in the suggestions for further reading at the end of this chapter. Many Christians have been greatly helped by Fr. Anthony de Mello, s.j.'s practical teachings in *Sadhana*, and I highly recommend it. You may also want to continue to explore body prayer by using CDs developed for this purpose. Instructional CDs by Episcopal priest, Nancy Roth, and Fr. Thomas Ryan, C.S.P. were developed specifically for use by Christians.

Bringing the Mind Back to the Body

The body is a great gift and a very good thing. De Mello has written, "When you pray with your body you give power and *body* to your prayer."[5] Although it diverges somewhat from the anthropology I have suggested, I love the story of the aboriginal man who was dying and whose spirit came back to thank

his body before it departed. A no less venerable Christian than
C.S. Lewis often spoke of what I have called the flesh-spirit/
body connection. For example, in *The Screwtape Letters* the
senior devil writes to his demon-in-training about human
beings, reminding him that they are animals and what they do
in their bodies affects their souls. In *Letters to Malcolm, Chiefly
on Prayer* Lewis writes "The body ought to pray as well as
the soul." "...but for our body one whole realm of God's
glory—all that we receive through the senses—would go
unpraised."[6] Unfortunately, we are often unfocused, stressed,
and unhealthy because we try to live as if we were disembodied
rather than the creatures of flesh God so lovingly fashioned.
The writer of Ephesians is correct when he writes, "We are
what he has made us." (Ephesians 2:10. And read again Psalm
139, especially verses 13–14.)

God gave us our flesh for our delight, and among other
things, as an aid to our life of prayer. The Apostle Paul had a
deep and mystical understanding of the fact that, because God
made the human body, the human body was both precious and
a fit receptacle for the life of God. Paul wrote, "Do you not
know that you are God's temple and that *God's spirit dwells in
you?*" (1 Corinthians 3:16) and "...glorify God *in your body*." (1
Corinthians 6:20) It is Paul who reminds us that coming back
to ourselves, coming back to our bodies, is one way to return
to God. "...it is no longer I who live, but it is Christ who lives
in me. And the life I now live *in the flesh* I live by faith in the
Son of God, who loved me and gave himself [his *body*] for me."
(Galatians 2:20. In all texts, italics are mine.)

Practically this means that the flesh can tell us a lot about
our psychological and spiritual state. As a vast psycho-physical
literature attests, we react somatically to danger, fear, affec-
tion, for example. So why don't we listen to our bodies? A
dramatic example of what I mean occurred several years ago
when, in the ladies' room before a meeting, I found a colleague
taking a hand full of aspirin. I inquired if she were sick and
should go home. "No," she said, "these are prophylactic

aspirin. This meeting always gives me a headache." Her body was trying desperately to tell her something about herself in relation to that particular meeting, and she was just shutting it up with pills.

The body doesn't lie. It tells us when we are endangered and when we are safe. It also tells us when we have had enough, when we need more. But most of us need to re-attune ourselves to the subtle signals of the flesh. What I call "taking our physical temperature" is an important way to find out how we are. Fleshly life and spiritual life are intrinsically connected because God in God's wisdom and mercy and generosity and humor (don't believe me? look at yourself naked in the mirror!) made us this way. It's time we paid attention to our *selves*, our bodies as they are. Our body sense has been corrupted by advertising. It takes some practice for most of us to have *awareness* of body rather than judgement of body.

So let's take your "body temperature." Right now, how are you breathing? Deep and slow? Shallow and rapid? Panting? Right now, how does your abdomen (your "gut") feel? Relaxed? Tight? Hurting? How are you sitting? Straight and alert? Slouched? Check your neck and shoulder muscles. Are they tight? What does what you have noticed, what you are *feeling in your flesh,* tell you about your spiritual or heart state? If not right this moment, some time soon take time really to experience the parts of your body. You can do this standing or sitting or lying down. Begin with your feet and move up to your head. How much can your really feel? The soles of your feet in your shoes? Your socks on the top of your feet? The pull of your stockings at your ankles? Progress as slowly as possible up your body noticing as many sensations in as many places as you can. Don't be afraid to notice the ones you might have been taught are "naughty." The sensation isn't naughty, though how you react to it, or act on it, could be. But we aren't reacting or acting, just feeling. When you have finished this survey note how you feel over all. Perhaps you have discovered where you store your tension or stuff your anger. This is useful information. You might want to record it for future use.

It is also revealing (!) to visualize your body both externally and internally in as much anatomical detail as possible. If it's been a long time since you've looked at a picture of your internal organs, you might want to do so. It's useful to know where your stomach really is! As you continue your internal scan, don't judge, just sense or feel. Get inside yourself. Note places of stasis and relaxation and places of tension and pain. What messages are your innards trying to give you?

Finally, befriend your body. Go back "through" and thank the various parts of your body and the systems of your body for what they do for you. I know it seems silly, but try it anyhow. Any exercise in attention and in gratitude is a step toward deeper prayer. And most of us are ignorant of or unaware of or downright abusive to our bodies. No wonder they act up. It is profoundly contemplative (more on that word in the chapters 8 and 9) to develop an attitude of kindness to your body. Give your flesh healthy food. For a lot of people this process takes some time because they have dulled their taste buds with chemical "foods" and sugars, so learning to taste again is required. Give it sufficient relaxation and rest. Studies show that we are chronically under slept, with terrible health consequences. Exercise the flesh. You don't have to be Mr. or Ms. Atlas. Gentle stretching and a leisurely walk are a good beginning. The body was made to move. Learn again to delight in sensation. Babies do. Watch them; it's evident they are enjoying their bodies. Take pleasure in sensual, incarnate life. God made your wonderful body that by means of it you might enjoy and know and serve the God of Life.

A very long time ago St. Ignatius of Antioch wrote that the glory of God was the person fully alive. (*Gloria Dei, vivens homo.*) Full aliveness means living in the flesh, enjoying it, not just putting up with it. And to be attentive to the body, which is the point of these exercises in "taking your body temperature," is to be present, and being present is absolutely necessary to knowing the God Who reveals the Divine Self as I AM.

Breath Exercises

We have already thought together a bit about breath, breathing and prayer. Chapter 4 closes with a breath exercise, and the Jesus Prayer requires one to coordinate words with breath. Breath is the stuff of life, the matrix in which we live, the matrix of the sacred. Chapter 4 pointed out that "spirit" and "breath" are the same word in Greek and in Latin. St. Teresa of Avila is reported to have said that most of our problems in prayer arise from thinking that God is somewhere else. We search for God like a fish searching for water. God is as close as our next breath. Sr. Vilma Seelaus, o.c.d. wrote "...every breath that we draw is a reminder of the union with God that is already ours. Life is God's gift and our breathing is a sign of life..."[7]

According to Genesis, everything that is originates with God's breath. "In the beginning when God created the heavens and the earth, the earth was a formless void and darkness covered the face of the deep, while a wind from God [or "while the spirit of God"] swept over the face of the waters. Then God said, 'Let there be light;' and there was light." (Genesis 1:1–3) God comes as spirit/wind to create. When God speaks, emits a breath, a word, a puff of wind, things happen, things come to be. As we have noted, God animates the human person with breath. (Genesis 2:7) Daniel made a similar point when speaking with King Belshazzar when he spoke of God "in whose power is your very breath." (Daniel 5:23) Breath is a direct "transfusion" from God. Even in his suffering Job remembered this. "But truly it is the spirit in a mortal, the breath of the Almighty, that makes for understanding..." (Job 32:8) Fr. Anthony de Mello suggests we think of air as "charged with the power and presence of God."[8]

To pray is to be in communication with God, the God Who

made us by divine breath. Therefore, a first step toward
praying is breathing properly. If you are a singer or if you have
taken Lamaze classes, you have probably been taught deep
breathing, what I call "bottom to top" breathing. Remember
each lung has two lobes, a lower and an upper. Now, sit or
stand up with your upper body relaxed, but your spine
straight. Exhale gently, but as completely as you can. Now
inhale deeply, filling the lower lobes of the lung first, then
drawing air into the upper lobes. It helps when you are
learning to do this to push out your abdominal muscles to
help the process. The inhale comes reasonably normally. The
surprise comes on the exhale. Empty the *lower* lobes of the
lungs first, then the upper lobes. This is "bottom to top"
exhaling. Collapsing or contracting the abdominal muscles
helps expel the "lower air" first. If you are "deep breathing"
correctly, it is your abdomen, not your chest, that rises and
falls with your breath. Watch a baby at rest. This is how the
baby naturally breathes; its little tummy rises and falls with
the breath.

Simply taking several deep, slow breaths of this "bottom to
top" type is a wonderful way to "re-collect," to come back to
your self. Wherever we are, we can use our breathing to quiet,
center and focus ourselves. And, the medical evidence is that it
is very good for you; as a practice it can lower blood pressure
and help dissipate all sorts of stress. But we are interested here
in breathing as prayer. So let me suggest some specific ways to
make a prayer practice of breathing.

Recall how you have seen an ember glow when someone
blows on it. Isaiah must have had something like this in mind
when he wrote "...the breath of the Lord, like a stream of
sulphur, kindles..." (Isaiah 30:33) Imagine you have an ember
or a coal or a spark in your solar plexus. (No! Don't think
"heartburn"!) Inhale gently and deeply, imagining that ember
glowing as it is aerated. This is an image of the Divine Light
within you which you are fanning into a flame.[9] When you
exhale, you are "giving back," returning the light generated to

the world. Every breath you take can nurture God's life within you, and every exhale can be a blessing. This was how the risen Christ bestowed blessing in St. John's Gospel. "Jesus said to them again, 'Peace be with you. As the Father has sent me, so I send you.' When he has said this, *he breathed on them* and said to them, 'Receive the Holy Spirit.'" (John 20:21–22, italics mine) Breath can rekindle God's flame within us and can be a means of blessing those around us.

You might want to add the words of the great Easter Vigil acclamation to your breath practice by inhaling, "The light of Christ" and exhaling, "Thanks be to God." This kind of breath prayer is an icon of our reality. We live in reciprocity, receiving and giving. We take life from the world, and give it back. An Islamic (remember *islam* means "surrender") prayer practice teaches one to breathe in acceptance and to exhale surrender to God. At the end of chapter 4 I suggested that when we inhale, we expand and receive; when we exhale, we contract and give back. On the basis of that image, I close this section with a quotation from the German poet, Goethe ("Life Lines" 55): "There are two graces in breathing: drawing in air and discharging it. The former constrains, the latter refreshes: so marvelously is life mixed. Thank God when he presses you, and thank him again when he lets you go."

Heart Exercises

Chapter 4 noted that "heart" in biblical anthropology is more than the affective center of a person, the seat of the emotions. It is the center of the whole person, the locus of thought, understanding and will. "Heart" is the central bodily organ, the root of physical vitality and of intellectual and spiritual acuity. Heart, as Cynthia Bourgeault so beautifully says, is the "organ for the perception of divine purpose and beauty."[10] No wonder the heart is such a potent image in many Bible verses. Let me remind you of a few:

"Love God with all your heart..." (Deuteronomy 6:5)

"...the word is very near to you; it is in your mouth and in your heart for you to observe." (Deuteronomy 30:14)

"Create in me a clean heart, O God..." (Psalm 51:10)

"Trust in the Lord with all your heart..." (Proverbs 3:5)

"A new heart I will give you, and a new spirit I will put within you; and I will remove from your body the heart of stone and give you a heart of flesh." (Ezekiel 36:26)

"Return to me with all your heart..." (Joel 2:12)

"Blessed are the pure in heart, for they will see God." (Matthew 5:8)

"Out of the believer's heart shall flow rivers of living water." (John 7:38)

I believe that a fundamental Christian task is to live from a fully awakened heart, to bring heart space, that is the locus and intensity of the whole person, to bear on everything. Here's how I describe it in a poem called "The Task:"

> Bookshops are filled
> with "do-it-yourself" books,
> volumes and volumes
> depicting in excruciating detail
> how to do things
> I never aspired,
> or even thought, to do.

The task is simple,
much simpler
than I was taught,
and much more difficult.

It is to be
present where I am,
to bring heart space
to bear on everything,
to leaven the world's sodden lump
by the capacity
to celebrate and love it.

The only real failure
is failure to love
which alone offers hope
beyond reason.

We awaken our hearts in prayer. We "clean out" heart space for God. We treasure God's presence in our hearts.[11]

This next bit may be a bit esoteric for you, but bear with me if you can (and if you can't, skip to the next section on walking prayer). In the energy system of Asian medicine and many Eastern religions, the heart is in the exact middle of the seven energy centers of the body, fourth from the bottom and fourth from the top, right in the center of the chest. As I noted in the previous chapter, this place is very beautifully called the "point of tranquillity." Each of the body's energy centers is understood to have a sound that activates or stimulates it. If you say, hum or chant the sound, and are attentive to your flesh, you feel a vibration in the center being activated. This made sense to me when I read the following verse in 1 Corinthians: "There are doubtless many different kinds of sounds in the world, and nothing is without sound." (1 Corinthians 14:10) Obviously, "body" has sound. (Adolescent boys are normally fascinated by reproducing the cruder ones!)

The sound that activates the energy of the heart center is "AH," the same "AH" sound we make with a great sigh of contentment. What fascinates me about this is not so much that Buddhism teaches that AH is the seed syllable and source of all speech (which it does teach), but that AH is the root sound of the "Name" by which Jesus taught Christians to address God: Abba (AH-bAH) or even in English, FAH-ther. In daring to address God as Jesus taught us to do, we are, in fact, opening and stimulating the heart, the very core of ourselves. (Parenthetically, it might alleviate some of the current tension around the use of "Father/Abba" if we view it from the standpoint of energy rather than gender.) In a very literal way, God is in our hearts. No wonder Jesus suggests rivers of living water originate there. Perhaps you would like to say or chant on any tone comfortable for you "Abba" (extending the AH at the beginning and end of the word). Notice whether you feel the vibration under your breast bone. "Abba" is the prime invocation in the Christian tradition. And the AH sound is also evident in the Arabic word for God, *Allah* (AH-lAH).

When I began to think about it, I realized that the AH sound was also at the root of the Judeo-Christian traditions' two primary cultic acclamations: Alleluia and Amen. "Alleluia" comes from the Hebrew, "to praise:" praise (imperative) YAH (YHWH). It is an ancient form of giving glory to God, Israel's enthusiastic cultic shout of praise, and what Luther called "the eternal voice of the church." "Amen" comes from a verb that means "to take care," "to support." It is an affirmation of what is said, and, implicitly, a willingness to bear the consequences of that affirmation. It can literally only be said "from the heart." In the Revelation to John, "Amen" seems to be a title for Jesus Christ. (See 3:14.)

In terms of "heart exercise," it may deepen your communal worship to know that every time you use the traditional, Christian terms "Abba," "Alleluia," and "Amen," you are activating your heart center, opening your heart to God. You might even wish to devise for yourself a private prayer practice involving the repetition of one or more of those words. Chanting or repeating it/them in coordination with your breath is very powerful and deepening.

Walking Prayer

Living prayerfully is really about living with attention and focus, especially focus on the basic, simple aspects of life, making of them prayer. As such, the flesh is an asset to prayer, as I hope you glimpsed in the discussion of breath above. Walking is another ordinary activity than can become prayerful. "To walk" (*peripateo* in Greek) is a basic Pauline metaphor for how we live our lives. He writes that we are buried with Christ in baptism so that "we too might walk in newness of life" (Romans 6:4), that we "walk by faith, not by sight" (2 Corinthians 5:7). But Paul was not the first Jewish teacher to use the metaphor.

> "I will walk with integrity of heart within my house..." (Psalm 101:2b)

> "Happy are those whose way is blameless, who walk in the law of the Lord." (Psalm 119:1)

> "...walk in the way of the good..." (Proverbs 2:20)

> "Walk while you have the light..." (John 12:35)

Walking is a basic activity. It's how we move through life. We normally take it for granted, until we sprain an ankle, break a hip, or are diagnosed with arthritis. But walking can be a wonderful means of centering and focus. It can be for us a living, moving metaphor of God's guidance through life: "...when you turn to the right or when you turn to the left, your ears shall hear a word behind you saying, 'This is the way; walk in it.'" (Isaiah 30:21)

Really paying attention to our walking centers us because walking itself requires that we know our physiological center of gravity, that we be balanced. In fact it requires a dynamic equilibrium between balance and off-balance. To walk we are balanced, step forward out of balance, move back to balance. This is not as easy as it might sound. Ask someone who has had a stroke, an illness, accident or wound and had to re-learn to walk. Walking is the physical manifestation of the "straining forward to what lies ahead," the "pressing on toward the goal" of which St. Paul wrote so eloquently. (Philippians 3:13–14) Walking is another of those physical icons of the spiritual life. We receive and give with the breath. We are balanced and out of balance in walking. Fleshly and spiritual life have these patterns and rhythms. In walking we can move forward because we trust the off-balance moment will return to balance. That is the path of progress in the spiritual life, as well.

If you find this discussion intriguing, I highly recommend you read the beloved Buddhist teacher, Thich Nhat Hanh's book *Peace Is Every Step* which includes both practices and teachings about walking that are relevant to all people of good will.[12] Here follow some suggestions for walking prayers. The kind of walking I have in mind is not the cardio-vascular exercise kind, as important as that, too, can be. As with everything of which you wish to make a spiritual practice or prayer, you must slow down. In the life of prayer haste or speed often mean inattention. In prayer, attention is crucial. So, first, just take a leisurely walk around your room or your home or your garden. Concentrate on your body as you move. Does your body "flow"? Do you feel the grating in your joints as those of us of a certain age often do? Does your body feel stiff and jerky? How does your walking affect your breath? Your heartbeat? Can you locate your physiological center of gravity? (Hint: it's usually much lower than most people think, for most of us about a few inches *below* the navel and deep within.) What is your walking telling you about the state

of your flesh? Your spirit? Slow down, move more deliberately, and become aware of your breath.

You can add any of your breath prayer practices (the coordination of word prayers to your breathing) to your walking.
Walking prayer is usually a practice for *walking*. I find it most
fruitful when I walk outside, but I am fortunate to live near a
very beautiful park with developed walking paths. You could
pray walking on an indoor track, perhaps even at the Mall, but
both would require the mental concentration necessary to
block out other stimuli. Begin your prayer walk with a short
invocation and by dedicating the walk to God. Then start
moving slowly and deliberately. Become aware of your breath.
Now coordinate a certain number of steps with your inhale
and exhale. This is the essence of the practice. You might try 3
steps to the inhale and 3 to the exhale, or 2 and 3. I am told
that a longer exhale (more steps on the exhale) is very good
physically as it pushes out more stale air and toxins.

The point of this sort of prayer walking is not so much to
notice the beauty of nature (if one is outside), although that
can be a wonderful exercise in gratitude, but to bring the
mind to focus in the body. Walk at a steady pace while
concentrating on finding a sustainable rhythm of breath to
steps. You might wish to do no more than that. Simply
coordinate breath and steps. That keeps you "out of your head"
and "into your body." (By the way, you can do this practice if
you use a cane or a walker.) Or you might want to experiment
with using a brief prayer or a few words of Scripture ("Lord
Jesus Christ, have mercy" or "O God, make speed to save me"
or "Jesus, Master"), coordinating the syllables of the words
with your steps. Walk, listening with the ear of your heart for
the voice which says, "This is the way; walk in it."

Preparing the Body for Contemplative Prayer/Waiting

In the chapters that follow we will be exploring *contemplatio*,
what Christian tradition variously calls "contemplative

prayer," "centering prayer," or "the prayer of quiet," and
which I think of as "waiting prayer." Such prayer requires
serious concentration. One of the most effective ways to
become more focused and concentrated is to "come back to the
body," and especially, to allow the body to relax so that the
mind and heart can be attentive. Explanations of contemplation will follow in chapters 7 and 8, and a method for waiting
prayer will be introduced in chapter 9. The exercises in this
chapter are intended for use as a prelude to any form of prayer,
but especially the prayer of waiting. We are, as Screwtape
knew, animals, and what we do with our bodies affects our
souls. If we are scattered and unfocused in mind and/or heart,
relaxing the body can lead to greater clarity of mind. (The
walking prayer mentioned above is particularly good in this
regard.)

If you are reasonably fit and can safely stretch up and down
from a standing position, here is an exercise routine to prepare
for other sorts of prayer.

1. Standing comfortably erect with your feet more or
    less under your shoulders, relax and drop your
    shoulders, let your stomach "pooch out," and your
    leg muscles relax.
2. Inhale gently through your nose and exhale through
    your mouth several times. You might want to exhale
    on the AH syllable as explained in the "heart" sec-
    tion above.
    (If doing numbers 3 and/or 4 make you dizzy,
    obviously you mustn't do them.)
3. Now stretch your arms over your head and "col-
    lapse" them down to the floor, letting the arms
    dangle down as far as is comfortable for you. No
    need to touch the floor. The point is to relax. Enjoy
    the looseness of your arms for a bit, but don't get
    light-headed and fall over!
4. Stand up slowly, concentrating on each vertebrae

aligning itself on the one beneath it. Imagine stacking one on the other as we did with blocks as children.

5. When you are standing up again, roll your neck around gently. Do it gently because most of us carry a lot of tension in our necks and you don't want to cause a strain. Gently try to touch the right ear to the right shoulder, then the left ear to the left shoulder. Scrunch up your shoulders, drawing them up toward your ears, then drop them and feel the muscles relax.

6. Engage in any gentle movement you perceive that your body needs to do to relax. Then take two or three "bottom to top" (see "breath" above) breaths and settle in the position in which you will continue your prayer.

It is also possible to stretch and relax the body for prayer from a sitting position or a wheelchair. If possible, choose a comfortable, but straight chair so that your spine can be erect. Do as many of the following as are possible for you, omitting any that cause discomfort. The point is to relax, not strain. "No pain, no gain" doesn't apply here.

1. Take two or three deep breaths, inhaling through the nose and exhaling through the mouth as in 2 above.

2. Extend and gently circle your right arm, then your left arm, then both arms.

3. Reach your right arm up as far as possible and wiggle your fingers. Now really s-t-r-e-t-c-h the arm up. Repeat with the left arm. Then sit for a moment with your hands at rest in your lap.

4. Put your right hand on your right shoulder and your left hand on your left shoulder. Gently circle the shoulders forward and then back. Then press back as

if you were trying to bring your shoulder blades together. Again, rest your hands in your lap for a moment.

5. (If this makes you dizzy, don't do it.) Spread your legs slightly and lean forward through your legs, allowing your arms to dangle as far down as is comfortable. Then "rise up", stacking your vertebra as in 4 above.

6. Engage in any gentle movement your body needs to relax. Then take two or three "bottom to top" (see "breath" above) breaths and continue with your prayer.

If you have the opportunity to experience therapeutic massage or to attend a body-work retreat, or to try a yoga class, why not give it a go? Many people have found that T'ai Chi most wonderfully combines movement with a deeply prayerful attitude. Trust the promise of Isaiah and listen for the heart voice that tells you where to go and what to try. (Isaiah 30:21) Trust the Voice, and do *not* do anything that feels wrong for you.

Conclusion

The purpose of this chapter is really quite modest. It is to remind you that you are body, and that if you want to bring your whole self to God in prayer, you need to bring your flesh along. Whether or not you adopt or even try out any of the exercises is less important than that you revisit your own attitude toward your wonderful, beautiful, incarnate body. In the biblical tradition something is good if it serves the purposes for which it was created by God. Your body is good not to the degree that it is beautiful in a women's magazine or sports magazine sort of way, not to the degree that it is young and thin or old and not-so-thin, but to the degree that you are "it," your body, which God made for you as a path to God.

As I was working on this book I ran across an article entitled "Awakening in the Body" in the Buddhist magazine, *Shambala Sun*. Its author, Phillip Moffitt, points out that the body is the ideal mirror for learning spiritual truths. In this regard, he says "...it is your direct experience or felt sense that is important, not your judgements about your body..."[13] As a Christian, I found the article very helpful because it reminded me that, because it is "fearfully and wonderfully made" by God, my flesh is one of my best teachers, especially when I attend non-judgementally to what it is telling me. No less a master of prayer than St. Bernard of Clairvaux (1090–1153) said as much when he wrote, "The flesh is clearly a good and faithful partner for a good spirit ... it surely benefits and is by no means a burden."[14] I hope that might be the message you carry away from this chapter.

For Further Reading and Exploration

J. Philip Newell, *Echo of the Soul: The Sacredness of the Human Body* (Harrisburg, PA: Morehouse Publishing, 2000).

Stephanie Paulsell, *Honoring the Body: Meditations on a Christian Practice* (San Francisco: Jossey-Bass, 2002).

Thomas Ryan, C.S.P., *Prayer of Heart and Body* (New York: Paulist Press, 1995).

———. (ed.) *Reclaiming the Body in Christian Spirituality* (New York: Paulist Press, 2004).

Flora Slosson Wuellner, *Prayer and Our Bodies* (Nashville, TN: The Upper Room, 1987).

David Steindl-Rast, O.S.B., *A Listening Heart: The Spirituality of Sacred Sensuousness* (revised edition) (New York: Crossroad, 1983/1999).

Chapter 7

Prayer: Toward a Cosmology

...you are my God, I seek you, my soul
thirsts for you; my flesh faints for you...
(Psalm 63:1)

In Christ "...all things in heaven and on
earth were created, things visible and
invisible..." (Colossians 1:16)

We believe in one God, the Father, the
Almighty, maker of heaven and earth and
of all that is, *seen and unseen*...
(Nicene Creed, italics mine)

The previous chapter consisted of exercises, fleshly things to
do to prepare the body for quiet prayer, things to do to pray in
and with the body, the whole self. This chapter will be a bit
more like chapters 1 and 4. It is more theoretical. It introduces
two basic trajectories that have characterized Christian prayer
and then, building on our anthropology, our view of the
human person (chapter 4), it provides some notes toward a
cosmology of Christian prayer. That is, the latter part of this
chapter sets forth one praying Christian's view of the world,

her "cosmology," her view of the universe. I introduce this material at this point in hopes that it will give us a common vocabulary or point of reference as we move into what may be the more unfamiliar territory of *contemplatio,* contemplative prayer. And, again, I hope it might encourage you to develop your own cosmological views.

There is an historical reason why in the twenty-first century a chapter like this might be necessary. Post-Enlightenment Christians (even if they are also post-modern!), especially but not exclusively Protestants, tend also to be "head" people, rational in preaching, worship and prayer. (This observation may not be true of Pentecostals, charismatics and some varieties of Orthodox Christians.) We are all not only heirs of the Reformation with its stripping down of personal and corporate spirituality, but, in America, even in the "Established Church" (Church of England/Anglican) southern colonies, heirs of Calvinist, Puritan ancestors. It was spiritually a great blessing when Quakers and Catholics came to Maryland and Pennsylvania, when later waves of immigration brought more Roman Catholic and Orthodox immigrants to America and, with them, a fuller expression of Christian faith. Throughout this book I have been making a case for embracing the full resources of the Christian prayer tradition.[1] In this chapter, I am suggesting we re-examine, if not re-embrace, aspects of a pre-Reformation, pre-Enlightenment cosmology or view of the world.

It seems very rudimentary to say it, but prayer must be rooted in belief in the *reality* of God, of God's presence and power among us, even if it is not seen, not measurable in scientific terms. Such a cosmology, such a world view comes into conflict not only with eighteenth-century rationalism, but with the scientific methods that have characterized our intellectual and educational formation in the West since the early nineteenth century. It's time to admit up front that the fundamental reality for Christian people is not only material, but also spiritual, an unseen world that is as real and as influential among us as the things that are palpable in the physical world. As there are different levels and aspects of the physical world, there are different levels and aspects of the spiritual world. This is my cosmological premise, and it is what Christians confess in the Nicene Creed.

I believe with all my heart, and by God's grace I have received experiences in prayer that "proved" (scientific word!) to me that God is an active and living presence, a reality not only in my life, but in the lives of many, many people. And concomitantly, there are much less benign realities in the spiritual realm.[2] I keep my vital connection to God and to God's level of reality through my life of prayer. I am hungry and thirsty for it, my soul "pants" for it like the Psalmist's hart longing for water. If that in some way doesn't describe your conviction, or if it doesn't in some way intrigue you, this chapter will be heavy going for you, and you might want to skip to the next one. However, if you aren't at least slightly interested in unseen realities, I do wonder why you are reading a book on prayer.

I am going to say more about this multi-dimensional reality in a moment. But first I want to introduce two basic trajectories of Christian prayer because I have a hunch that most of us are naturally drawn to one or the other of them, that whether we are active Christians or contemplative Christians, Marthas or Marys (see Luke 10:38–42) to use traditional (and not entirely accurate) designations, is related both to our basic personality type and to one of these trajectories of prayer.

The Cataphatic and Apophatic Trajectories

Following the work of Carl Jung, the Myers-Briggs Personality Inventory (a much used instrument in institutional and church circles) suggests that people are basically either extroverts or introverts, that they are re-charged or energized either by being in company (extroverts) or by withdrawing into solitude (introverts). It's not that extroverts hate solitude or that introverts hate other people, but that each draws primary energy from either being in company (extroverts) or alone (introverts). Several studies have suggested that extroverts, the sociable and talkers among us, gravitate toward active, communal worship and verbal forms of prayer and that introverts, the "shy silent types," tend to prefer quieter communal worship (or no communal worship) and listening or more contemplative forms of prayer. This is not a matter of right and wrong, but of preternatural disposition. I suggest, however, that just as it is important to eat a variety of foods to stay healthy (neither all green vegetables nor all saturated fat leads to health), practicing a variety of forms of prayer makes for the most vigorous and healthy spiritual life.

Bearing in mind this idea of extrovert/introvert, remember that historically, Christianity has described spirituality as either cataphatic or apophatic. In cataphatic spirituality or prayer, the major strand in Western Christianity, one approaches God through what one can know and experience. Cataphatic theology is sometimes called "positive theology" since it asserts that we can know God through God's self-revelation, especially as it comes to us in Jesus, although Paul suggests it is available through nature and in other ways. (See Romans 1:19–20.) We approach God through what we can know and experience of God and, on that basis, make positive statements about God. The difficulty, of course, is that what we know about God, we know metaphorically. We know "about" God, not, except in most unusual cases, God in God's essence. We know God "analogically." Cataphatic prayer, then, includes the more active forms of prayer. It seeks to express God's majesty and implore God's assistance. Simplistically, you might think of it as vocal prayer, or "eyes open" prayer.

Apophatic spirituality is most clearly articulated in the Orthodox tradition of the church. Dionysius the Areopagite (*ca.* 500) speaks of the soul's entry into "darkness beyond understanding," and points out the inadequacy of all human

attempts to describe God and God's majesty. All the language
we make about God is partial and inadequate. All assertions
about God must be true in only a limited or qualified sense.
Apophatic theology is therefore sometimes called "negative
theology," an unfortunate term in English because the connotation of "negative" is, well, negative. Perhaps it would be
marginally better to think of apophatic theology as the
theology of "absence," in that it begins with what God is not,
although "absence" as a term works only if one can take the
term as neutral rather than negative (rather like "nothingness"
in Buddhist literature). In apophatic spirituality one sets aside
all the "content" *about* God in order to be open *to* God. The
difficulty here is a practical one. In setting aside the content,
one has a *need* to experience God's *presence*. The danger is that
what we feel or experience takes on too much importance. In
prayer, our desire for and availability to God is the point, not
what we feel. Apophatic prayer, then, includes the more passive forms of prayer, what is popularly called "meditation,"
and more technically called *contemplatio*. You might want to
think of it as "listening prayer" or "eyes shut" prayer.

There is an historical reason why apophatic thinking characterizes the Eastern Church. That branch of the family has
always valued wisdom over intellect or scientific knowledge.
The Eastern church did not, after the early and unified period
of the Church, pursue philosophical formulations of theology;
they excelled in spiritual theology. Orthodoxy did not
experience (suffer from?) Enlightenment thought, and so never
lost the experience of the unseen world. In his *Life of Moses* for
example, Gregory of Nyssa's (*ca.* 330–395) insistence on the
utter unknowability of God (the "obscure but certain presence") is to safeguard the absolute transcendence of God
against misrepresentation by human analogy.[3] While the
Eastern church insists that it is not possible to know the
essence of God, we can, through the gift of God's self-
disclosure, experience God's "energies." (See, for example, the
writings of Gregory Palamas, *ca.* 1296–1359, especially *The*

Triads.[4]) Apophatic theology and spirituality is also in evidence in the Western church, for example in St. John of the Cross, in *The Cloud of Unknowing*, and in monastic theology, recently that of Thomas Merton.

These two trajectories of spiritual theology/prayer represent "the wisdom of God in its rich variety." (Ephesians 3:10) Both cataphatic and apophatic prayer reach out to God, but by different means. Cataphatic spirituality actively seeks God. I think its active quality makes it especially amenable to American Protestants. Apophatic prayer, through waiting and listening, prepares the person to *meet* God; it awaits God's invitation and visitation. Again, the way we find most congenial is often related either to personality type or to the traditions in which we have been formed in prayer. (For more on this, see the opening pages of the previous chapter.) Unfortunately, the Reformation traditions of the Western Church have seldom been introduced to the riches of the apophatic way in Christendom, and thus sometimes associate it with cults or "Eastern religions," by which Hinduism or Buddhism is apparently meant since, having arisen in Asia, Christianity *is* an Eastern religion. The forms of prayer which we shall consider in the remainder of this book tend toward the apophatic.

Toward a Cosmology for Prayer

A serious life of prayer requires that we consider the human person in ways that are not common in our culture. Chapter 4 of this book introduced that discussion. The more apophatic ("mysterious"?) forms of Christian prayer require that we think about the world, or the cosmos in similarly unconventional ways for our time. In what follows, I introduce three cosmological ideas: that reality is multi-dimensional, that the human person is multi-dimensional, that methods of *contemplatio* move us toward the deepest levels of both. I make this introduction by means of three well-known (but insufficiently understood) sayings of Jesus: "...no one can see the kingdom of God without being born from above/anew" (in Greek, *anothen*, John 3:3); "...the kingdom of God is within/in the midst (*entos,* in Greek) of you" (Luke 17:21); "If any want to become my followers, let them deny themselves and take up their cross and follow me." (Mark 8:34)

1. Reality is multi-dimensional

One of the basic tensions in the gospel of John is that of "above and below." The evangelist reflects the assumption of Jesus that the world has an "above" and a "below." Jesus uses the Greek word *anothen* which can be translated both "anew" and "from above" to powerful effect, especially in the often quoted "...unless one is born *anothen*, he cannot see the kingdom of God." (3:3, RSV) Writing in Greek John the Evangelist has poor Nicodomus go for the wrong translation as evidenced by his astonishment about re-entering the womb. (I taught Greek for a while, and my students and I can commiserate with him!) But Jesus' point is cosmological; the world has an above, a below, and a "kingdom of God" which apparently spans the two. There is "this world" (which in John's gospel is often a negative metaphor) and other worlds. A caution is in order: beware of thinking of these only as geographical places; they are also realms of experience.

Jesus' words in John 3 reflect an ancient, biblical, tripartite cosmology: the cosmos was understood to be heaven, earth, and "under the earth." Each part had layers as, for example, is reflected in Paul's reference to the "person in Christ" who "was caught up to the *third heaven*—whether in the body or out of the body I do not know..." (2 Corinthians 12:2, italics mine) In the following ominous verse, the Ephesian letter reflects the same cosmology: "For our struggle is not against enemies of blood and flesh, but against the rulers, against the authorities, against the cosmic powers of this present darkness, against the spiritual forces of evil in the heavenly places." (6:12) (If you read chapter 4 you will immediately hear the resonances of "body" and of "blood and flesh.")

Except perhaps in theoretical physics, this biblical, multi-dimensional reality is not our modern cosmology. We tend to view as real or extant only what can be perceived by the five physical senses, what can be quantified and measured. But there are other realms and realities. Theologian Marcus Borg describes them as *"actual* even though non material."[5] Borg notes that "... in addition to the visible material world disclosed to us by ordinary sense perception (and modern science), there is another level of reality, a second world of nonmaterial reality, charged with energy and power ... the 'other world' is not simply an article of belief, by an element of experience .... It is not merely believed in, but *known*."[6] If we cling to a modern and scientific cosmology, we absolutely shut ourselves off from a whole realm of reality, indeed, from much of what God wants to give us and to make available to us.

In her wonderful book, *The Wisdom Way of Knowing*, Cynthia Bourgeault explains the "energetic continuum" that runs through all creation, and is the instrument through which the divine life becomes perceptible to itself.[7] (In this her thought resembles that of the Greek Fathers.) She speaks of the divine consciousness surrounding us, which makes itself present by meaningful patterns of "coincidence."[8] Modern Christians interested in exploring the "unseen realities" can do no better than to begin with this clear work by a Canadian Anglican priest.

Just as there is a material realm of reality, there is a spiritual realm of reality. The material realm is rationally perceived; the spiritual realm is spiritually perceived. Paul wrote about this in 1 Corinthians 2. He spoke of a wisdom not "of this age or of the rulers of this age" which "God has revealed ... through the Spirit..." (1 Corinthians 2:6, 10) Paul speaks of "interpreting spiritual things to those who are spiritual," and explains that there are things that the unspiritual cannot understand "because they are spiritually discerned." (1 Corinthians 2:14)

It is a fascinating chapter, and it makes just this point: that there are spiritual realities, and that if you want to know about them, you must at least entertain the possibility that they exist, and be willing, as Borg suggests, to *experience* them.

The biblical worldview, and, indeed, Jesus Himself assumed the existence of this "other world," and that it exerted influence over this world. This has been the cosmological premise of all the great adventurers in prayer in the Christian tradition. One finds it clearly articulated in the writings of recent English classics like the works of Evelyn Underhill,[9] C.S. Lewis (especially in his trilogy of space novels), and in his friend, Charles Williams' novels, particularly in *Many Dimensions*. Shakespeare was right. There *is* more in heaven and earth than is normally dreamed of in "our philosophy."

2. The human person is multi-dimensional

Once upon a time the Pharisees, good and scholarly Second-Temple Jewish leaders whom modern Christians often wrongly think ill of since we see them as Jesus' interlocutors, asked Jesus about the Kingdom of God; in effect, about the substance of His preaching. Jesus responded that it wasn't observable (that is, it's not a material reality, known by the senses). "...the Kingdom of God is in the midst of/within [*entos*] you." (Luke 17:20–21) Here is another of those glorious words like *anothen* which can be translated correctly in two ways. (Greek students love this!) *Entos* can mean "among" or "in the midst of" and thus it suggests a communal reality, or it can mean "within," suggesting a psycho-spiritual reality.

We are more than we appear to be. We have an outer and an inner life. What goes on externally may or may not reflect what is going on internally. Spiritual maturity consists, among other things, in coherence between these two realms of life. We are "soul sick" when inner life and outer life aren't consistent, and that spiritual sickness is often manifested psychologically or somatically. The psychologist Carl Jung is reported to have said that he never saw anyone over fifty whose basic problem wasn't spiritual. I often wonder how many physicians, if they are tuned in, might say something similar.

Normally, we can be much more congruent than we are, indeed, much *more* than we are. But we are not encouraged by our culture, especially by our economic and political systems, to "go beyond," and particularly to "go within." If people begin to do their "internal work," they discover how shallow and, in fact, absurd are many of the shoulds, oughts, and must-haves that the media and advertising feed us. If we discover decay at the core, most of us are very likely to cut it out. The modern West suffers terribly from a great lack of interiority, an interiority we once had and lost. In the contemplative forms of Christian prayer we begin by seeking to recover this lost interiority, by "going within." Contemplative prayer can foster healthy alliances among prayer, theology, psychology and medicine.

Let me say a bit more about the self, what chapter 4 called "body." Nobody (!) much would disagree about the existence of an "inner life." But even at the level of the internal, the self can be true or false, "little s" self or "big S" Self. Thomas Merton has written with great clarity about this in chapters 5–10 of *New Seeds of Contemplation,*[10] and my discussion here owes much to him and to his interpreters, especially William Shannon.[11] Our "little s" self, what psychology calls the "ego,"[12] is shaped by parents, environment, profession, tribe/nation/culture, religion. It is the socialized self, often who the world tells us we are. But this may have little to do with our God-given identity, our "big S" Self. "Little s" self, ego, is the surface layer of inner identity, not the depth or totality of the Self God created us to be. Nor is it the aspect of personhood in which deep prayer occurs. And this is why Jesus said we must be born from above/anew. (John 3:3) We are someone other than the socialized, theologized, temporal and limited self out of which most of us operate. There is, deep in our hearts, another Source from which we are to draw and live Life, the life Jesus says He came to give in abundance. (John 10:10)

Contemplative prayer deals with "big S" Self, human transformation at the deepest levels. Writing in his book *Prayer of Heart and Body*, Thomas Ryan says, "The goal of the spiritual journey is to shift our point of identification from this conditioning which represents our personal ego, our self (small s), to our real Self, capital S, that is one with God, one with Spirit."[13] This process is what Christianity has traditionally called "conversion" or "repentance" (*metanoia*, literally, "turning around"). It is the process of turning from the false, "little s" self toward the true, "big S" Self. So conversion is more than a moral matter, more than a turn from bad to good action. It involves ontological change, a change in who we *are* which leads to a change in what we do.

Prayer as we shall be discussing it in the remainder of this book deals with this "kingdom within." (Luke 17:21) To enter into the deepest life of prayer, one must be convinced that Christ lives within, what Paul describes variously as "Christ in you the hope of glory" (Colossians 1:27) and the life "hidden with Christ in God." (Colossians 3:3) Paul asks us to think of God as a "place" or a "destination." The idea is metaphorical, and expressed with great clarity in Psalms 61, 62 and 63. In Psalm 61 God is the "rock that is higher than I," "the refuge" under whose wings the Psalmist shelters. In Psalm 62 God is the "rock" and "fortress" and "refuge." In Psalm 63 God is the "place" the Psalmist seeks "as in a dry and weary land where there is no water." (63:1) That Place is within. There is within us a Reality greater and more powerful than the individual. We are invited by Christ to wade in those waters. In the words of the Persian psychologist friend of Thomas Merton's, A. Reza Arasteh, prayer is the means of doing so; prayer is "the instrument of detaching one's self from social reality and relating one's self to human destiny."[14] Arasteh quotes M. Iqbal who says that prayer is "...a normal vital act by which the little island of our own personality suddenly discovers its situation in the large whole of life."[15]

Of all the figures known to the West, it is perhaps Jesus

who most clearly understood and lived this. It is what characterizes His life. In psychological terms we would say that for the True Self to blossom, the ego ("little s" self) must die. In the Garden of Gethsemane, we overhear Jesus praying, "not my will, but Thine be done." (Mark 14:36) It is the pattern of His life outlined in the great Christ Hymn which Paul quotes in Philippians 2:6–11. It is certainly what in Mark 8:34 Jesus taught His disciples they must do: deny self (not personhood, or body, but "little s" self), take up their cross (which, in His day no one did except to go and die; the cross wasn't a nice piece of jewelry or a life inconvenience like arthritis or a bad mother-in-law, but a terrible means of capital punishment whose deterrent was its horror), and follow Jesus (the technical term in Mark for doing as the teacher does). As Thomas Ryan notes, "If we want to know a new life centered on God, we must accept the death of the old life that is centered on self."[16] This is the great Easter drama of death to life. Practically it means that the death of the ego, the "little s" self, is resurrective. In fact, I think the very point of Incarnation is Resurrection. Contemplative methods of prayer lead us through this resurrective process.

3. *The methods of* contemplatio *move us toward and into the deepest levels of existence*

At this point a *caveat* is in order. It is very important to understand that when we move into the realm of mystery in Christian prayer we are moving into the realm of the very deepest aspects of human personality. This necessitates that we face our "stuff," all the psychic junk we have shoved down there as if it were a forgotten cellar. When the Christian opens the deep recesses of the heart by means of contemplative prayer, there is likely to be some psycho-spiritual fall out. One of the best things one can do as the True Self begins to emerge, as the process of resurrection takes hold in the heart, is to seek psychological help or short-term therapy should it be necessary. One thing is absolutely true about the stuff in the cellar;

it stays there until you actively cart it up and pitch out what is useless junk.

In *contemplatio*, then, we are stepping into the "universal stream." We are aligning our Selves with all human beings made in God's image, with everybody. The deepest longing of the human heart is to recover that image in ourselves, to "clean the mirror" so that we can reflect it to others. Deep prayer has a necessary byproduct, what traditional Christianity calls "evangelism," calling others to Christ and into the community of those in search of True Self. In the resurrective process others will be drawn to the One who is more and more clearly seen through us. We attract people to Him by becoming more who *we* are, more authentic, living more fully the freedom God gives us in Christ Jesus. This is precisely what Jesus did perfectly. He set ego, "little s" self aside. The Christ Hymn in Philippians 2:6–11 says He "emptied (*ekenosen* in Greek) himself." And being empty of self, He became a perfectly empty receptacle for God. It is a material as well as spiritual truth, that you can't fill what is already full. If we are "full of ourselves," there will be little room for the Divine Life within us. We, too, need to participate in a *kenotic* process. This is precisely what contemplative prayer in all its forms intends to help us do: empty out the "stuff" of self in order to be filled by God. In part this is volitional; we choose it. But it is also gift; we *are* chosen *for* it. And this is a great mystery about which I can say nothing at all.

Conclusion

In this chapter we have entertained the idea that our mode of prayer is intrinsically related to our basic personality, that the two traditional trajectories of Christian prayer are the cataphatic and the apophatic, and that the Christian cosmology embraces seen and unseen worlds. Not only the world, but the human person is external and internal, phenomenal and cosmic. The complexity of the world without is matched (if not exceeded) by the complexity of the world within. The human heart *is* a mystery, but as even King Nebuchadnezzar recognized, our God is "a revealer of mysteries" (Daniel 2:47) and more than that, a bestower of grace and gifts.

Contemplative prayer and its insights and consolations are manifestations of God's grace. They aren't something we earn by practicing some technique or other. As we have noted, Genesis records that from time to time, God came down to walk in the garden in the cool of the evening with Adam and Eve. God still longs to come to us and to dwell ("pitch his tent" according to John 1:14) with us. This is entirely at God's initiative. It is a gift of God's love to us. The best we can do is clean out our inner junk so that the place is ready for God. We can dispose ourselves toward God's arrival, open our deepest hearts to its possibility, but what happens is entirely God's choice and God's doing. Thomas Ryan is exactly correct that "True contemplation is not a psychological trick, but a theological grace. It can come to us only as a gift and not as a result of our persevering use of spiritual techniques. Grace, mercy, faith are not earned commodities, but constantly renewed gifts. The life of the Spirit in our hearts is renewed from moment to moment, directly and personally by God as an expression of God's love for us."[17] *Contemplatio*, to which we now turn, makes us aware of and disposes us to receive this great gift. Whether or not we do is, finally, God's business.

Perhaps the best summary of the ideas in this chapter is my poem "Fiery Impulse."

> There is a fiery impulse
> at the heart of prayer,
> not saying prayers,
> but primal prayer,
> the self's radical
> turning toward God
> in Whose incendiary gaze
> ego's dross is consumed.

The essence left
after the conflagration
wears only the garb of light,
a radiance that passes
from soul to soul.
Glimpsed, not taught,
it illuminates a dark world
with a searing love
that beckons, burns,
ignites a fiery impulse.

For Further Reading and Exploration
If you are interested in the basic spiritualities in Christendom,
you might find the volumes on Christian Spirituality in the
Crossroad Press "World Spirituality" series and Arthur Holder
(ed.) *The Blackwell Companion to Christian Spirituality* (Oxford:
Blackwell Publishing, 2005) very helpful. All these works
provide extensive bibliographies.

Two particularly clear and remarkably contemporary
introductions to Christian spiritual life and cosmology are
Evelyn Underhill's *Concerning the Inner Life* (Oxford: One
World, 2000, talks originally given to English clergy in 1926)
and *The Spiritual Life* (Harrisburg, PA: Morehouse, 1955, four
talks originally broadcast on BBC radio 1936).

Also of interest is Jonathan T. Pennington and Sean M.
McDonough (eds.), *Cosmology and New Testament Theology*
(London: T & T Clark, 2008).

Chapter 8

Prayer: Toward Contemplatio

For thus said the Lord God, the Holy One of Israel: in returning and rest you shall be saved; in quietness and trust shall be your strength. (Isaiah 30:15)

Introduction

When we speak of prayer, most people imagine some sort of conversation, "speaking with God." And, indeed, that is one sort of prayer, an important one which we considered in earlier chapters. At the outset of this book, we made the distinction between "saying prayers" and "praying," and in chapter 1 spoke of prayer as a "mode of being." In *Thoughts in Solitude* Thomas Merton wrote that prayer is "...not just a formula of words, or a series of desires springing up in the heart—it is the orientation of our whole body, mind and spirit to God in silence, attention, and adoration."[1] There are ways of prayer in the Christian tradition that foster this "orientation" and have more to do with listening than with talking, prayer that is primarily about "seeing" in the sense that St. John uses that term: understanding, but not discursive understanding, spiritual perception. There are forms of prayer that lead us to what Cynthia Bourgeault calls "wisdom ways of knowing."[2] A general term for these forms of prayer is "contemplative prayer."

Contemplative prayer is a little hard to talk about because it is more an attitude or a spiritual disposition toward life in general than a method to learn. Here is how Merton introduces contemplation:

> Contemplation is the highest expression of ... intel-lectual and spiritual life. It is that life itself, fully awake, fully active, fully aware that it is alive. It is spiritual wonder. It is spontaneous awe at the sacred-ness of life, of being. It is gratitude for life, for awareness and for being. It is a vivid realization of the fact that life and being in us proceed from an invisible, transcendent and infinitely abundant Source. Con-templation is, above all, awareness of the reality of that Source.[3]

I think that the best we can do is to dance around an understanding of this aspect of the life of prayer. And this is as it should be because at some level, contemplation comes to us as a gift. Perhaps the fourteenth-century English work *The Cloud of Unknowing*, which is the root work in English on contemplative prayer, says it best by saying simply, "In itself, prayer is nothing else than a devout setting of our will in the direction of God..."[4] Contemplative prayer is "a simple steadfast intention reaching out towards God."[5]

The Contemplative Way Exemplified in Isaiah 30:15

It has occurred to me that all the aspects of the alternative way of being in the world that *contemplatio* encapsulates appear in Isaiah 30:15: "*For thus said the Lord* God, the Holy One of Israel: in *returning* and *rest* you shall *be saved;* in *quietness* and *trust shall be* your *strength*." (Italics mine.) It begins with the familiar, prophetic messenger formula, "Thus said the Lord," reminding us that what follows is a command of God, a direct word of God to us. "Returning" suggests there was something we already had, something lost or misplaced, an original intention gone astray. We must go back to something that was there before.

But this is not exactly a command to "do" something. "Rest" suggests something other than our usual hurry and activity. "Rest" is a way of speaking about inactivity, leisure, stillness. It is in this doubling back and inactivity that we will *be saved.* Note the passive voice. This is something that is done to us, not something we do. As we have noted, in Scripture the use of the passive voice, the Divine Passive, is a way of indicating that the actor is God. God is going to "save" us when we return to rest. Of course theologically we Christians know that salvation is something we cannot do for ourselves, and that, in Jesus, God has provided for our salvation. But it is helpful to know that in Greek the word for "save" and for "heal" is the same (*sozo*). God acts to liberate and rescue us, but also to bring us wholeness, health, healing. It will be done for us through our receptivity to it in our returning, rest, quietness and trust. This aspect of "saved" is not about talk or doing, but about listening and being. "Quietness" comes from *quietare* "to set free," "to calm." In Isaiah 30:15, tranquillity, peace and relaxation lead to strength. So does "trust," which implies dependence upon someone else. We "trust in" someone or something, in the case of contemplation, in the God of "shall be."

The contemplative way summarized in this verse from Isaiah is about returning to something once possessed, about rest or leisure, about quietness or listening, about "trust in," allowing ourselves to *be* "saved," liberated and/or healed. Isaiah 30:15 gives us a hard assignment: to accept a gift which we do nothing to deserve. It is about "strength," but strength understood very differently from its common connotations of force or physical power. Contemplative strength is about a different kind of power than we normally encounter. It is the

"power made perfect in weakness" of which the Lord spoke to
St. Paul. (2 Corinthians 12:9) Contemplative strength is the
strength of yielding to what God wants to do for us. It takes a
very strong person to accept an extravagant gift. We see Jesus
do exactly this when He accepts the gift of the anointing
woman. (Mark 14:3–9) *Contemplatio* is about the strength of
voluntary surrender.

Contemplation: Etymology and "Dancing Around Description"

The word "contemplation" comes from the Latin *con*, "with,"
and *templum*, "temple." The *templum* was originally the space
marked out for the observation of auguries. In the Roman
world, the *templum* was the place were augurs or diviners read
omens seen in the stars or in the entrails of animals. Animals
were ritually killed, and the pattern of their entrails inter-
preted. By much less grisly comparison, the temple is the
place where we read the intentions of God. Etymologically,
then, contemplation is the sacred space marked out for the
consideration of "inside things." Thus Thomas Ryan in his
book *Prayer of Heart and Body* calls it "the actual *looking* at the
insides of reality."[6]

To pray contemplatively is to attend to the "insides of
reality." To contemplate something is to view it with careful
attention. It has come to mean concentration on the spiritual
life or perhaps even mystical awareness of and communication
with God. As such contemplation in the many, many forms it
can take usually involves some combination of the following:
solitude, silence, open-ness, and focus or centered-ness. But it
involves something that many of us would prefer to avoid:
waiting, not ordinary waiting, to be sure, waiting in hope and
expectancy. It is the psychological condition of Advent waiting, or more dramatically, the child's waiting for Christmas,
the newly married couple for the wedding night, the parents
for the birth of their child. Contemplation involves

expectancy, but waiting none the less, and this is because it is gift and not achievement or accomplishment.

Jesus Himself commands us to "wait, watch, pray." Over and over again at the end of His life, Jesus tells His disciples "keep alert" or "watch." (See Mark 13:5, 9, 23, 33.) The word *blepete* is variously translated "be alert" or "beware." It is the imperative form of "see, look consider." It frequently occurs with the word translated "watch," *agrupneite* imperative of *agrupneo*, "chase sleep away," "be watchful." The word implies alertness, but not activity. These word pairs occur in Jesus' final long teaching, Mark 13, and in His last request to the disciples in Gethsemane. (Mark 14:34, 37, 38)

"Watch and pray" are Jesus' words to us. (Mark 14:38) But they are part of a very ancient biblical tradition of "seeing" and "waiting," often in silence and darkness.

> Wait for the Lord; be strong, and let your heart take courage; wait for the Lord! (Psalm 27:14)

> Be still before the Lord, and wait patiently for him. (Psalm 37:7)

> For God alone my soul waits in silence. (Psalm 62:1)

> I wait for the Lord, my soul waits, and in his word I hope;
> my soul waits for the Lord more than those who watch for the morning,
> more than those who watch for the morning. (Psalm 130:5)

> O Lord, we wait for you; your name and your renown are the soul's desire.
> My soul yearns for you in the night, my spirit within me earnestly seeks you. (Isaiah 26:8b–9a)

This kind of waiting comes with a promise: "those who wait for the Lord shall renew their strength,/they shall mount up with wings like eagles/they shall run and not be weary/they shall walk and not faint." (Isaiah 40:31)

This sort of waiting was well known in the Medieval courts of Europe where there were ladies and gentlemen "in waiting." Their job was to await the desires of the royalty, to be ready to do their will. This is our position *vis-à-vis* God in contemplative prayer. We await God's summons. "Wait" contains another interesting suggestion. The English word comes from an old high German word, *wahta*, which means "a guard." The spiritual idea of guarding is very positive. We Christians are guarding the knowledge of the positive outcome of history that we await. St. Paul says we "wait for the revealing of our Lord Jesus Christ." (1 Corinthians 1:7) Contemplative prayer teaches us to wait for Christ's revelation in history (the public/communal sphere of life) but also in our own hearts (the private/individual sphere of life). To wait is to be ready for what is coming, to remain in expectation of it. This attitude is part of the point of the parable of the wise and foolish virgins who had to wait, but had work to do before they settled down to their waiting. (See Matthew 25:1–13 which ends "Keep awake, therefore...") To wait, then, is to serve, or to visit a superior to pay respects or ask a favor. I hope you will revisit and consider all of all these interesting notions about waiting when I introduce a method for the prayer of waiting in the next chapter.

As you now know from having gotten this far in the book, I believe that prayer is always a response to the prior activity of God. God is always seeking us out. The paradigmatic biblical narratives are Genesis 3:8ff in which God comes down to walk with Adam and Eve in the Garden of Eden and Luke 15:1–32, the story of the prodigal son which is really the story of the seeking father. Many of Jesus' parables of the Kingdom are stories of seeking (lost sheep, lost coins, lost children) and finding with great joy. Jesus can tell us to ask and seek and knock because He knows that God is there waiting to respond. (Matthew 7:7–11) We wait on God, but oh how much more seriously God has been waiting on us! According to Thomas Merton, contemplation is "the response to a call: a call from Him Who has no voice, and yet Who speaks in everything that is, and Who, most of all, speaks in the depths of our own being: for we ourselves are words of his."[7]

The premise of contemplative prayer, indeed, of the whole Christian life is that in every situation the love of God is seeking us for good. Indeed in *Contemplative Christianity* Aelred Graham says that faith, itself is "an awareness beyond sense-perception that the power behind the universe is not neutral, but gracious and beneficent."[8] Our *experience* of the very deepest response to God's seeking initiative is where contemplative prayer begins. Thomas Merton says "It is not we who choose to awaken ourselves, but God Who chooses to awaken us."[9]

Contemplative prayer, then, involves waking up, aliveness, gratitude. It is not a method to be mastered or a doctrine to be learned. In fact it has little to do with the intellectual function. It is not the *cogito ergo sum* of Descartes. In fact, thinking can get in the way of this sort of prayer in which the intuitive function of the human person is more active than reason. Contemplative prayer understands "thinking with the heart" of which we spoke in chapter 4. As the *Cloud of Unknowing* says God "may be loved but not thought."[10] Nor is contemplative prayer a function of the external self; it is not really something we "do." Therefore it is not "saying prayers" or the liturgical life, though both of those can feed it if it exists or stimulate the desire for it if it does not yet exist. Contemplative prayer can't really be taught. It is the personalized response of an individual soul whom God calls as He calls no one else. It has to do with the private language of love by means of which each of us, very individually, communicates with God. We "open into" contemplative prayer, return to its rest, quietness and trust, accept it as a gift from God, relax into what it is for each

of us and agree to go where it takes us. We become like
Abram, who at 75 was given promises and told by God to
"go" but not given the destination. (Genesis 12:1–3) My poem
"Abram at Haran" serves as a good summary to this point.

> He was seventy-five years old
> and God's first word to him
> was "Go."
>
> I think of Abram
> when my plans go awry,
> when happenstance
>
> pries my fingers loose
> from the grasping illusion
> of control over life.
>
> "Go," God said to Abram,
> giving no address,
> disclosing no destination.
>
> Taking an unruly family,
> trusting God to show the way,
> Abram went.
>
> On that wild journey
> he, too, had fingers pried loose,
> heard Sarai laugh, learned
>
> the blessing comes
> in the going
> and the letting go.

It goes without saying, then, that contemplative prayer
concerns the interior life. It is an awareness or an experience of
God in the interior life, and thus it has to do with our identity

as persons in Christ. To use a New Testament phrase that I hope is familiar, contemplative prayer is about opening up to the God who "dwells with you and will be in you." (John 14:17) Contemplative prayer is about coming to know God, to experience God's reality, as opposed to knowing things *about* God. Again, few people have articulated this as well as Thomas Merton, who wrote, "There exists some point at which I can meet God in a real and experimental contact with His infinite actuality . . . . Within myself is a metaphorical apex of existence at which I am held in being by my Creator."[11] As such, *contemplatio* is a gift, not an achievement. It is something God, in infinite generosity gives us, the ability to know our lives in the Divine Life, in Paul's words "Christ in us, the hope of glory." (Colossians 1:27) ". . . contemplation is the sudden gift of awareness, an awakening to the Real within all that is real. A vivid awareness of infinite Being at the roots of our own limited being. An awareness of our contingent reality as received, as a present from God, as a free gift of love."[12]

To pray contemplatively is to experience the all-pervasive presence of Christ in ourselves and in the world around us. In his book *Silent Music: The Science of Meditation,* William Johnston says that "Christian contemplation is the answer to a call and the response to a vision." It "begins with the belief, the conviction, the experience of God's love for me . . . Christian contemplation is the experience of being loved and of loving at the most profound level of psychic life and of spirit."[13] This is why the language of the mystics is so often the language of erotic love. Our life with God is a love story, a passionate and embodied love story. Contemplative prayer is a romance in which we are, first, the object of Another's Love.

Perhaps you are becoming weary of my "dancing around" descriptions of *contemplatio.* The task of describing contemplation is a difficult one because contemplative prayer is not one thing, but many things. It is not some esoteric practice available only to those who go off to the woods to wear robes, eat weeds, and stare into space all day. It is the ordinary Christian's whole-hearted response to God's love for him or her in Jesus Christ, the awareness of that love at the core of being itself. To pray contemplatively is to put ourselves in an environment, a state or a space whereby we can best experience this love. Contemplation is listening with the whole of our being for the voice of the Beloved, waiting, living in hopeful expectancy that the Beloved will, indeed, come to us.

Aspects of the "Methods" of Contemplative Prayer

> Contemplative prayer is a deep and simplified spiritual activity in which the mind and will rest in a unified and simple concentration upon God, turned to Him, intent upon Him and absorbed in His own light, with a simple gaze which is perfect adoration because it silently tells God that ... He alone is important to us, He alone is our desire and our life, and nothing else can give us any joy.[14]

This quotation from Thomas Merton begins to suggest something of the methodologies of contemplative prayer. The metaphor is of sight; the environment is one of silence. We gaze on God, concentrate on God, desire God alone; this is the essence of the contemplative way. There are many forms of contemplative prayer. What they have in common is a turning away from all that is not God, especially from the noisy, exterior, and goal-oriented, and turning inward or God-ward, focusing on and centering in God's reality. "...in this inward urge you have no real thought for anything less than God, and ... your desire is steadily and simply turned toward him."[15] "Return to me with all your heart" (Joel 2:12) is a command and an invitation.

As Isaiah 30:15 suggests, we receive the gift of contemplation; we don't earn it or achieve it by our own activity, so we can't really learn it like a technique. But there are things that we can do to dispose ourselves to receive the gift. The conditions in which we open ourselves to receive the gift of contemplation, which is nothing more than the gift of God Himself, involve silence, solitude, focus, and a return to "being," that is, open-ness, or pure passivity, or however we would describe the opposite of doing or achieving. It is important to bear in mind that these are not necessarily exterior conditions, so much as states in the interior life. (See the previous chapter.) It is possible, although perhaps not easy, to maintain an inner quietude and detachment while driving the kids to soccer practice or dealing with the plumber! If our intention is to be open to God, we are, no matter what else is going on.

In the following chapter I am going to introduce one of the many forms or methods of contemplative prayer. I call it "the prayer of waiting," but you may have encountered it as some form of "transcendental meditation," or "centering prayer," or "the prayer of quiet." As all of these methods require some measure of silence, solitude, focus and passivity, I close this chapter with brief remarks on each of these conditions for contemplative prayer.

1. *Silence*[16]

A *New Yorker* cartoon (by "BEK") which I have never forgotten depicts a man talking on the telephone. The caption reads, "I'm not trying to say anything—I'm just talking." That, alas, is true of 95 percent of our use of language. Nobody I know of will argue with you if you say, "we live in a polluted environment." But I have come to think that the most dangerous pollutant in our society is not bad air or dirty water, but noise. We are a people who have lost our interiority, because we have become a people who cannot bear silence. And people who cannot bear silence have a very difficult time hearing God. The average person wakes up to a radio alarm clock, goes into the kitchen and turns on the radio or television while making the coffee, listens to the radio while showering or shaving in the bathroom. In the car on the way to work, she turns on the radio or puts in a CD. In the bus on the way to work, he listens to an MP3 player. At work there is "muzak" and the noise of the workplace. The same noise is generated on the way home, where one turns on the television and leaves it on until bedtime. When did God (or anybody else!) have an opportunity to "get a word in edgewise", as my mother used to say? What are we so afraid of that we cannot be in silence? I think that generation of so much noise (and activity) is a symptom of fear. A parallel is the endless stream of chatter, the mindless production of words which has completely devalued language so much that in some circles "bad" connotes "really good."

The Bible provides us with a very different set of imperatives. Some important ones include "Be still before the Lord, and wait patiently" (Psalm 37:7) and "Be still and know that I am God." (Psalm 46:10) The Bible is quite explicit about the matter of noise. We cannot experience God if our ears are full and our tongues are constantly in motion. Isaac of Nineveh wrote that "Many are avidly seeking, but they alone find who remain ... in silence ... If you love truth, be a lover of silence. Silence like the sunlight will illuminate you in God and will deliver you from the phantoms of ignorance. Silence will unite you to God..."[17]

The quest for exterior silence is difficult enough for most of us. But it is only the beginning and the easy part. If we have the courage to turn off all our technological distractions and toys and can find a "quiet corner," we will still have our interior din to cope with. Kallistos Ware writes that true silence "is not merely a cessation of sound, a pause between words, but an attitude of openness, receptivity, of attentive waiting upon God .... True silence is nothing else than God-awareness."[18] For many of us the real noise problem is interior noise, the running commentary we have going in our heads all the time. I once heard a Buddhist teacher call this "monkey mind," and it seemed just right. To pray contemplatively we are going to have to find and use the "off" switch to this interior noise. Happily, some suggestions will follow in the next chapter.

2. *Solitude*

Just as silence isn't absence of external noise, solitude is not necessarily being physically isolated or alone. Many of us live in families or religious communities. Most of us work in densely populated environments. But we can still develop the ability to dwell in what the early monastics called "the cave of the heart," no matter where we are. We can carry our solitude and quietude with us. Silence and solitude go hand in hand. One reason we make noise is to convince ourselves we are not alone. Far too many people are afraid of themselves. From my point of view, the greatest social danger we face is not terrorism, but our lack of interiority. As a result of it, we can't see ourselves as others see us, can't understand the responses to us and have no resources to deal with negative ones and to be gracious about positive ones. We cope by incessant chatter.

Let us be clear that contemplation does not seek solitude to be anti-social. We don't go away just to escape the nasty people in our lives. That wouldn't do us any good because we would still be taking the nastiest person with us ... our ego, our "little s" self. (See the previous chapter.) Thomas Merton says "We do not go ... to escape people but to learn to find them..."[19] To seek solitude to escape others is doomed to failure because it is self-oriented. It carries the world along "as an implicit standard of comparison. The result would be nothing but self-contemplation, and self-comparison with the negative standard ... one had abandoned."[20] "Isolation in the self, inability to go out of oneself to others, would mean incapacity for any form of self-transcendence."[21] And self-transcendence is a primary goal of Christian life. *Contemplatio* urges us not to be self, but to be God-oriented. And anything that is God-focused, by our Lord's definition, passes through the neighborhood of other people. Of the true contemplative, the anonymous fourteenth-century writer of *The Cloud of Unknowing* said "...when the soul is wholly turned to God all people are equally dear ... for he feels no other cause for loving God than God himself. So all are loved simply and sincerely, for God's sake as well as his own."[22]

True solitude has to do with an opening in the soul, a turning to the deepest mystery of God within our hearts. And, ironically, when we do that, we find our commonality with others, true *koinonia*. Only in solitude can I discover my identity in God. And only when I have discovered that identity, only when I have "known myself" (to use the phrase of Plato and of Augustine) *in* God, am I ready to be in relationship to others. One reason so many of our relationships are so unfulfilling, and so brittle and easily broken, is that we are using them to fill our own emptiness. People use others to gain an identity and validity that, in actuality, only comes from God. In order to be able to be deeply related to others, we must first learn to live with ourselves, to know ourselves as the locus of God's life.

3. Focus

Multi-tasking may be a good thing if you are a computer, but it is a terrible thing in the life of prayer. Like Martha of Bethany, most of us have to learn from the Lord that "one thing only is necessary." (Luke 10:42) Or perhaps we need to say one thing at a time. Doing three or four (or five or six!) things simultaneously mostly means we are doing none of them with attention. Most of us need to re-learn to be present where we are and to be attentive to the "now" moment. I sometimes wonder if this isn't part of what Jesus meant when He told us we must become like little children. (Mark 10:13–16) Children who haven't been ruined by being overly entertained are present where they are and able really to focus. Watch children at play in a sand box or on the beach and you will see REAL focus and concentration.

Focus has to do with living fully in the present moment,

which is the only one we have. And focus is what brings tranquillity. When we are agitated about many things, we don't have peace of heart. When we are simply doing what we're doing, life is so much easier, less complex and stressful. One means of lowering stress, and a very simple means of re-focusing, is paying attention to the breath, perhaps by using the techniques I described in chapters 4 and 6. I will have a good deal more to say about focus in the next chapter.

4. Passivity

Contemplation is as much something that happens to us as something we do. God seeks us and gives us this gift of God's self. *The Cloud of Unknowing* advises, "...let this thing deal with you, and lead you as it will. Let it be active, and you be passive. Watch it if you like, but let it alone."[23] One liberating lesson of silence and solitude is that the world can go on without us. It is God and not my efforts that makes the sun rise and set. Truly to understand this is a great relief, a matter of immense liberation. But as Merton notes, "The absence of activity in contemplative prayer is only apparent. Below the surface, the mind and will are drawn into the orbit of an activity that is deep and intense and supernatural, and which overflows into our whole being and brings forth incalculable fruits."[24]

I recently spent a quiet morning with the women clergy in my town. We met, had a cup of coffee, and then were quiet together for two hours. Some of us read, some prayed, some "just sat." When we spoke briefly about the experience before our closing prayer, many confessed they had told their secretaries they were going to a program, because otherwise it seemed they were "doing nothing." Even (especially?) the clergy feel guilty about "returning and rest." I suspect most people equate interior passivity with "nothing." (If so, it is the "populated" nothing of which Buddhism speaks.) But contemplation is far from a waste of time. It may be the most important thing we don't do!

Creative waiting, passivity are not part of our culture. We
are raised to be "doers." And this isn't a bad thing. It means we
have done a lot of good (and, to be honest, great evil, as well).
But overactivity can protect us from ourselves and be a hindrance to the deepest kind of prayer that we can experience.
Sometimes "nothing" is the right thing to "do." Sometimes we
need to let things come to us, rather than rushing to them.
Practically this approach works really well with children and
animals, both, I think dear to God. It may, therefore, also work
well with God! Sometimes acting is the wrong thing to do.
Sometimes the best thing to do is just sit. I learned this from
my Dad who loved to sit on the porch at night. He didn't read
or talk or listen to the radio. He just sat on the porch listening
to the night sounds (and sometime my talkative mother!). Dad
was a natural contemplative, taciturn and observant, and when
he said something, it was worth hearing.

Conclusion

I close this rather rambling chapter on contemplation with a
brief story from the desert Christians of the fourth century,
men and women who had gone out into the desert precisely to
seek God contemplatively. The account summarizes what I
have been trying to say in this chapter.

> A brother asked one of the elders: What good thing
> shall I do, and have life thereby? The old man replied:
> God alone knows what is good. However, I have heard
> it said that someone inquired of Father Abbot Nisteros
> the great, the friend of Abbot Anthony, asking: What
> good work shall I do? And that he replied: Not all
> works are alike. For Scripture says that Abraham was
> hospitable and God was with him. Elias loved solitary
> prayer, and God was with him. And David was hum-
> ble, and God was with him. Therefore, whatever you
> see your soul to desire according to God, do that thing,
> and you shall keep your heart safe.[25]

For most of us the contemplative way will be marked out by someone who has walked it ahead of us, an "older one" leading a "younger one." Merton wrote, "I do not think contemplation can be taught, but certainly an aptitude for it can be awakened." That aptitude, Merton felt, was awakened by being with a real contemplative: ". . .it is a question of showing . . . in a mysterious way by example how to proceed. Not by the example of doing, but the example of being. . ."[26] The impulse toward contemplation will have great respect for personal vocation and call. There is no arbitrary uniformity in contemplative prayer. Paradoxically, we find a teacher, and we find our own way. *Contemplatio* has to do with interior sight, with what Ephesians calls having the "eyes of the heart enlightened." (Ephesians 1:18) Contemplation gives us understanding of interior realities. And it requires focus, the "one thing" of the soul's desire. The heart will come to rest in God when it has found and is pursuing the primary reason for its existence, its great desire, when it hears the word God speaks deep within. We listen for that word in silence, solitude, with focus and passivity. We find it in and receive from it returning, rest, quietness, confidence and a strength that nothing in this world can stand against. In the next chapter, I shall suggest a way to dispose ourselves in that direction.

For Further Reading and Study

Cynthia Bourgeault, *The Wisdom Way of Knowing* (San Francisco: Jossey-Bass, 2003).

N.A., *The Cloud of Unknowing* (New York: Penguin, 1961/71).

Anthony de Mello, the section of *Sadhana* entitled "Awareness and Contemplation."

Thomas Merton, O.C.S.O., *Contemplative Prayer* (New York: Doubleday/Image, 1971).

Thomas Merton, O.C.S.O., *New Seeds of Contemplation* (New York: New Directions, 1961).

Chapter 9

Praying Contemplatively: The Prayer of Waiting

Wait for the Lord; be strong, and let your heart take courage; wait for the Lord!
(Psalm 27:14)

For God alone my soul waits in silence...
(Psalm 62:1a)

O God, you are my God, I seek you, my soul thirsts for you;
my flesh faints for you, as in a dry and weary land where there is no water. (Psalm 63:1)

O Lord, be gracious to us; we wait for you.
(Isaiah 33:2a)

Introduction

I have sought to introduce the three basic trajectories of prayer in the Christian tradition. *Oratio*, is the prayer of speech, that movement of the heart that leads one to speak with God in one's own words, or those of the Psalmist, or of a prayer book, or another's voiced prayers. *Meditatio* is the prayer of thought, that movement of the heart that ponders the mysteries of Scripture, of creation, of the liturgy, of the Divine Self. Finally, we come to *contemplatio*, the prayer of waiting, the quieting of the heart to rest in joy in the presence of God. There are many ways of prayer in each of these categories, and this is no less true of *contemplatio* than of *oratio* and *meditatio*, which we have examined earlier. In fact, as noted earlier, both *lectio divina* and the Jesus Prayer can lead one into *contemplatio*.

The common word used for *contemplatio* is "meditation," and, I dare say, the practice is often associated with Zen meditation or Transcendental Meditation or, in Christian circles, with "Centering Prayer," the method of prayer described in the Western church in the fourteenth-century work *The Cloud of Unknowing*, popularly introduced by English Benedictine, John Main, and to Americans by Thomas Merton, and widely taught by his brother Cistercian monks Fr. Thomas Keating and Dom Basil Pennington. Let me say at the outset that if you have an opportunity to take a Centering Prayer workshop, I hope you will do so. "Contemplative Outreach," the organization associated with Fr. Keating, offers many workshops and retreats. You will find their teachers/ leaders well equipped to lead you in this sort of prayer. And they can help you locate other people in your area who meet to pray together in this way.[1]

Several cultural observers have noted that meditation as a form of prayer was popularized especially in the U.S.A. after the Second World War and the Vietnam War, as people who had encountered various forms of "Eastern" prayer brought them home. Certainly the rise of Zen meditation centers in America seems to follow this pattern.[2] But long before the 1960s, Western Christians and especially monastics serving in Asia had encountered and begun to dialogue with Asian religious practitioners about prayer. The popularity of Anthony de Mello, S.J.'s work and those of William Johnston, S.J.,[3] are part of the fruit of that dialogue, as are the publications that have arisen from the work of the Monastic Inter-religious Dialogue group. So pervasive was the phenomenon of Western persons practicing various forms of Buddhism that a scholarly society, the Society for Buddhist Christian Studies, arose in the 1980s to facilitate interchange between the religions. A number of Buddhist-Christian dialogues have been held.[4] And this is to note only Buddhist-Christian conversation, not Hindu-Christian which is much older.[5] Perhaps for this reason, on October 15, 1989 (ironically the feast of St. Teresa of Jesus) the Congregation for the Doctrine of the Faith of the Roman Catholic Church promulgated the cautionary "Letter to the Bishops of the Catholic Church on Some Aspects of Christian Meditation."

What I want to point out is that when we begin to explore contemplative prayer, whether or not we are personally engaged in it, we necessarily do so in the context of cross-religious dialogue and all the baggage pro and con that comes with it. The phenomenon of *contemplatio* is not confined to Christianity. However, what I present in this chapter is a basic form of meditation for Christians. A less esoteric setting for learning about *contemplatio* than the one I experienced is hard to imagine. I was taught to "meditate" in the spring of 1976 in one of a number of Lenten course offerings at an Episcopal parish church. The teacher was a newly minted (and pregnant as I recall?) Episcopal parish priest, and we met in a (slightly musty) basement choir room. The setting was hardly threatening! What I learned in that very ordinary way proved extraordinary for me, and it is not too dramatic to say it revolutionized my understanding of prayer and my own life of prayer.

Before providing some theological and biblical foundations and teaching a method for this sort of prayer, let me tell you why I call it "the prayer of waiting." It is precisely because, as I have just noted, rightly or wrongly, "meditation" is often associated in the popular mind with non-Christian methods of prayer. "Centering Prayer" is the term used by a particular contemplative movement in contemporary Christianity, and while I once (at a Buddhist-Christian gathering) received instruction from Fr. Thomas Keating and very much admire his work, I am not technically associated with that movement. When I think about what characterizes the form of *contemplatio* that I know best it is, very simply, waiting. We prepare ourselves for God's arrival and wait. Over and over again the Psalmist and the prophets speak of "waiting for God." And so I like to call this way of praying "the prayer of waiting." (You might want to read the section on waiting in the previous chapter if you skipped it.)

Theological and Scriptural Foundations

Because this form of prayer is often narrowly and wrongly associated with non-Christian religions, before we learn the method, let us ground ourselves in our own theological and scriptural traditions, something I tried to do in the previous chapter. The prayer of waiting is a non-verbal prayer of awareness. As opposed to "saying prayers to" or "speaking to" a God "out there," the prayer of waiting helps us to become aware of God within. This, in actual practice, is the individual, spiritual essence of "Emmanuel," "God with us." (Matthew 1:23, 28:20; Isaiah 7:14) Clearly, its theological assumption is the omnipresence of God, that God is everywhere all the time. Psalm 37:7a perfectly describes this prayer: "Be still before the Lord, and wait patiently for him..." There are any number of ways to characterize this sort of prayer, but let me do so with four metaphorical participles: inviting, listening, beholding, loving.

The prayer of waiting is a radical invitation. In practicing (another important participle about which more will be said) this sort of prayer I am both asking God to come and asking the God who is already present to become manifest, to allow me to be aware of the Divine Presence. The prayer of waiting is Paul's prayer *Marana tha*, "Our Lord, come!" writ large in the human heart. (1 Corinthians 16:22) It is the "Search me, O

God, and know my heart; test me and know my thoughts" of
the Psalmist. (Psalm 139:23) I am not speaking of Quietism, a
teaching proposed by Miguel de Molinos and condemned by
the Roman Catholic Church in 1687, that one can "cause"
mystical experiences by quieting the senses.[6] I may desire
contemplatio, and I may request it, but I cannot cause it to
happen. As with all invitations, I issue it and wait for the
response. Or, perhaps more accurately, God offers me an
invitation and awaits my response.

The prayer of waiting is also the listening side of prayer.
We have noted (perhaps too frequently!) that prayer is often
understood as a conversation with God. If so, this is the
"listening" side of the conversation, the side of conversation
that few of us are good at either with our friends or with God:
stilling our interior noise, then accurately, openly and lovingly
receiving the word of the other—*not* thinking about or preparing our own response, just listening. The prayer of waiting
creates an empty space for God to fill. It creates an interior
silence into which the Word can be spoken, which is important because John's Jesus states categorically, "Whoever is
from God hears the words of God." (John 8:47) And, not to
put too fine a point on it, God declares at the Transfiguration
of Jesus, "This is my Son, the Beloved; listen to him!" (Mark
9:7) Mark's gospel has a remarkable number of occurrences of
the verb "listen" in the imperative. This prayer is one way of
obedience to that command.

Another way to think of the prayer of waiting is to think of
it as "beholding God" or a "state of pure beholding."
"Beholding" is an old-fashioned word. In the southern
mountains where I grew up to be "beholden" to someone was
not good; it was to owe them something, to be indebted. We
are, of course, all beholden to God. This is the natural result of
God's grace to us. "Behold," however, in this context means to
apprehend through careful looking, to gaze at (lovingly or
with awe), carefully to observe. I have written a poem which
tries to describe such "beholding."

Prayer is not
scrabbling together
a few paltry words,
flinging them like stones
at the windows
of ineffability.

It is *Gelassenheit,*
letting go,
being carried on a current
toward a vast ocean,
deep beyond imagining;

sitting silently,
gaze firmly fixed
on one golden,
inscrutable face,
waiting
with the patience of love;

pouring out life,
that alabaster vial
of costly ointment,
at the feet of One
Who washes others
with His tears.

Prayer is
asking nothing,
desiring nothing
but this,
only this.

Older translations of John 1:14, the Christmas gospel, read
"we beheld (Greek, *etheasametha,* the root of which can be
translated "contemplate") his [Jesus'] glory..." Those who

were with Jesus looked carefully and awefully at it. "Behold-ing" suggests that the prayer of waiting is a way of looking, a way of seeing. I suggest that it asks us to stop (or at least slow down) and experience what is *already* here, to be present in the present. It fulfills the command of the Psalmist, "Look to him [God], and be radiant." (34:5) Reflect the glory of the God you "see." This seemed to be what happened to Moses on Mount Sinai. He glowed with the glory of the One with Whom he had been. (Exodus 34:29) In this form of prayer we are the servant looking to the hand of the master, the maid looking to the hand of her mistress. (Psalm 123:2)

Perhaps my favorite way to think of the prayer of waiting is to think of it as the prayer of loving; it is a love affair between the one who prays and God. It is a trysting place. What I know about love could be written on the head of the proverbial pin. Alas. But what I *do* know of myself in love is that I have a great desire to be with and fully present to the beloved, to paraphrase the Shema (Deuteronomy 6:5), heart, soul, strength, mind, and, yes, body. The prayer of waiting is the prayer of the one who loves God in this way, who understands that Reality is dynamic and personal. As we move toward It/God, It/God moves toward us, like God to Adam and Eve in the Garden of Eden, like the father to the penitent son in the Prodigal Son parable. When we love someone, we want to be with him or her. That is true of us and, amazingly, it is true of God, too. God loves us and wants to be with us. The prayer of waiting is a way of making ourselves available, fully available, to God's loving approach. It is our response to the invitation "O taste and see that the Lord is good..." (Psalm 34:8) The prayer of waiting engages the whole person (remember chapter 4) in receptivity to God. It presumes that God is seeking us and tries to help us arrange ourselves so that we are most likely to be found. As Gerald May has written, this requires two psychological qualities, "an unfocused openness ... one is simply present to what is," and *"centeredness in the present moment."*[7] (Italics May's.)

Finally, the prayer of waiting is a very direct way by which we can encounter what John calls the "Spirit of Truth." It is a way of being held in the matrix that is God. In John 14 Jesus promises that the Father will give the Advocate (the Holy Spirit) to be with us forever. (John 14:16) "This is the Spirit of truth, whom the world cannot receive, because it neither sees him nor knows him. You know him, because he abides with you, and he will be in [or, in another translation, "among"] you." (John 14:17) The prayer of waiting is a way of knowing with the heart the One Who already abides with and in us. It is a way of honoring the One Who abides within us.

A Method

The most important thing to remember as you begin to experiment with the prayer of waiting is: *you can't do it wrongly*. This form of prayer is, in some sense, a skill to be acquired. More profoundly, it is a gift to be received. Just as those who love us carefully choose gifts that will give us pleasure, gifts that suit us in particular, God chooses to come to us in ways that are individuated, particular to us. So the ways that we dispose ourselves to receive God will be individual to us. As with all the methods of prayer presented in this book, the one presented here is *suggested*. Use what suits you. Ignore what doesn't. I'm not checking up on you, and it won't be on the final exam! The point is to be ready to receive the God who is lovingly desiring you. That said, I have found the following "four Bs" helpful in practicing the prayer of waiting: be quiet; be comfortable; be focused; be passive.

1. Be quiet
In the previous chapter I spoke about silence and the great danger of noise pollution. In order to practice the payer of waiting, one needs to find a reasonably quiet place, an environment as free from the racket of life as is possible. The

degree to which one can do this depends very much on one's life circumstances. But if you are going to listen, you need to be able to hear. So find a quiet corner in your home or apartment, the public library, or your church. As difficult as it may be to find a quiet external environment, it will probably be more difficult to create a quiet *internal* space. In order to listen for God, which is the point of this silence, we need to still the internal monologue that runs in our heads, especially the "shoulds," "oughts," "if onlys" and "what ifs." One way to begin to do this is to practice breath prayer like that introduced in chapter 6 to "quiet down and settle in." Another is to have a focus of attention. More on that in a moment.

Being quiet is really for the purpose of being able to hear, not just with our physical ears, but with the ears of the heart. Periods of quietude help us to be more attuned to the very subtle movements of God. Gerald May has written that "most of us become desensitized or *habituated* to the especially delicate experiences of life. Most of us live in a world of overstimulation and sensory overload."[8] Silence is deliberately chosen and practiced as sensory deprivation for a spiritual end. In his book *The Other Side of Silence* Morton Kelsey says it is "discovering the way inward."[9]

2. Be comfortable

The meditative traditions of yoga are known for the challenging bodily positions assumed by their practitioners. Happily, that is not necessary for us in the prayer of waiting. (My middle-aged hip sockets couldn't assume the lotus position if my life depended upon it!) But as we discussed in chapter 4, we *are* "body," incarnate, so, in order to dispose the whole of ourselves toward God, we need to attend to our body in prayer. In the quiet environment you have found for yourself, arrange your body in a comfortable, but *alert* position. I recommend you sit in a supportive and not-too-soft chair with your spine straight (so that your lungs can work properly and your internal organs are unhindered by kinks) and your feet flat on the floor (so that your feet and lower legs don't go to sleep). You may find it natural to rest your hands in your lap or on your knees. The *mudras* (hand positions) of Hindu and Buddhist meditation are meaningful for many, but not necessary for the prayer of waiting. Sit in a way that is comfortable, not stiff, and so that you are able to breathe deeply. Be relaxed, but alert and expectant. Don't fidget, but sit still. If you find you can't sit still, you are probably not comfortable. Remember, the body doesn't lie. Try another position. The point is the prayer. As Blessed Paul Giustiniani noted, "By tranquillity of the body, we can acquire tranquillity of mind."[10]

A word of caution: if you really do experiment with this form of prayer, and get quiet and comfortable and breathe deeply you may find you go right to sleep. Don't worry and certainly don't feel guilty. The sleep is a gift and a message. It is your body telling you that you aren't getting enough rest, that you need to allow more time for your flesh to relax and recuperate. If the prayer of waiting puts you to sleep, but you feel it may be very fruitful for you, stop doing it for a week or so and during that time sleep an extra hour or two every day, then go back and try this method of prayer again.

3. Be focused

While it may be restful and psychologically beneficial to sit comfortably and quietly, it is not yet the prayer of waiting, especially if your mind is "running wild," swinging through your mental trees like a pack of monkeys. The prayer of waiting is a prayer of great internal focus and quietude. Thomas Keating has called it "the discipline of interior silence," and Stephen Batchelor refers to a form of it as "a centered stillness." You are one-pointedly waiting for God. To do this, some point of focus is usually helpful. The most simple is the breath. Focus on your breathing, using the deep breathing technique I suggested in chapter 6. You can focus on "fanning the flame within," or, even more simply, on the breath as it enters your nostrils (cool) and exits your nostrils (warm). Sit quietly, alertly, and breathe and wait. (And don't worry too much if you nap occasionally!)

Many people find that having a brief word or a phrase (called a *mantra* in some religious traditions) to repeat helps them focus the mind. You might choose a snippet of Scripture or a phrase like "Come, Lord Jesus;" "Lord, have mercy;" "Kyrie eleison," or a word like "peace." I use the Name "Jesus" in my own practice of this form of prayer for reasons you can deduce from reading chapter 5. Choose a very short phrase or a word that has deep meaning for you, and simply and gently repeat it mentally. Every time your mind wanders, just return ever so gently to the repetition of your phrase or word. The point is not to engage with it intellectually, to puzzle out its deepest meanings, but to use it as a way to bring your mental and emotional self to one point or focus, as a magnifying glass refracts beams of light into one, intense, beam.

Some people find a point of focus other than the verbal is more helpful. They focus on a candle flame, an icon, a phrase of music. In this case, the person who prays is using the senses to go beyond them, just as using a word uses a mental construct to go beyond the intellectual. Writing to Malcolm, C.S. Lewis noted that "I think the mere fact of keeping one's eyes focused on something … is some help towards concentration. The visual concentration symbolises, [sic] and promotes, the mental. That's one of the ways the body teaches the soul."[11] Again, when the thoughts wander, return to the focus of attention. You can experiment to see what is most helpful to your concentration and focus. Naturally, you can change what you use, but my experience has been that, in the beginning, it is best if you choose a method to focus your attention and use it consistently until the practice of this form of prayer takes hold, or you decide it isn't for you.

Focusing is actually a way of emptying out your "stuff" to provide a space for God to inhabit. It is clearing away the internal junk to find that God is already there, although previously crowded into a dark corner. Focusing the self in this way, that is, by setting aside one's normal mental clutter and furnishing, mirrors the kenotic "emptying" of Jesus, who also "set himself aside" (See Philippians 2:6–11) for God's purposes. Henri le Saux, o.s.b. (Abhishiktananda) writes that "the mind is so fascinated by sensible objects that the first essential discipline in the spiritual life is to free oneself from the appeal of the external world."[12] That is what "focus", as I am speaking of it here, helps us to do.

Another word of caution: when you open up your interior life, what's in there will rise up. Any time we move toward interiority, we move into both a psychological and a spiritual milieu. Practically, this means that the prayer of waiting can uncover a good deal of psychic clutter, especially things we have repressed. Thus, if you undertake the prayer of waiting with seriousness, I recommend you do so with the companionship of a spiritual director or someone who has a good deal of experience with this form of prayer.[13] He or she will help you winnow the mental grain from the chaff and will help you decide if a period of psychotherapy might be useful. Improved psychological health can be a byproduct of prayer. Just as we would seek medical help with a "fleshly" problem, we should not be ashamed to seek expertise to address a psychological one.

4. Be passive
At the outset most people struggle with silence, bodily stillness and, especially, keeping the mind focused. It is not physically taxing, but hard work none the less. It takes effort and fortitude and commitment and, like any other skill, practice. But the most difficult aspect of this form of prayer is the "doing nothing" and keeping a passive attitude. Most of us were trained to be "doers." I was probably not the only child to be raised with proverbs like "Idle hands are the devil's playground," or the command to "get busy." Passivity and waiting are not our natural modes, but they are essential to this form of

prayer in which nothing *seems* to be happening, but so much is going on.

In the prayer of waiting we have nothing to gain or accomplish. We are disposing ourselves to receive God's visitation. We are, as the Psalmist so often describes, "waiting for the Lord." Often, with a little practice of this way of preparing for God's "visit," we experience the Divine Presence. Extraordinary graces do often seem to be given to beginners, in order to encourage their lives of prayer. When one receives a visitation, the Divine Presence, this form of prayer can become a "resting in God." It is a little difficult to describe, and I expect each person experiences it differently, but in practicing the prayer of waiting we find an internal "door" which we can enter and be in God's presence, not to speak, but to be present in mutual love. As Jesuit Walter J. Ciszek wrote, every true prayer begins by placing self in the presence of God. ". . .true prayer, is communication—and it occurs only when two people, two minds, are truly present to each other in some way."[14] The prayer of waiting is a way of being "truly present" to God.

Here is how *The Cloud of Unknowing* introduces this form of prayer:

> . . .when you feel by the grace of God that he is calling you to this work, and you intend to respond, lift your heart to God with humble love . . .. And think no other thought of him. It all depends on your desire. A naked intention directed to God . . . is wholly sufficient . . . .
> . . . take a short word, preferably of one syllable, to do so . . . A word like '*God*' or '*love*.' . . . And fix this word fast to your heart, so that it is always there come what may.[15]

Note that the author of *The Cloud* presumes God chooses one for this form of prayer. Volitionally, one responds in humility and love and by means of intense focus.

In slightly expanded form here is my method for the prayer of waiting.[16] First and foremost, very simply ask God if you are to undertake this form of prayer. You may have to listen a while for a response. If it is positive, then choose a sacred word or words or some focus of attention as a symbol of your intention to be focused only on and open to God's presence. You might want to use some of the exercises in chapter 6 to help you settle your body for prayer. Choose a quiet place or environment and sit comfortably, but alert, perhaps, if you use a word or phrase for focus, with your eyes closed to prevent external distractions. Take a few deep, gentle, centering breaths, and keep breathing gently and slowly. Focus yourself, your whole body, to receive God. When you become aware that your thoughts have wandered from this "empty expectation," return gently to your sacred word/words or point of focus. Be still. Rest. Wait. When you have "finished" your prayer (perhaps 10 to 15 minutes as you begin this practice), take a little time to return to your ordinary awareness and external senses. Don't jump right up, you may fall right over! The body is at rest as well as the heart and mind. Gentle stretching and movement will "wake you up" kindly. (Incidentally, many medical studies have shown that this form of prayer is very good for the flesh as it produces a physiological state of deep relaxation, lowering metabolic, heart and respiration rate and blood pressure.)

It is probably most helpful at the outset to practice this form of prayer for only 10 or 15 minutes or so. As you find you are able to be more still and focused, increase the time. Most teachers of Christian *contemplatio* suggest that 20 to 30 minutes of this type of prayer twice a day (morning and evening) is ideal. Practically those who employ other modes of daily prayer as well (*lectio* or a period of intercession or the use of the Daily Offices), find one daily period of this prayer to be most realistic and workable. Fleshly and interior stillness is a discipline, and it normally takes some time to acquire. Really to know if this is a fruitful mode of prayer for you, you should practice it daily for a month or so. Then you will be in a position to make an informed decision about whether it's for you or not.[17]

Practical Suggestions

Four Bs introduced the method of the prayer of waiting: be quiet; be comfortable; be focused; be passive. My practical suggestions come under the heading of "killer Ps:" patience, pride, perseverance, practice, and passivity (again).

The person who practices the prayer of waiting must be patient. Like the lady or gentleman in waiting, one, well, *waits*. As are the practices of *lectio divina* and the Jesus Prayer, the prayer of waiting is prayer for the long haul, not a quick fix. One simply practices it with focus and expectancy. It is, I think, the personal equivalent of the liturgical season of Advent in which we await what we know is coming but which isn't here yet. Oddly enough the prayer of waiting is often most effective when nothing seems to be happening. In the prayer of waiting "we are content simply *to be*, with our gaze turned inwards and our ears attuned to inner silence, attending to one thing only, that *God is*."[18] (Italics Abhishiktananda's)

Although I dislike being judgmental (because I struggle so against it in myself!), I do have to say that I think the total inability simply to be patiently and passively open to God is, at root, pride. So very little depends upon us, and so much is really God's business and not ours. Many of us who want to pray seriously can very easily become spiritual busybodies, intruding ourselves (usually our "little s" self) where we are not needed. The world is not here for us to fix, and the sense that one must be *constantly*, busily active, even (especially?) in good works, is a mark of pride, of *hubris*, of missing the mark, overstepping the boundaries and appropriating to ourselves what is really God's. The more carefully we pray, the more clear we will become about what we are and are not to undertake.

There is another aspect of pride that can arise when we practice the prayer of waiting. We can begin to think we have reached the masters level or are the Ph.D.s of praying. *"Those* poor Christians can *only* pray with words. *We* know the prayer of waiting. *We* are contemplatives, closer to the heart of God than anybody else." Phooey. If you enter into *contemplatio* with this attitude, you are very much like the Pharisee in Jesus' parable in Luke 18:9–14. The fact is that our most fruitful method of prayer is as much a matter of our psychological disposition as of our spiritual maturity. Some of us pray best verbally, and some mentally, and some by dancing or singing our prayers. Some of us will be "at home" in the prayer of waiting, and others of us will bear much fruit in *oratio*. As I indicated at the outset, our prayer is as individuated as we are. When we deeply and sincerely want to pray, to respond to the God Who is reaching out to us, we will find the way that most suits us and our relationship to God. Even fumblings toward prayer are prayer when our intention is God-ward. God provides as many ways to pray as there are people. Beware of thinking your way is best, or normative. That leads directly to the pitfall of pride. If you find yourself thinking this way, pray the Psalmist's prayer: "...cleanse me from my secret faults./ Above all, keep your servant from presumptuous sins;/let them not get dominion over me..." (Translation from the *Book of Common Prayer*.)

Develop patience. Despise pride. Develop perseverance. Because the prayer of waiting is a form unfamiliar to many modern Western Christians, and because it is just so hard for many people to shut up and sit still, the tendency is to give up on this kind of prayer before it has been given a real chance to take root in our interior landscapes. I really do think one needs to work with it for a month to six weeks before deciding to go on or give up. Another reason we need perseverance is that so few of us have developed any real control over our thought processes, and we are just beginning to do that as we learn to focus in this form of prayer.

Most Christians understand that they have control over their bodies. They can (with difficulty?) appropriately direct their sexual impulses. They can decide to exercise or not. They can choose to eat moderately and healthily or to overindulge. Some Christians even understand that we have volitional ability in our emotional lives. Unless there are clinical, diagnosable difficulties (and there can be), we have more choice over being "happy, sad, mad, glad" than most of us exert. Very few Christians outside the monastic community seem to have developed much control over their thoughts. We can *choose* what we think or don't think. I believe that's what Jesus is suggesting in the "antithesis" section of the Sermon on the Mount, Matthew 5:21–48. Jesus is concerned about what people think because their actions grow from their thoughts. The prayer of waiting asks us to exert a kind of control over our mental processes that is seldom taught outside monastic formation. Control of one's thoughts (what monastic literature might call "custody of the mind"), on the other hand, is fundamental to most Buddhist devotional practice. I love the cartoon by one P. Byrnes in which one Asian monk asks another, "Are you not thinking what I'm not thinking?"

In fact, in traditional Christian writing on prayer there is a lot of writing about our unfocused minds. The fluctuations of the mind, the inability to focus, the seemingly unwilled intrusions into our attempts to be focused, are, in the literature called "distractions." Everyone who prays seriously very quickly comes face to face with distractions. It may be as simple as realizing that you have stopped really praying the Office of Evening Prayer and are reading the words while thinking about what you'll have for supper. It may be that you settle down seriously to intercede for a situation, and find yourself thinking about something else altogether. It may be that the focus required by the prayer of waiting seems an impossible dream. It may be that in the prayer of waiting you are uncomfortably aware of watching yourself pray. Thomas Keating has characterized the sort of thoughts that intrude themselves into the silent focus of this sort of prayer as "superficial" (mental "perpetual motion"), "brilliant" (when we have great intellectual or theological insights), "pious delight" and "interior purification" (the surfacing of deep-seated psychological issues.[19] Whether our thoughts in the prayer of waiting are intrusions, illuminations or consolations, they are all distractions to be set aside for the period of the prayer of waiting.

Almost every teacher on prayer responds to the problem of distractions by saying something like, "yes, we all have them; notice them; gently return to your point of focus; don't get too tied up in knots about it." For example in his "Admonitions on Prayer" Evagrius, using "unclean thoughts" as his example says if they "should enter your mind, do not be upset; just refuse to consent to them: do not accept them or allow them any place in your mind, then they will leave all of a sudden and run off..."[20] Thomas Merton's advice about distractions is simple and practical and, not surprisingly, echoes Evagrius. Distractions should be accepted "idly and without too much eagerness."[21] In a series of conferences on prayer given in Alaska at the end of his life Merton quipped "What do you do with distractions? You either simply let them pass by and ignore them, or you let them pass by and be perfectly content to have them. If you don't pay attention to then, the distractions don't remain."[22] "If you don't wrestle with distractions wildly and just let them go by for a while, they get less and less, and after a while there is nothing much left."[23] This is another reason why perseverance is required; one needs to practice the prayer a bit before one *knows* that ignored distractions "evaporate."

Martin Smith has another important insight about distractions. He suggests that prayer is God's way of "getting you to meet the cast of characters you call your distractions." "Prayer will always be mess ... . Those distractions are our mess, they're the mess we are in .... Maybe what you call your distractions are really the main event."[24] Perhaps those "ideas" which and "persons" who distract us during our persevering practice of the prayer of waiting *are* the prayer.

In any skill one learns, practice is essential. While, just as some people have a natural aptitude for sports or for music, some have a natural disposition toward interior stillness and silence, the ability to focus the mind. The rest of us have to practice just as we have to practice pitching really to enjoy playing baseball or practice scales really to enjoy playing the piano. Practice does make perfect, and in the spiritual life perspiration as much as inspiration is required. In fact many who write on this form of prayer suggest the main difficulty with it "is lack of practice."[25] Blessed Paul Giustiniani said "...the greatest obstacle to spiritual activity and the greatest difficulty in mental prayer is lack of practice. Nothing makes us so ready and eager for it as habitual practice."[26]

This leads me to our final "killer P," passivity. Even at prayer most of us are pragmatists. (another "P"!) We want the sense that, if *only* spiritually (!), we are "doing something" that might just get results. We think of prayer as an activity, don't we? Writing of centering prayer Basil Pennington noted that most of us think God couldn't get things done if we didn't do them.[27] Without words, without Scripture, with only empty expectancy, the prayer of waiting seems to be "doing nothing." Big time. Well, yes, exactly. In *Contemplative Life in the World* M.A. Bouchard wrote that, for the contemplative, all else is subordinate to the call to contemplation. The contemplative's "sole motive ... is docility to God."[28] Mostly we aren't very good at being docile. Docile doesn't get you anywhere in the world. True enough. But it may be the Christian's best preparation for eternal life. Abhishiktananda writes "...even in things concerning the Kingdom, we ordinarily work through our bodies and minds, the contemplative works in the Rest of God ... Those who live within the Rest of God are already engaged on what will be their occupation in eternity."[29]

I suppose you might think of the prayer of waiting as practice for heaven where, as the glimpses we get of it in the

Revelation to John suggest, we shall be forever adoring the Divine eternally present to us. Everything about the prayer of waiting is difficult for most modern Christians. Being quiet. Sitting still. Waiting. But the "doing nothing" part may be most difficult of all, and, therefore, spiritually most important. It is a reminder in my body, the whole of myself, that the universe does not depend upon me, but upon God, that my role in it all is to be completely and totally open to and docile before God. May I remind you that it was precisely that openness and availability in Mary of Nazareth that ultimately was most useful to God? Blessed Paul Giustiniani says that "usually prayer is truer and more efficacious when we ask nothing whatever of [God]."[30]

The practical among you may ask "why engage in this sort of prayer?" My simple answer is "for love." When I think about the people I have *really* loved, I know I just wanted to be with them. I didn't necessarily want to "do" anything. I just wanted to be where they were, to enjoy their presence. If someone came to me for spiritual direction and, in the course of our conversations, revealed himself to be utterly incapable of even allowing for the possibility of the form of prayer I have introduced in this chapter, I would want him to look very hard at whether he really loves God. It is quite possible to believe in God, to be obedient to God, to serve God, without loving God. I think it that is missing the best part.

Conclusion

You can probably tell that I am very enthusiastic about this kind of prayer. I hope that you will try it, or try something like it. There are many forms or methods of this kind of prayer in addition to the one I have outlined here. Knowing that this kind of prayer is an option for every praying Christian is valuable. However, I tend to agree with Dom Jean LeClercq that finally, it is "... vain and superfluous to seek a method of mental prayer; but the best method is to pray without a method. The Holy Spirit is an incomparable master in this art and we need only let Him guide us without looking backwards to find out by what path He is leading us."[31] If you are able with the intention to be open to God's visitation, to be still and focused, the Holy Spirit will show you "what to do," and it will be the most important possible "non-doing." It will awaken you to the deepest present Reality. C.S. Lewis was so correct that "we may ignore, but we can nowhere evade, the presence of God. The world is crowded with Him .... . The real labour [sic] is to remember, to attend. In fact, to come awake. Still more to remain awake."[32]

The life of prayer is a life of "attending" (waiting), of continual awakening, and of great synchronicity, so I am not surprised to be writing this chapter in mid-Advent. As part of my Advent preparation I am using a leaflet of reflections by Henri Nouwen. The selection chosen for Friday of the first week of Advent is remarkably appropriate for the conclusion of this chapter because it addresses both the matter of passivity and docility in the prayer of waiting and also its "practicality" or "usefulness." It also presents us with a challenge that I find directly relates the prayer of waiting to the (terrible) situation of the world. Here it is:

> We consider waiting a waste of time, perhaps because our culture is always saying, "Get going! Do something! Show you are able to make a difference! Don't just sit there and wait!" Waiting seems a dry desert between where we are and where we want to be .... . We want to move out of it and do something worthwhile. Waiting is even more difficult because we are so fearful—not just as individuals but as whole communities and nations. Fear explains why it is so hard to wait and how tempting it is to act. That is the root of a "first strike" approach to others. Those who live in a world of fear are more likely to make aggressive, hostile, destructive responses than people who are not so

frightened. The more afraid we are, the harder waiting becomes.[33]

For Further Reading and Exploration

Lawrence Freeman (ed.), *John Main: Essential Writings* (Maryknoll, NY: Orbis, 2002).

Lawrence Freeman, *Light Within: The Inner Path of Meditation* (NY: Crossroad, 1987).

William Johnston, S.J., *Silent Music: The Science of Meditation* (New York: Harper and Row/Perennial Library, 1974).

Thomas Keating, O.C.S.O., *Open Mind, Open Heart: The Contemplative Dimension of the Gospel* (New York: Amity House, 1986). (Sounds True has produced a 3 CD set of Fr. Thomas Keating's important and accessible teachings called "Contemplative Prayer." *www.soundstrue.com*)

Thomas Merton, O.C.S.O., *Contemplative Prayer* (New York: Doubleday/Image, 1969/71).

M. Basil Pennington, O.C.S.O., *Centering Prayer* (New York: Doubleday/Image, 1982).

Thomas Ryan, C.S.P., *Prayer of Heart and Body* (New York: Paulist Press, 1995).

Summary Notes

For freedom Christ has set us free. Stand firm,
therefore, and do not submit again to a yoke of
slavery. (Galatians 5:1)

...nothing ... will be able to separate us from
the love of God in Christ Jesus our Lord."
(Romans 8:39)

I opened this primer on prayer confessing that I am not an expert on prayer and suggesting that, when it comes to prayer, one is always a beginner. If you have read the whole book, you now know how true those statements are! So "conclusions" seems an inappropriate ending for a work of this sort. You can hardly draw definitive conclusions about a subject in which you are a neophyte! So instead of a tidy summary, I have appended some "summary notes." This last chapter will do three things; remind you of the territory we have traveled together, introduce five final practical suggestions about prayer and, since "by their fruits ye shall know them," five "observable results" of a life of prayer.

The Territory Traveled

The landscape we have traversed includes the three traditional trajectories of Christian prayer, *oratio* (voiced prayers), *meditatio* (prayer of thought and intellect) and *contemplatio* (prayer of quiet, rest and waiting). We began in chapter 1 with the suggestion that prayer is not so much "saying prayers" as a way of being, a mode of life that is characterized by attentiveness. That does not mean that one shouldn't "say prayers." Chapter 2 introduced a variety of types of voiced prayer and suggested some ways to organize one's said prayers. Because serious Christians are often scripturally oriented, chapter 3 introduces a traditional way of praying the Scriptures called *lectio divina*. *Lectio* involves reading, thought and voiced prayer as well as a movement into more contemplative modes. *Lectio* asks us to take the mind into the heart. To better understand that invitation, chapter 4 presents a Christian anthropology, a view of the human person as "body." I suggested "body" is composed of flesh, spirit/soul and mind, and that these are held together by "heart," the core of personhood. All authentic prayer begins and ends in the heart, the locus of identity and the dwelling place of God within.

Chapter 5 introduced the Jesus Prayer which originated in the Eastern Church and which has been called "the prayer of the heart" in the Christian tradition. Because the Jesus Prayer invites us to attend to breathing and heartbeat, it seemed appropriate to follow that teaching with a chapter on praying with the body. Chapter 6 discusses praying with the whole of the person and suggests some exercises to engage one's body in prayer, perhaps as a way of preparing for other modes of prayer. It is followed in chapter 7 with a cosmology, a discussion of the human person and his or her many levels in the wider context of the whole creation. Building on this cosmology, chapter 7 highlights how important it is that contemporary Christians understand that reality is both material and spiritual. Without this understanding it is difficult to move into more contemplative forms of prayer. Chapter 8 introduces some aspects of the many forms of prayer that might be called "contemplative," and chapter 9 teaches a form of contemplative prayer I called "the prayer of waiting."

We noted that one's particular mode of prayer is very individualized, that no one way of praying is "best" or "most advanced." In fact, our most comfortable and habitual way of praying will probably have a lot in common with our basic personality type. In any case, most of us will pray in a variety of ways at any given point in and throughout our lives. Writing to Malcolm, C.S. Lewis noted that "heaven will display far more variety than hell."[1] That heavenly variety characterizes Christian prayer as well. It is important not to assume there is only one correct way to pray or to get stuck in one way of praying. Indeed, the traditional liturgical year, itself, presents us with a variety of modes and "atmospheres" of prayer.[2] Contrary to what commercial culture suggests, Advent is a contemplative time, a quiet season of waiting and "going inward." Christmas is celebratory, a time for praise and feasting. Epiphany is the season of enlightenment and the manifestation of God in the Incarnation. It invites us to meditation, thought and greater understanding. Lent is the season of self-examination, penitence and confession as preparation for Easter, a time of both mystery and joy. "Ordinary time" (as if any time were ordinary!) is a time of active growth and exploration of the life and ministry of Jesus. And at every time and season, profound gratitude characterizes the Christian's prayers.

I have tried to present a variety of ways of praying in the hopes that one or another of them might help you to draw closer to God. I believe with Jean Pierre de Caussade, s.j. that when we are seeking God *how* we find God is a matter of indifference.[3] My attempts to share with you something of what I have learned about Christian prayer may be miserable, but they have at least quoted some of the great teachers of Christian prayer. Cassian, Evagrius, St. Benedict, St. Basil, John Climacus, John of the Cross, Teresa of Avila, Brother Lawrence, *The Cloud of Unknowing*, John Calvin, and closer to our own day, Evelyn Underhill, Metropolitan Anthony, Thomas Merton, Thomas Keating and David Steindl-Rast—they all know vastly more about prayer than I do. If you have met any of them for the first time in this book, then I am content, knowing that the suggestions for further reading that close the chapters and the bibliography at the end of the book may be of the most service to you.

Five Final Suggestions

As I said at the outset, this book does not claim to be comprehensive. I have only written about forms of prayer with which I have had experience, and that has limited the contents significantly. I wanted this to be a book in which I shared my experiences in prayer in the much greater light of Scripture and Christian tradition. I "do not claim to be wiser than [I am]." (Romans 12:16) That being the case, I want to share five final bits of practical advice or information under the headings of "conscience," "feelings," "perseverance," "individuality," and "freedom."

1. Conscience

As I mentioned earlier, when you are learning about prayer and experimenting with various modes of prayer, it is important that you *never* transgress against your own conscience. There are many forms of prayer and not every one of them is for every person. If you are deeply uneasy with a particular type of prayer, don't use it. As we noted in chapter 6, the body doesn't lie. If you are getting "no," signals, pay attention to them. There may be some spiritual or psychological reason why this form of prayer is not for you at a particular point in time. In Romans 14, writing about the matter of clean and unclean food, Paul teaches "that nothing is unclean in itself; but it is unclean for anyone who thinks it unclean." (Romans 14:14) His final word is that "those who have doubts are condemned if they eat, because they do not act from faith; for whatever does not proceed from faith [another translation would be "conviction"] is sin." (Romans 14:23) The principle applies to prayer: if it seems wrong to you, don't do it.

But one must be discerning. It is important to make distinctions among "theologically/spiritually wrong," "aesthetically unpleasing," and "unfamiliar." It is easy to condemn (something Paul also warns against in Romans 14) what is essentially only unfamiliar. That might make unavailable to you a prayer practice that would be of real value. Once again, discernment with a spiritual director or spiritual friend or prayer partner is of great help. (See note 31 of chapter 5 for information on spiritual direction.) My real point is that the spiritual life is both very resilient and very delicate. It is nearly impossible to quench a great thirst for God. And, in any case, God is always seeking *us*. But, to change the metaphor, one can wander off the path or be led into dead ends. Never allow your conscience, your heart, to be run rough shod over. In the life of prayer it is, in the long run, better to move slowly than to race willy nilly into a quagmire. In the life of prayer, the laurels often go to the tortoise rather than the hare.

2. Feelings

It is harsh but true that how we feel in the life of prayer is absolutely unimportant. This is one reason why it's important to have a clear anthropology; one knows the difference between "conscience/heart" as used above and feelings which are, at best, ephemeral. The feeling of God's presence and closeness, deep peacefulness or contentment in prayer are traditionally called "consolations." Consolation in prayer is wonderful when it comes, but a very minor byproduct and hardly the point. It is true that God often graces beginners in prayer with great consolations. I think perhaps this is an encouragement to a deeper life of prayer. But no less an expert than Teresa of Avila describes prayer as a "mixture of boring effort and intermittent consolation."[4] The real "proof of the pudding" in one's prayer life comes when the consolations dry up. Some of our greatest saints had very difficult experiences of prayer as Mother Teresa of Calcutta's book *Come Be My Light* (and, more classically, the writings of St. John of the Cross) makes perfectly clear.

Apparently Mother Teresa's greatest apostolic accomplishments came during the fifty years when she herself had no sense of the presence of God.[5] The apparent absence of God is a great trial in the life of prayer, but one many, many great Christians have experienced and survived.

Emotion, the level of "feeling," is a very surface level of life. (See chapters 4 and 7 of this book.) Thus how we feel in prayer is secondary because prayer is not about us. Prayer is about God, a response to God, a gift of God. No matter how we feel, we continue to pray. And our prayer may be most fruitful and deep precisely when God seems absent, and we feel nothing. In the life of prayer perseverance is a great, indeed a crucial, virtue. Keeping our prayer discipline is essential. When you have found your way to pray, keep doing it until (with your spiritual advisor or friend) you are absolutely sure God is calling you to another method.

3. *Perseverance*

At the outset of this book I suggested that there is no wrong way to pray. Some ways may be more fruitful for us, and some less, but we can't get it wrong when our desire is for God and for prayer. Writing in the dark days of the First World War, P.T. Forsyth said simply, "the chief failure of prayer is its cessation."[6] As long as you are praying, you are doing the right thing. But, prayer is also an activity in which, once you have set your hand to the plow, it isn't very useful to look back. (See Luke 9:62.) You must keep praying. One learns how to plow, how to keep the rows straight and the furrows the proper depth, by plowing. One learns how to pray by praying. There are no short cuts and no quick fixes. Prayer requires practice. Blessed Paul Giustiniani was speaking of mental prayer, but it is true that in general "that prayer is not subject to any method, except the method of preparatory discipline."[7] Prayer is, in this sense, an experimental activity. We learn it by the same kind of disciplined practice that we learn other activities. One tries various forms of prayer until the one which most quickly and deeply responds to God's very personalized invitation is found. We find a method that connects us to God, and we use it until it no longer is serviceable, and then we begin again to search for a different mode of prayer for a new season of life or altered circumstances.

In this process it can be difficult to discern whether our way of prayer should change or whether we should just keep on with it a while longer. Once again, a good spiritual director can be of invaluable assistance. Most importantly, if you are having difficulty in prayer, I encourage you not to give up on prayer itself. Be like the "little engine that could" in the children's book. If you *believe* you can pray, you *can* pray. To quote another childhood proverb, "if at first you don't succeed, try, try again." A great deal in the life of prayer is not unlike the rest of life. One continues to put one foot in front of the other, "keeps on keeping on." We continue to water dry earth, and, mysteriously, one day the seed germinates and the flower blossoms. We practice, and the practice itself "makes perfect." How it all works, I don't know. But I am profoundly sure that prayer is for everybody because God is reaching out to everybody, to each one, in very particular ways.

4. *Individuality*

In his "Admonitions on Prayer" Evagrius articulated very clearly what I have been trying to say: "...choose a way of life that suits your feeble state; travel on that, and you will live, for your Lord is merciful and he will receive you, not because of your achievements, but because of your intentions..."[8] We desire fellowship with God and so find a mode of prayer that suits us, and we continue faithfully to practice it, and God responds to our intention. As Episcopal priest Margaret Guenther so wisely notes, "The way we choose to pray is not as important as where it leads us: the point is to focus on being open to God and not to make an idol of the method."[9] Again, I remind you that I cannot teach you how to pray because your "God language" will be yours alone. There was, is and never will be another you. Just as you have a "God-shaped" hole in your heart that nothing else can fill, God has in the Divine Heart a "you-shaped" place. You are the only one who can fill it. God is reaching out to you in ways that are uniquely yours. Your response, your prayer, will be unique and individualized. Some of the methods in this book may help you to respond. (I pray that none of them will hinder you!) But your response is yours alone.

Henri le Saux, o.s.b. (Abhishiktananda) writes very practically about finding a spiritual guide, one who "has himself attained to the Real, and who knows by personal experience the path that leads there; one who is capable of giving the disciple the essential introduction to this path." This guide "never does more than initiate."[10] A spiritual guide initiates you, perhaps facilitates the beginning of your journey, but, as Abhishiktananda says "the last stage of the pilgrimage and the discovery of the door to the innermost shrine has to be achieved by each one alone."[11] That is because each one is so individually loved by God, so personally summoned and awaited. Prayer is perhaps the most individualized and intimate of our activities. In his study of John of the Cross and Teresa of Avila, Gerald May notes that "both say that God deals with each soul with 'esteeming love,' addressing each of us with profound respect for who we are and what we need and can bear. And though the process of this soul journey cannot be rigidly categorized ... it *is* going somewhere."[12] (Italics May's.) "Whatever form it takes, the movement of the soul and God is always finding its way toward freedom."[13]

5. Freedom
Essentially prayer is the very individualized and intimate relationship of an individual and God. As such, it *must* be characterized by freedom, ultimate, radical freedom, the freedom Christ came and lived and died to give. Perhaps more clearly than anyone since his time, the Apostle Paul understood that the Christ event was about freedom. "Jesus Christ,"

he writes in Romans, "has set you free." (Romans 8:2) Freedom is the climax toward which the theological argument in Galatians moves. And to the Galatians, "For freedom Christ has set us free; stand fast therefore, and do not submit again to a yoke of slavery." (Galatians 5:1) I have heard numerous Galatians sermons on the Law vs. Faith (a good many of them remarkably anti-Semitic), but none on Galatians 5:1: "for freedom Christ has set us free." "Where the Spirit of the Lord is, there is freedom," writes Paul in 2 Corinthians 3:17. It is a good litmus test for prayerfulness. Where you find freedom in the Christian community, you will also find people of deep prayer. Where you find servitude, narrowness, legalism, you are unlikely to find authentic prayerfulness. Your own most fruitful ways of prayer will be the ones that free you.

Prayer moves us directly into the realm of radical freedom, not the freedom that is "an opportunity for self-indulgence," but, paradoxically, freedom to "through love become slaves to one another." (Galatians 5:13) Our freedom is not to become a "stumbling block" to others (1 Corinthians 8:9), but to liberate us for service. The ultimate freedom of prayer is the freedom of love, which joyfully puts the good of others before our own. Indeed, this is perhaps the most potent byproduct of prayer in our lives. When you have met God in the ground of your own being and had even the faintest glimpse of God's great and personalized love for you (and for everybody), the various servitudes proffered by contemporary culture very quickly lose their appeal. To take but one example, who would want to use make-up and fashion, pump iron and sculpt the flesh, swagger or wiggle around according to the current (and therefore, by definition, fleeting) mode in order to attract love (for, let us be honest, this is what fashion is about, looking as you are supposed to so other people will accept/love you) when real and permanent and divine love (from which true human love springs) is available? When prayer has ushered you into even the antechambers of an unspeakably beautiful eternity, the rather tawdry and ephemeral (and usually fake) goods offered by advertising, commercialism, the "accepted way," are shown up for the rubbish they are. Prayer liberates you from them, and, ever so gently, asks you to liberate others.

Oddly enough, I think this may be one reason why a great many very good Christian people don't really pursue a life of prayer. Freedom frightens them. Freedom is a great deal more difficult than cultural servitude.[14] If prayer sets us free, perhaps we'd better give it a wide berth. Reflecting on faith and art, Madeleine L'Engle noted that we are afraid of what we can't control, so we draw boundaries that limit what we can know and understand.[15] Prayer is very dangerous in that it introduces us into a level of Reality over which we have absolutely no control. (Remember chapter 7.) We *choose* to protect ourselves from this arena of Reality by refusing its existence. We beaver away at setting limits (which can be manifested as working away to change the world, perfecting things from the outside, "fixing" creation), and all the while God is trying to set us free! L'Engle says it is not possible to be a Christian while refusing to be vulnerable.[16] Prayer, I would suggest, is the chosen vulnerability to God that sets us free, the "truth" that makes us free. (John 8:32) I don't suggest that this doesn't have an element of fear and risk. It does. But I can attest that it is also incomparably wonderful when you can "let go" into it.

Results of a Life of Prayer

In speaking of freedom, we have begun to think about the consequences of prayer in our lives. I want to stress that, fundamentally, we pray for God alone. As the writer of *The Cloud of Unknowing* warns, "Lift up your heart to God with humble love: and mean God himself, and not what you get out of him."[17] Any "results" of prayer, even freedom, are byproducts, perhaps quite wonderful ones, but secondary none the less. And yet, our tendency is to want results, isn't it? We want toothpaste that makes our teeth noticeably whiter (fewer cavities seems to have taken second place to cosmetic appeal!) and gasoline that gives greater mileage. And so our minds are set to ask "What will prayer do for me? How will I change/ improve?" These are honest and perhaps reasonable questions. But let me shift the focus ever so slightly. The teachings of Jesus in the gospels generally warn us against being judgmental because, in the final analysis, judgement is God's business. If Jesus gives us a principle of evaluation, it is fruitfulness. "You will know them by their fruits," He says in Matthew 7:16 and 20. This is His primary metaphor in Matthew 7:16–21 and 12:33. So let us note some of the "fruits" of prayer.

I have already spoken of the most luscious, and dangerous, fruit of prayer: freedom. This freedom allows us to live "from the inside out" rather than from "the outside in." It allows us to be persons of authenticity and choice rather than reactivity. We quietly refuse to be manipulated by unexamined convention and assumptions, cultural trends, even political and religious givens. We become autonomous, realized persons —and, therefore, dangerous! To live from the inside out is to assume the freedom of the daughters and sons of God. Let me suggest five fruits of prayerfulness: a life without illusion; a life without defenses; a life in solidarity; a life of hope; a life exhibiting "the peace that passes understanding."[18]

1. Prayerfulness leads to a life without illusion

Prayerfulness leads us to something like Paul's experience when he was visited by Ananias (the bravest man in the New Testament?): "something like scales fell from his eyes, and his sight was restored." (Acts 9:18) Prayer helps us to see things as they really are, not as we would like them to be, and not as political and cultural systems, advertising, and perhaps even religious institutions tell us they are. Most importantly, I have found that prayer prevents me from having too high an opinion of myself, my abilities, my importance in the Great Scheme of Things. In the book *Primary Speech: A Psychology of*

Prayer Ann and Barry Ulanov write, "prayer protects us from our pretensions to omnipotence..."[19] Indeed. But the same lesson can be learned from Jesus Himself as we watch Him in Gethsemane. What P.T. Forsyth wrote many years ago is still true: "nothing would do more to cure us of a belief in our own wisdom than the granting of some of our eager prayers."[20]

Prayerfulness brings the world into proper focus and shows me to myself as I am. Often the picture is not pretty. What I see in prayer's mirror is alienated, broken, judgmental of others (so I won't seem so bad to myself), in short what the Bible calls "sinful." The prayer of blind Bartimaeus in Mark 10:51, "Lord, let me see," when sincerely prayed, has staggering consequences. But seeing what is really there is the first step toward freedom, toward living the truth. In graduate school I had a poster of a rag doll being squeezed through an old wringer washing machine which offered a "spin" on John 8:32. The caption read, "the truth will set you free, but first it will make you miserable." On the positive side, seeing what is there is also viewing the beauty of creation, the loveliness and courage and kindness of people, the longing of the whole created universe for what God created it (including us) to be. And that is a very positive experience. So while, initially the clarity of sight prayer offers may be an alarming experience, it is an important step on the road to freedom.

2. Prayerfulness leads to a life without defenses

Modern psychology, and our own experience, tells us how much life energy is devoted toward defense, protecting ourselves. This is true in both the public and private arenas. In 2007 my own country spent on defense something in the neighborhood of ten times the amount the next highest spending country did. And I noticed no greater sense of security and serenity among my neighbors. If anything, the constant talk of the need for defense made people edgy and frightened. And frightened people are ready to concede their decision-making power to those who promise to protect them.

Whether privately or corporately, fear is a very bad motivation for action.

On the personal level, since prayerfulness shows us things as they are, it shows me as I am. "...by prayer we acquire our true selves."[21] Prayer asks me to be honest with myself. If I cannot hide my own, true condition from God (and of course, I can't, and shouldn't because I am as God made me), Who accepts me as I am and encourages me to be all I was meant to be,[22] why should I try to hide it from others? Prayer reveals to us our acceptability, and bestows the security of knowing ourselves ultimately acceptable, thereby setting us free from the tyranny of self-concern to be of liberating service to others. Prayerfulness teaches me that I do not have to "defend myself," because, in Jesus Christ, God has taken on that assignment. I can live an open, available and honest life. As Metropolitan Anthony notes, "only if we stand completely open before the unknown, can the unknown reveal itself, Himself, as he chooses to reveal Himself to us *as we are today*."[23] (Italics mine.) To "know God," and thus who we are, is a great freedom. We can, indeed, "let go and let God."

3. Prayerfulness leads to a life in solidarity

The more I know of the world and of myself through honest prayerfulness, the more I realize my essential relatedness to others. At prayer I learn that nothing human is alien to me. Since prayer opens the heart, the one who prays becomes profoundly attuned to the needs and sufferings, the accomplishments and joys of others. This can be a cause for celebration, but also a terrible burden. As Theodore Jennings, Jr. wrote, "...an existence formed by prayer is an existence that is worldly—one that is fully in the world, in solidarity with the world's cry, longing and need."[24] Most of the great teachers of prayer in the Christian tradition make the point that, rather than isolating us, prayer profoundly connects us to others. Prayer makes us great lovers! Here is how the author of *The Cloud of Unknowing* put it: "...when the soul is wholly turned to God all people are equally dear . . . for [one] feels no other cause for loving than God himself. So all are loved simply and sincerely, for God's sake. . ."[25]

Often our lived experience is slightly different. How many times I have heard pastors lament the fact that their "sheep" view the time they spend in prayer or on retreat as wasted or unnecessary! If we decide seriously to commit ourselves to lives of prayer, to spend time in prayer, we will very quickly face those who tell us to "get busy and 'do'," as if prayer were not the work of eternity. Sometimes our own attitude toward others is like that of Peter and the disciples toward Jesus in Mark 1:35–39. We hunt people down who have gone away to pray, and we tell them bluntly that they have work to do. Only a culture that worships at the idol of activism exhibits this attitude. Prayer may be the very best thing that we can "do" in many situations. How frequently the unselfaware rush in and act and cause even greater distress.

Often, I personally am not wise enough to know either what is the right or most helpful thing to do, or am powerless to do anything directly. At this point, for me prayer, especially confession, intercession and lamentation, is action. I have suggested earlier, and remind you now, that prayer *is* social action. (Remember those women I told you about who gather to pray their way through the newspaper?) Only those who do not really believe in God's power and God's benevolence would think prayer is impotent. Again, how it works, I can't tell you. *That* it works I can attest. But more than producing observable (albeit sometimes surprising) results, prayer rights the spiritual balances. A prayerful, reflective person's energy serves to balance the aggressive and selfish energy of the evil, or simply unenlightened and blundering.

4. *Prayerfulness leads to a life of hope*
I have tried to be honest with you about prayer. It is absolutely true that the opening of the heart that follows from an authentic desire for and life of prayer can, initially, be very

disturbing. As Thomas Keating has written, "the spiritual journey is not a career or a success story. It is a series of humiliations of the false self that become more and more profound. These make room inside us for the Holy Spirit to come and heal."[26] Happily he continues, "every movement toward the humiliation of the false self, if we accept it, is a step toward interior freedom and interior resurrection."[27] It is hard to admit who we are, painful to see the world as it is. Prayerfulness involves risk and vulnerability and requires great courage. But after its initial disruptions (and they may be extended over a long period of time), prayerfulness opens the door of hope. We wouldn't bother to persevere in prayer if we didn't believe in God and in God's power to effect change, would we? Prayer implies expectations for the future. And anyone who has an expectation for the future has at least nascent hope. Hopeless people are the most dangerous, and the most in need of our prayers.

Throughout this book I have insisted that prayer is always a response to God's invitation and initiative, and that, itself, is a reason for hope. God continually calls us to prayer, awakens in us the desire for it, issues us a personal invitation to it. People still desire prayer. And this is existential proof that God has not abandoned us. The chilling phrase that Paul uses to such effect in Romans 1, "God gave them up," does not universally apply, for which I am unspeakably grateful. Prayer, itself, is a reason for hope. And the witness of those who pray prayers of intercession and petition is that prayers of this sort *are* answered, although perhaps not as expected. It is very instructive to keep a little intercession/petition notebook and to record answers to prayer as you see them. Over time, you will, I think, recognize many more answers to prayer because you will have a better understanding of what you are looking for. (See 1 above.) What one formerly thought was chance, in the light of prayer is seen as synchronicity and even God's providence. And this is another reason for hope.

5. Prayerfulness leads to "the peace that passes understanding"

St. Paul summarizes Philippians 4:4–7, one of the most important teachings on prayer in the New Testament, "And the peace of God which surpasses all understanding, *will* guard your hearts and your minds in Christ Jesus." (Italics mine.) This is a great promise, but it requires some unpacking. First, Paul assumes that all peace is of God (see, for example, Romans 15:33, 16:20), but God's peace is not the absence of conflict. It is a quality of heart, and therefore of living, that one possesses in whatever circumstances she finds herself. Second, this peace "surpasses" or "passes" (the Greek means "is superior to") "understanding," what in chapter 4 we called *nous* or "mind." God's peace is superior to, ungraspable by, human intelligence, and it will protect the whole person ("heart") *and* his rationality ("mind"). This peace is the gift of God in whom, or *within* whom, the prayerful person "lives and moves and has being." It is the same peace Jesus promises in John 14:27 which is "not as the world gives."

If you meet a person who is centered, calm, serene, you are probably meeting a person who has a disciplined life of prayer, whose connection to the Divine is deep and strong. As we have just noted, praying keeps us aware that things don't ultimately depend upon us, that, in fact, very little that is of real consequence does, and this brings tremendous relief from guilt and stress and worry. And, on the positive side, it releases in us great energy for good. It sets us free. Deep and prayerful freedom is not frenetic but serene. It knows what it knows and is unshakeable. The quiet conviction, the serenity of a person of prayerfulness changes things both by what she or he does and by the godly energy that he or she brings to bear on everything.

Finally...

As I come to the end of this little book what I am most aware of are its lapses, lacunae and inadequacies. The best I can do in closing is to remind you that the New Testament teaches us that we have Divine assistance in prayer. The Holy Spirit and the Risen Christ Himself aid us in our attempts at prayer. Indeed, when we cannot pray, they pray on our behalf. Much of Jesus' Farewell Discourse to His disciples in John 14–17 revolves around the promised help of the Holy Spirit which God will send. The Spirit will teach everything, remind us of what Jesus has taught (14:26) and guide us in the truth. (16:13) St. Paul writes in Romans 8 of this same Spirit who "helps us in our weakness; for we do not know how to pray as we ought, but that very Spirit intercedes with sighs too deep for words . . . intercedes for the saints according to the will of God." (Romans 8:26–27) Paul continues, "Jesus Christ . . . is at the right hand of God, who indeed intercedes for us" (8:34) and from whom nothing can separate us. (Romans 8:31–39) The writer of the Letter to the Hebrews also believes that the Risen Christ "always lives to make intercession" for "those who approach God through him." (Hebrews 7:25) Christ "entered into heaven itself, now to appear in the presence of God on our behalf." (Hebrews 9:24) He is our "advocate with the Father" of whom John writes in 1 John 2:1. In my own struggles with prayer, when I feel inadequate or unable to pray at all, I rest in the Greater Prayer which is going on all the time and at every level of reality and in which, from time to time, I participate by prior invitation.

In the life of prayer, we respond to a deep invitation, a longing in the heart's core. We begin where we are and are led to places we couldn't imagine. Usually, our prayer life begins, as do most relationships, with *oratio*, grateful conversation with the Beloved. Voiced prayer begins in gratitude and moves toward adoration, and adoration moves toward silence, what we called *contemplatio*, the deep joy of waiting on, being in the presence of, the Beloved. Loving and knowing ourselves loved so deeply is profoundly liberating. We are freed to be ourselves, and from the calm assurance that we are chosen and loved arises both the desire and the power to serve the liberation of others. In no other way can the world ultimately be changed for the better except by this disinterested, egoless, "from-the-inside-out" way of living and serving. Finally, prayerfulness is power, the gentle and eternal power of Love which is in hidden ways now, and one day dramatically on the stage of history will, re-create what it first created. Through our prayerfulness, we are given the mysterious privilege of participating in the process.

Prayer

In the early days,
in the first flush
of feeling its power
flow freely,
one stands
with audacious confidence
lisping a litany of
"give, give."

A lifetime,
myriad gifts later,
their immensity
obscures the Giver.
One kneels
in heart-deep silence,
whispers, trembling,
"take, take."

Notes

Introduction

1. Quoted in Gerald G. May, M.D., *The Dark Night of the Soul* (San Francisco: HarperSanFrancisco, 2004) 9–10.

2. Noteworthy and recommended exceptions include Richard J. Foster, *Prayer: Finding the Heart's True Home* (San Francisco: HarperSanFrancisco, 1992), Margaret Guenther, *The Practice of Prayer* (Boston: Cowley Publications, 1998) and Tony Jones, *Soul Shaper* (Grand Rapids, MI: Zondervan, 2003: written for youth but widely applicable). See also Anthony de Mello, S.J., *Sadhana* (New York: Doubleday/Image, 1984).

3. Quoted by David Steindl-Rast, O.S.B. in "Man of Prayer" in *Thomas Merton, Monk* Br. Patrick Hart, O.C.S.O. (ed.) (New York: Sheed & Ward, 1974) 84–85.

4. Thomas Merton, O.C.S.O., *New Seeds of Contemplation* (New York: New Directions, 1962) 221, 224.

5. *Rumi: Fragments & Ecstasies* Daniel Liebert (ed.) (New York: Omega Publications, 1999) 26.

6. *Rumi* 53.

7. David Steindl-Rast, O.S.B., *Gratefulness: The Heart of Prayer* (New York: Paulist Press, 1984) 42–43.

8. A good test question for me in appropriating other religions' prayer practices has been "does this compromise the Lordship of Jesus in my life?" If the answer is "yes," then I have declined to participate in the practice.

9. Lynn Szabo, "The Sound of Sheer Silence: A Study in the Poetics of Thomas Merton," *The Merton Annual* 13 (2000) 208.

Chapter 1: Prayer: Toward a Definition

1. An earlier version of this material was serialized in *Spirituality* volume 10, numbers 52 and 53, 2004. I am grateful for permission to incorporate that material here.
2. Anthony Bloom (Metropolitan Anthony), *Beginning to Pray* (New York: Paulist Press, 1970).
3. Ibid.
4. Jean Danielou, *Prayer: The Mission of the Church* (Grand Rapids, MI: Eerdmans, 1996).
5. Ibid.
6. Stanley J. Grenz, *Prayer: The Cry for the Kingdom* (Peabody, MA: Hendrickson, 1998).
7. Ann and Barry Ulanov, *Primary Speech: A Psychology of Prayer* (Atlanta: John Knox, 1982).
8. John Skinner (transl.), *Julian of Norwich: Revelation of Love* (New York: Doubleday/Image, 1997) 17.
9. Quoted in John Kirvan, *Raw Faith* (Notre Dame, IN: Sorin Books, 2000) 21–22.
10. Thomas Merton, o.c.s.o., *New Seeds of Contemplation* (New York: New Directions, 1961) 34–35.
11. Merton, *New Seeds* 37.
12. Danielou 12, 15, 16.
13. Danielou 19.
14. George Foot Moore, *Judaism* (Cambridge: Harvard University Press, 1954) II: 223.
15. Hilkot Tefillah 4, quoted in Moore II: 224.
16. Quoted in Sebastian Brock (transl.), *The Syriac Fathers on Prayer and the Spiritual Life* (Kalamazoo: Cistercian Publications, 1987) 71.
17. Blaise Pascal, *Pensées* (William F. Trotter, transl.) (New York: Washington Square Press, 1965) 85.
18. N.A., *The Cell of Self Knowledge* (New York: Crossroad Press, 1981) 89.
19. Margaret Y. MacDonald, *Colossians and Ephesians* (Sacra Pagina) (Collegeville, MN: Liturgical Press, 2000) 141.
20. Kirvan 32.

21. Dale Allison, *The Silence of Angels* (Valley Forge: Trinity Press International, 1995) 37.
22. David Steindl-Rast, O.S.B., *Gratefulness: The Heart of Prayer* (New York: Paulist Press, 1984) 211, 212.
23. Jean-Pierre de Caussade, S.J., *Abandonment to Divine Providence* (New York: Doubleday/Image, 1975) 96.
24. Norman Pittinger, *Praying Today* (Grand Rapids, MI: Eerdmans, 1974) 24, quoted in David Willis, "Contemporary Theology and Prayer," *Interpretation* 34 (1980) 253.
25. Gustavo Gutiérrez, *A Theology of Liberation* (New York: Orbis, 1973) quoted in Willis 257.

Chapter 2: *Oratio*: Praying with Words

1. For a discussion of this see James Barr, "*Abba* isn't 'Daddy'," JTS 39 (1988) 36.
2. For an extended discussion of this see Vernon MacCasland, "'Abba' Father," JBL 72 (1953) 81.
3. Quoted in Charles Talbert, *Reading the Sermon on the Mount* (Columbia, SC: University of South Carolina Press, 2004) 114.
4. Ann and Barry Ulanov, *Primary Speech: A Psychology of Prayer* (Atlanta: John Knox, 1982) 29.
5. Robert Wicks, *After Fifty* (New York: Paulist Press, 1997) 24.
6. For an accessible introduction to St. John of the Cross' thought see Gerald G. May, M.D., *The Dark Night of the Soul* (San Francisco: HarperSanFrancisco, 2004).
7. N.A., *The Cell of Self-Knowledge* (New York: Crossroad Press, 1981) 69.
8. Steven Chase, *The Tree of Life: Models of Christian Prayer* (Grand Rapids: Baker Book House, 2005) 45.
9. Richard Foster, *Prayer: Finding the Heart's True Home* (San Francisco: HarperSanFrancisco, 1992) 81.
10. C.S. Lewis, *Letters to Malcolm, Chiefly on Prayer* (London: Collins/Fontana, 1964/66) 90, 93.

11. Lewis 91.
12. David Steindl-Rast, *Gratefulness: The Heart of Prayer* (New York: Paulist Press, 1984) 201.
13. Steindl-Rast 12.
14. Jean-Pierre de Caussade, S.J., *Abandonment to Divine Providence* (New York: Doubleday/Image, 1975) 27.
15. Stanley J. Grenz, *Prayer: The Cry for the Kingdom* (Peabody, MA: Hendrickson, 1988/1991) 21.
16. Sr. Mary Ellen Rufft, C.D.P., "The Silver Rule" in *Providence Alive!* (Autumn, 2007) 11.
17. Quoted in Patrick Hart, O.C.S.O. (ed.), *Thomas Merton, Monk* (New York: Sheed & Ward, 1974) 88.
18. Thomas Merton, O.C.S.O., *Thoughts in Solitude* (New York: Farrar, Straus, Giroux, 1956) 89.
19. Abhishiktananda, *Prayer* (Norwich: Canterbury Press, 1967/2006) 66.
20. Chapter 2 of Richard Foster's *Prayer*, "Prayer of the Forsaken," while brief, clearly maps the terrain of this sort of prayer.
21. Kathleen Norris from "Preface" to *The Psalms* (New York: Riverhead Books, 1997) xiii.
22. See, for example, the discussion in Chase 64 and in Grenz 20–23.
23. I copied this quotation from Romano Guardini's *Prayer in Practice* on a card and have long since lost the full citation. I would be happy to correct this omission in future editions of this book.
24. Anthony Bloom (Metropolitan Anthony), *Beginning to Pray* (New York: Paulist Press, 1970) 31.
25. Grenz 21.
26. Steindl-Rast 83.
27. Grenz 43.
28. Grenz 41.
29. Grenz 40.
30. Rowan Williams, *A Ray of Darkness* (Cambridge: Cowley Publications, 1995) 118–119.

31. Quoted in Kyu Nam Jung, "Prayer in the Psalms," in D.A. Carson (ed.), *Teach Us to Pray* (Grand Rapids, MI: Baker Book House, 1990) 36. You might find Fr. Murphy's book *The Gift of the Psalms* (Peabody, MA: Hendrickson, 2000) an accessible introduction to the Psalter.

32. Thomas Merton, O.C.S.O., *Praying the Psalms* (Collegeville, MN: Liturgical Press, 1956) 31.

33. Norris viii, ix.

34. Walter Brueggemann, *Praying the Psalms* (Winona, MN: St. Mary's Press, 1993) 25.

35. I have found these books on praying the Psalms particularly helpful: Walter Brueggemann, *Praying the Psalms* (Winona, MN: St. Mary's Press, 1993); John C. Endres and Elizabeth Liebert, *A Retreat with the Psalms* (New York: Paulist Press, 2001); C.S. Lewis, *Reflections on the Psalms* (London: Collins/ Fontana, 1958/61); Thomas Merton, O.C.S.O., *Praying the Psalms* (Collegeville, MN: Liturgical Press, 1956).

36. Her series, entitled "Singing the Psalms," is available from Sounds True, P.O. Box 8010 Boulder, CO 80306.

37. Quoted in Kathleen Norris, *The Cloister Walk* (New York: Riverhead Books, 1996) 91.

38. C.S. Lewis, *Reflections on the Psalms* (London: Collins/Fontana, 1958,61) 43.

39. Quoted in Dom Jean LeClercq, *Alone with God* (New York: Farrar, Straus and Cudahy, 1961) 113.

Chapter 3: Praying the Word: *Lectio Divina*

1. David Steindl-Rast, O.S.B., *Gratefulness: The Heart of Prayer* (New York: Paulist Press, 1984). See the chapter "Prayers and Prayerfulness."

2. A good collection of introductory essays about the Ignatian Exercises is John E. Dister, S.J. (ed.), *A New Introduction to the Spiritual Exercises of St. Ignatius* (Collegeville, MN: Liturgical Press, 1993 and re-issued by Eugene, OR: Wifp and Stock, 2003). The Institute of Jesuit Sources (3700 West Pine

Blvd., St. Louis, MO 63108) can provide you with further
information and publications.

3. Luke Dysinger, o.s.b., "Accepting the Embrace of God: The
   Ancient Art of *Lectio Divina,*" *Valyermo Benedictine* 1/1
   (Spring, 1990) 33.
4. Marcus J. Borg, *Reading the Bible Again for the First Time*
   (New York: HarperCollins, 2001) 32.
5. M. Basil Pennington, o.c.s.o., *A Place Apart* (New York:
   Doubleday, 1983) 84.
6. This quotation is from a handout I received at a workshop on
   lectio divina.
7. Esther de Waal, *Seeking God: The Way of St. Benedict* (Collegeville, MN: Liturgical Press, 1984) 33.
8. Timothy Fry, o.s.b. (ed.), *The Rule of St. Benedict* (Collegeville, MN: Liturgical Press, 1981) 447.
9. Pennington 82.
10. de Waal 43.
11. Pennington 80.
12. Pennington 77.
13. Fry, *Rule* 157.
14. See M. Basil Pennington, o.c.s.o., *Lectio Divina* (New York:
    Crossroad, 1998). Steven Chase, *The Tree of Life: Models of
    Christian Prayer* (Grand Rapids, MI: Baker Book House,
    2005) 106.
15. Dysinger 37.
16. Anthony de Mello, s.j., *Sadhana: A Way to God* (Anand,
    India: Gujarat, Sahitya, Prakash, 1978) 103.
17. Fry, *Rule* 217.
18. C.S. Lewis, *Letters to Malcolm, Chiefly on Prayer* (London:
    Collins/Fontana, 1964/66) 23).
19. Pennington 79.
20. Dysinger 35.
21. de Waal 42.
22. Dysinger 36.
23. Actually, one can engage in *lectio* by using spiritual books or
    poetry. Sometimes this can be very helpful when one is stale

or stuck in Bible reading. In this chapter, I stress the use of the Bible because the prayer form arose in connection with the Bible.

24. de Waal 52.

Chapter 4: Prayer: Toward an Anthropology

1. Blaise Pascal, *Pensées* (William F. Trotter transl.) (New York: Washington Square Press, 1965) 79.

2. W. Norris Clarke, s.j., "Living on the Edge: The Human Person as 'Frontier Being' and Microcosm," *International Philosophical Quarterly* 36/2 (issue 142) (1996) 183.

3. Ibid.

4. Clarke 189.

5. Evelyn Underhill, *The Spiritual Life* (New York: Harper & Bros., n.d.).

6. L.J. Kreitzer, "Body," in *Dictionary of Paul and His Letters* Gerald Hawthorne and Ralph Martin (eds) (Downers Grove, IL: InterVarsity Press, 1993) 72.

7. James Keenan, s.j., "Current Theology Note: Christian Perspectives on the Human Body," *Theological Studies* 55 (1994) 330.

8. Anne Lamott, *Traveling Mercies* (New York: Anchor, 2000) 206.

9. For a good study of this matter see Jerome Neyrey, "Body Language in 1 Corinthians," *Semeia* 35 (1986) 129–170 and John A.T. Robinson, *The Body: A Study in Pauline Theology* (Philadelphia: Westminster Press, 1952).

10. So Rudolf Bultmann and John A.T. Robinson. But for a different view see R.H. Gundry, *Soma in Biblical Theology* (Cambridge: Cambridge University Press, 1976).

11. R.Y.K. Fung, "Body of Christ" in *Dictionary of Paul and His Letters* 81.

12. Quoted in Keenan, p. 332. And see Rudolf Bultmann, *Theology of the New Testament* 1.192–203.

13. So Bultmann, quoted in R.J. Erickson, "Flesh" in *Dictionary of Paul and His Letters* 305.

14. Erickson 305.

15. Erickson 306.

16. E. Schweizer, *"Pneuma"* in *Theological Dictionary of the New Testament* (Abridged in One Volume) Geoffrey W. Bromiley (ed.) (Grand Rapids, MI: Eerdmans, 1992) 889. Hereafter TDNT.

17. E. Schweizer, *"Sarx* in the New Testament," *TDNT* 1006.

18. Schweizer 889.

19. Schweizer 890.

20. E. Jacob, *Psyche,* TDNT 1342, 1343.

21. N.W. Porteous, "Soul," in *The Interpreter's Dictionary of the Bible* G.A. Buttrick (ed.) (Nashville, TN: Abingdon Press, 1962/85) 4: 428.

22. A brief example by E. Schweizer is found in TDNT (Abridged) 1350–1351.

23. Writing in the TDNT (Abridged) H. Kleinknecht notes "In contrast to *nous* (mind), which resembles the calmer medium of light, *pneuma* (spirit) is a dynamic term suggesting the forceful movement of air that seizes us with elemental power and catches us up into tension or movement." 876.

24. J. Philip Newell, *Echo of the Soul: The Sacredness of the Human Body* (Harrisburg, PA: Morehouse Publishing, 2000) 9.

25. Jacob 1345.

26. Quoted in J.K. Chamblin, "Psychology," *Dictionary of Paul and His Letters* 769.

27. Quoted in Richard Foster, *Prayer: Finding the Heart's True Home* (San Francisco: HarperSanFrancisco, 1992) 32.

28. Porteous 429.

29. Kallistos Ware, "How Do We Enter the Heart?" in *Paths to the Heart: Sufism and the Christian East* James S. Cutsinger (ed.) (Louisville, KY: Fons Vitae Press, 2002) 7.

30. David Steindl-Rast, o.s.b., *Gratefulness: The Heart of Prayer* (New York: Paulist Press, 1984) 27, 29, 31.

31. Thomas Merton, o.c.s.o., *Thoughts in Solitude* (New York: Farrar, Straus, Giroux, 1956/77) 46–47.

32. Keenan 332.

33. For more on this see Michael Bradford, *The Healing Energy of Your Hands* (Berkeley: Crossing Press, 1993), Barbara Ann Brennan, *Hands of Light* (New York: Bantam Books, 1988) and Donna Eden, *Energy Medicine* (New York: Jeremy P. Tarcher/Putnam, 1998).

34. To explore this more you might consult Swami Amaldas, *Christian Yogic Meditation* (Wilmington, DE: Michael Glazier, Inc. 1983); Michaelle, *Yoga and Prayer* (Westminster, MD: Christian Classics, 1980); Nancy Roth, *An Invitation to Christian Yoga* (New York: Seabury Books, 1989/2005) this work includes an instructional CD; Thomas Ryan, C.S.P., *Prayer of Heart and Body* (New York: Paulist Press, 1995).

35. Thomas Ryan, C.S.P., *Prayer of Heart and Body* (New York: Paulist Press, 1995) 144.

36. It is well worth a Christian's time to take a lesson or two from a really good Zen teacher. Thich Nhat Hanh's book *The Miracle of Mindfulness!* (Boston: Beacon Press, 1975) is an accessible introduction to breath prayer. And Richard Rosen's *The Yoga of Breath* (Boston: Shambala, 2002) may also be of interest. If you are really interested in praying with the breath, you should have a teacher to assist and guide you.

37. I apologize to those of you who are asthmatic or have lung disease. You, most of all, understand how breath is life!

Chapter 5: Praying the Name: The Jesus Prayer

1. Mary Jo Weaver, *Springs of Water in a Dry Land* (Boston: Beacon Press, 1993) 113.

2. Thomas Merton, O.C.S.O., *New Seeds of Contemplation* (New York: New Directions, 1961) 37.

3. Tito Colliander, *Way of the Ascetics* (Crestwood, NY: St. Vladimir's Seminary Press, 1985) 65.

4. Anthony Coniaris, *Introducing the Orthodox Church* (Minneapolis, MN: Light and Life Publishing, 1982, 207.

5. Timothy (Kallistos) Ware, *The Orthodox Church* (New York: Penguin Books, 1963/76) 73.

6. Quoted in John Meyendorff, *The Orthodox Church* (New York: St. Vladimir's Seminary Press, 1981) 203–204.

7. Nicholas Zernov, *Eastern Christendom* (London: Weidenfield & Nicholson, 1961) 130.

8. Quoted in Elisabeth Sehr-Sigel (transl. Fr. Steven Bigham), *The Place of the Heart: An Introduction to Orthodox Spirituality* (Torrance, CA: Oakwood Publications, 1992) 168.

9. I have written more extensively about the Name in early Christianity in chapter 4 ("The Name" in Acts 1–10) of my book *Spiritual Life in the Early Church* (Minneapolis, MN: Fortress Press, 1993).

10. Ware 313.

11. Thomas Merton, o.c.s.o., *Contemplative Prayer* (New York: Doubleday/Image, 1969/71) 22.

12. Ibid.

13. Fr. Thomas Ryan, c.s.p., *Prayer of Heart and Body* (New York: Paulist Press, 1995) 36.

14. Meyendorff 205.

15. Merton, *Contemplative Prayer* 22.

16. *The Way of a Pilgrim* (Helen Bacovcin, transl.) (New York: Doubleday/Image, 1978) 19.

17. *The Way of a Pilgrim* 40.

18. N.A., *The Jesus Prayer* (Crestwood, NY: St. Vladimir's Seminary Press, 1987) 96.

19. Ware in Sehr-Sigel 158.

20. Quoted in Abhishiktananda, *Prayer* (Norwich: Canterbury Press, 2006) xii.

21. Quoted in Kallistos Ware, "How Do We Enter the Heart?" in *Paths to the Heart* James S. Cutsinger, (ed.) (Louisville, KY: Fons Vitae Press, 2002) 3 and 5.

22. Quoted in Ware, "How Do We Enter" 5.

23. Quoted in Ware 313.

24. John Meyendorff (ed.) (Nicholas Gendle, transl.), *Gregory Palamas: The Triads* (New York: Paulist Press, 1983) 107.

25. Quoted in Sehr-Sigel 159.

26. Abhishiktananda 99–100.

27. Abhishiktananda 98.
28. Quoted in Sehr-Sigel 151.
29. Abhishiktananda 101.
30. Rama Coomaraswamy, *The Invocation of the Name of Jesus as practiced in the Western Church* (Louisville, KY: Fons Vitae, 1999) 9.
31. If you are unfamiliar with spiritual direction an accessible introduction is Margaret Guenther, *Holy Listening: The Art of Spiritual Direction* (Boston: Cowley Publications, 1992). The text book on the subject is Carolyn Gratton's *The Art of Spiritual Guidance* (New York: Crossroad,1992/2000). Other helpful studies include Joseph J. Allen, *Inner Way* (Grand Rapids: Eerdmans, 1994); William J. Barry, S.J., *Spiritual Direction and the Encounter with God* (New York: Paulist Press, 1992); Gerald G. May, M.D., *Care of Mind/Care of Spirit* (San Francisco: HarperSanFrancisco, 1992; Martin Thornton, *Spiritual Direction* (Boston: Cowley Publications, 1984).
32. *The Jesus Prayer* 94.
33. Gerald O'Collins and Edward Farrugia (eds.), *The Concise Dictionary of Theology* (New York: Paulist Press, 1991) 91.
34. Quoted in Coniaris 205.
35. Br. David Steindl-Rast, O.S.B., *A Listening Heart: The Spirituality of Sacred Sensuousness* (New York: Crossroad Press, 1993/99) 6.

Chapter 6: Praying with the Body: Some Exercises

1. James Keenan, S.J., "Christian Perspectives on the Human Body," *Theological Studies* 55 (1994) 333.
2. Keenan 332.
3. For recent reflections on this issue you might find Robert C. Fuller's review article "Faith of the Flesh: Bodily Sources of Spirituality," *Religious Studies Review* 33/4 (2007) 285–290 and Meredith B. McGuire, "Why Bodies Matter: A Sociological Reflection on Spirituality and Materiality,"*Spiritus* 3 (2003) 1–18 of interest.

4. Anthony de Mello, s.j., *Sadhana: A Way to God* (Anand, India: Gujarat Sahitya Prakash, 1978) 41.

5. de Mello 40.

6. C.S. Lewis, *Letters to Malcolm, Chiefly on Prayer* (London: Collins/Fontana, 1964/66) 19.

7. Vilma Seelaus, o.c.d., "The Contemplative Dimension Uncompartmentalized," *Spiritual Life* 30/2 (Summer, 1984) 90.

8. de Mello 32.

9. For a similar practice see Jennifer Derryberry, "The Heart Meditation," *Spirituality & Health* (Jan./Feb., 2000) 74–75.

10. Cynthia Bourgeault, *The Wisdom Way of Knowing* (San Francisco: Jossey-Bass, 2003) 33.

11. For another reflection on the "heart" which includes some exercises, see Gil Hedley, "Your Whole Heart," *Spirituality and Health* 11/3 (May/June, 2008) 48–51.

12. Thich Nhat Hanh, *Peace Is Every Step* (New York: Bantam Books, 1991).

13. Phillip Moffitt, "Awakening in the Body," *Shambala Sun* 16/1 (September, 2007) 46.

14. Bernard of Clairvaux, *On Loving God* (Kalamazoo, MI: Cistercian Publications, 1995) 32.

Chapter 7: Prayer: Toward a Cosmology

1. The following books address the spiritualities of particular branches of Christianity: N.A., *Orthodox Spirituality* (Crestwood, NY: St. Vladimir's Seminary Press, 1978), Donald L. Alexander (ed.), *Christian Spirituality: Five Views of Sanctification* (Downer's Grove, IL: InterVarsity Press, 1988), Richard P. McBrien, *Catholicism* (Oak Grove, MN: Winston Press, 1981) chapter 28 "Christian Spirituality;" Karl Rahner (ed.), *The Teaching of the Catholic Church* (Cork: Mercier Press, 1967) chapter 9 "The Sacraments;" Frank C. Senn (ed.), *Protestant Spiritual Traditions* (New York: Paulist Press, 1986).

2. C.S. Lewis writes with great clarity and very sensibly about

the "darker realm." You might want to read the chapter entitled "The Invasion" in *Mere Christianity* or the very entertaining (and sobering) allegorical novel *The Great Divorce* in which a busload of residents of hell visit heaven.

3. An accessible edition is Abraham J. Malherbe and Everett Ferguson, *Gregory of Nyssa: The Life of Moses* (New York: Paulist Press, 1978).

4. An accessible edition is John Meyendorff (ed.) *Gregory Palamas: The Triads* (New York: Paulist Press, 1983.)

5. Marcus J. Borg, *Jesus: A New Vision* (New York: Harper & Row, 1987) 26.

6. Ibid.

7. Cynthia Bourgeault, *The Wisdom Way of Knowing* (San Francisco: Jossey-Bass, 2003) 45, 53.

8. Bourgeault 25.

9. Of particular interest in this context are *Concerning the Inner Life* (Oxford: One World, 2000), *Practical Mysticism* (New York: Dutton, 1960), *Abba* (New York: Vintage, 2003), and *The Spiritual Life* (Harrisburg, PA: Morehouse Publishing, 1955).

10. Thomas Merton, O.C.S.O., *New Seeds of Contemplation* (New York: New Directions, 1961).

11. See especially *Thomas Merton's Dark Path* revised edition (New York: Farrar, Straus, Giroux, 1987).

12. For classic, but very different, treatments of this construct see Sigmund Freud, *The Ego and the Id* (New York: W. W. Norton, 1962) and Jean-Paul Sartre, *The Transcendence of the Ego* (New York: Noonday Press, 1957).

13. Thomas Ryan, C.S.P., *Prayer of Heart and Body* (New York: Paulist Press, 1995) 23.

14. A. Reza Arasteh, *Growth to Selfhood* (London: Arkana, 1990) 23.

15. Quoted in Arasteh 22.

16. Ryan 30.

17. Ryan 102.

Chapter 8: Prayer: Toward *Contemplatio*

1. Thomas Merton, O.C.S.O., *Thoughts in Solitude* (New York: Farrar, Straus, Giroux, 1958) 48.
2. Cynthia Bourgeault, *The Wisdom Way of Knowing* (San Francisco: Jossey-Bass, 2003).
3. Thomas Merton, O.C.S.O., *New Seeds of Contemplation* (New York: New Directions, 1961) 1.
4. N.A., *The Cloud of Unknowing* (New York: Penguin, 1961/71) 98. Hereafter *Cloud*.
5. *Cloud* 53.
6. Thomas Ryan, *Prayer of Heart and Body* (New York: Paulist Press, 1995) 43.
7. Merton, *New Seeds* 3.
8. Aelred Graham, *Contemplative Christianity* (New York: Seabury Press, 1974) 68.
9. Merton, *New Seeds* 10.
10. *Cloud* 60.
11. Merton, *New Seeds* 37.
12. Merton, *New Seeds* 3.
13. William Johnson, S.J., *Silent Music: The Science of Meditation* (New York: Harper & Row, 1976) 117.
14. Merton, *New Seeds* 243.
15. *Cloud* 93.
16. A particularly helpful exploration of contemplative silence is Thomas Merton's "Creative Silence" found in *Love and Living* (Naomi Burton Stone & Br. Patrick Hart, eds.) (New York: Harcourt Brace Jovanovich, 1985) 38–45.
17. I have used this quotation a great many times and, unfortunately, lost track of its source, for which I beg pardon of Isaac of Nineveh.
18. Kallistos Ware, "How Do We Enter the Heart?" in James S. Cutsinger (ed.), *Paths to the Heart* (Louisville, KY: Fons Vitae Press, 2002) 19.
19. Merton, *New Seeds* 80.
20. Thomas Merton, O.C.S.O., *The Wisdom of the Desert* (New York: New Directions, 1960) 22. Hereafter *Wisdom*.

21. Merton, *Wisdom* 17.
22. *Cloud* 85.
23. *Cloud* 93.
24. Merton, *New Seeds* 243.
25. Merton, *Wisdom* 25–26.
26. Quoted from a letter in William Shannon (ed.), *The Hidden Ground of Love: Letters of Thomas Merton* (New York: Farrar, Straus, Giroux, 1985) 367.

Chapter 9: Praying Contemplatively: The Prayer of Waiting

1. An excellent introduction to the Centering Prayer movement is found in Joseph G. Sandman, "Centering Prayer: A Treasure for the Soul," *America* (Sept. 9, 2000) 12–14, and the Summer/Fall 2001 (10/1) issue of *Hungryhearts*, a publication of the Office of Spiritual Formation of the Presbyterian Church (U.S.A.) was devoted to Centering Prayer.
2. For more on Eastern Spirituality in America see Robert S. Ellwood (ed.), *Eastern Spirituality in America* (New York: Paulist Press, 1987). Two interesting and very different personal accounts of this journey are Diana L. Eck, *Encountering God: A Spiritual Journey from Bozeman to Banaras* (Boston: Beacon Press, 1993) and David Toolan, s.j., *Facing West from California's Shores* (New York: Crossroad Press, 1987).
3. See, for example, his *Christian Zen: A Way of Meditation* (San Francisco: Harper & Row, 1971/79).
4. The proceedings of several of these dialogues have been published. In chronological order by publication date, four volumes of interest are *A Zen-Christian Pilgrimage* (The Fruits of Ten Annual Colloquia in Japan 1967–1976) (Hong Kong: Pearl Island Typesetters, 1981); Susan Walker (ed.), *Speaking of Silence: Christians and Buddhists on the Contemplative Way* (New York: Paulist Press, 1987); Donald W. Mitchell and James Wiseman, o.s.b. (eds), *The Gethsemani Encounter* (New York: Continuum, 1998); Patrick Henry (ed.), *Benedict's Dharma* (New York: Riverhead Books, 2001).

5. See, for example, Shirley du Boulay (ed.), *Swami Abhishik-tananda: Essential Writings* (Maryknoll, NY: Orbis, 2006); Bede Griffiths, *Return to the Center* (Springfield, IL: Templegate, 1977); Thomas Matus (ed.), *Bede Griffith: Essential Writings* (Maryknoll, NY: Orbis, 2004); Ramundo Panikkar, *The Unknown Christ of Hinduism* (Maryknoll, NY: Orbis, 1964/81). And an interesting introductory study on meditation in a several religions is Daniel Goleman, *The Varieties of the Meditative Experience* (New York: E.P. Dutton, 1977).

6. For more on this see M. Basil Pennington, O.C.S.O., *Centering Prayer* (New York: Doubleday/Image, 1982) 214–215.

7. Gerald G. May, M.D., *The Dark Night of the Soul* (San Francisco: HarperSanFrancisco, 2004) 108.

8. May 150.

9. Morton T. Kelsey, *The Other Side of Silence* (New York: Paulist Press, 1976) chapter 10.

10. Quoted in Dom Jean LeClercq, *Alone with God* (New York: Farrar, Straus and Cudahy, 1961) 76.

11. C.S. Lewis, *Letters to Malcolm, Chiefly on Prayer* (London: Collins/Fontana, 1964/66) 85.

12. Abhishiktananda, *Prayer* (Norwich: Canterbury Press, 2006) 42.

13. For more on spiritual direction see chapter 5, footnote 31.

14. Walter J. Ciszek, S.J., *He Leadeth Me* (Garden City, NY: Doubleday/Image, 1975) 66.

15. Clifton Wolters (tranls.), *The Cloud of Unknowing* (New York/London: Penguin, 1961/71) 61.

16. Another extremely good and brief explanation of how to pray this way is found in "Focus on Centering Prayer" p. 63 in Thomas Keating (*et al.*), *Finding God at the Center* (Still River, MA: St. Bede Publications, 1978). Chapters 5 and 6 in Ryan's *Prayer of Heart and Body* are also helpful.

17. Thomas Ryan in *Prayer of Heart and Body* devotes chapter 4 to "Is Contemplative Prayer for Everyone?" Reading it may help your discernment about this matter.

18. Abhishiktananda 40.

19. Thomas Keating, "Cultivating the Centering Prayer" in *Finding God at the Center* 30–31. And see chapters 6 and 8 in *Open Mind, Open Heart: The Contemplative Dimension of the Gospel* (New York: Amity House, 1986).
20. Quoted in Sebastian Brock (transl.), *The Syriac Fathers on Prayer and the Spiritual Life* (Kalamazoo, MI: Cistercian Publications, 1987) 72.
21. Quoted in Christine Bochen (ed.), *Thomas Merton: Essential Writings* (Maryknoll, NY: Orbis Press, 2000) 83.
22. Quoted in Robert Daggy (ed.), *Thomas Merton in Alaska* (New York: New Directions, 1988) 138,
23. *Merton in Alaska* 139.
24. I encountered this quotation in a diocesan prayer calendar in England. The citation was simply Martin Smith, *Compass and Stars*.
25. LeClercq 129.
26. Blessed Paul Giustiniani in LeClercq 130.
27. M. Basil Pennington, "Centering Prayer—Prayer of Quiet," *Finding Grace at the Center* 15.
28. M.A. Bouchard, *Contemplative Life in the World* (St. Louis: B. Herder, 1959) 177. (The work is a translation of *La Vie Contemplative, est-elle possible dans le monde?* Paris, 1952.)
29. Abhishiktananda 54.
30. Quoted in LeClercq 121.
31. LeClercq 120.
32. Lewis 77.
33. Henri Nouwen quoted in James E. Adams (ed.), *Living in Hope* (Fenton, MO: Creative Communications for the Parish, 2007) 8. The editor notes the quotation is from Nouwen's *Finding My Way Home* (New York: Crossroad, 2001).

Summary Notes

1. C.S. Lewis, *Letters to Malcolm, Chiefly on Prayer* (London: Collins, Fontana, 1964/66) 12.
2. Thomas Merton's book, *Seasons of Celebration* (New York:

Farrar, Straus, Giroux, 1950/77) has a series of wonderful essays on the spirituality of the various liturgical seasons.

3. Jean Pierre de Caussade, S.J., *The Sacrament of the Present Moment* (New York: Harper & Row, 1982) 29.

4. From *The Interior Castle* quoted in Mary Jo Weaver, "A Whistling Shepherd and a Little Lost Otter: An Essay on Prayer," *Spiritus* 7 (2007) 20.

5. A brief, popular account of this by David Van Biema, "Her Agony," appeared in the September 3, 2007 *Time Magazine*. Gerald G. May's book *The Dark Night of the Soul* (San Francisco: HarperSanFrancisco, 2004) is a modern psychiatrist's view of the experience of "dryness" and "absence" in prayer.

6. P.T. Forsyth, *The Soul of Prayer* (London: Independent Press, Ltd.,1916/51) 17.

7. Quoted in Jean LeClercq, *Alone with God* (New York: Farrar, Straus and Cudahy, 1961) 122.

8. Quoted in Sebastian Brock (transl.), *The Syriac Fathers on Prayer and the Spiritual Life* (Kalamazoo, MI: Cistercian Publications, Inc., 1987) 67.

9. Margaret Guenther, *The Practice of Prayer* (Boston: Cowley Publications, 1998) 61–62.

10. Abhishiktananda, *Prayer* (Norwich: Canterbury Press, 2006) 82, 83.

11. Abhishiktananda 83.

12. May 130.

13. Ibid.

14. A challenging study of this point is Brian J. Walsh and Sylvia C. Keesmaat, *Colossians Remixed: Subverting the Empire* (Downers Grove, IL: IVP Academic Press, 2004).

15. Madeleine L'Engle, *Walking on Water: Reflections on Faith and Art* (Wheaton, IL: Harold Shaw Publishers, 1980) 161.

16. L'Engle 189.

17. N.A., *The Cloud of Unknowing* (New York: Penguin, 1961) 53.

18. The first four of these categories were suggested by Theodore

W. Jennings, Jr., "Prayer: The Call for God," *The Christian Century* (April 15, 1981) 410–411. I have adapted them somewhat, but am grateful to Jennings for the clarity of his categories.

19. Ann and Barry Ulanov, *Primary Speech: A Psychology of Prayer* (Atlanta: John Knox Press, 1982) 101.

20. Forsyth 28–29.

21. Forsyth 20.

22. "We are already all that we are to be." "When [God] comes to our prayer he brings with Him all that He purposes to make us." Forsyth 25.

23. Anthony Bloom (Metropolitan Anthony), *Beginning to Pray* (New York: Paulist Press, 1970) 45.

24. Jennings 413.

25. *The Cloud of Unknowing* 85.

26. Thomas Keating, O.C.S.O., *The Human Condition: Contemplation and Transformation* (New York: Paulist Press, 1999) 38.

27. Keating 42–43.

Select Bibliography

Abhishiktananda (Henri le Saux, O.S.B.), *Prayer* (Norwich: Canterbury Press, 1989)

Alexander, Donald L. (ed.), *Christian Spirituality: Five Views of Sanctification* (Downer's Grove, IL: InterVarsity Press, 1988)

Allison, Dale, *The Silence of Angels* (Valley Forge: Trinity Press International, 1995)

Amaldas, Swami, *Christian Yogic Meditation* (Wilmington, DE: Michael Glazier, Inc., 1983)

Arasteh, A. Reza, *Growth to Selfhood* (London: Arkana, 1990)

Bacovcin, Helen (transl.), *The Way of a Pilgrim* (New York: Doubleday/Image, 1978)

Barry, William J., S.J., *Spiritual Direction and the Encounter with God* (New York: Paulist Press, 1992)

Bernard of Clairvaux, *On Loving God* (Kalamazoo, MI: Cistercian Publications, 1995)

Bianchi, Enzo, *Praying the Word* (Kalamazoo, MI: Cistercian Publications, 1992)

Bloom, Anthony (Metropolitan Anthony), *Beginning to Pray* (New York: Paulist Press, 1970)

Bochen, Christine (ed.), *Thomas Merton: Essential Writings* (Maryknoll, NY: Orbis, 2000)

Borg, Marcus J., *Jesus: A New Vision* (New York: Harper & Row, 1987)

_____. *Reading the Bible Again for the First Time* (New York: HarperCollins, 2000)

Bouchard, M.A., *Contemplative Life in the World* (St. Louis: B. Herder, 1959) du Boulay, Shirley (ed.), *Swami Abhishiktananda: Essential Writings* (Maryknoll, NY: Orbis 2006).

Bourgeault, Cynthia, *The Wisdom Way of Knowing* (San Francisco: Jossey-Bass, 2003)

Brand, Paul and Philip Yancey, *Fearfully and Wonderfully Made: A Surgeon Looks at the Human and Spiritual Body* (Grand Rapids, MI: Zondervan, 1980)

Brock, Sebastian (transl.), *The Syriac Fathers on Prayer and the Spiritual Life* (Kalamazoo, MI: Cistercian Publications, 1987)

Bromiley, Geoffrey W. (ed.), *Theological Dictionary of the New Testament* (Abridged in One Volume) (Grand Rapids, MI: Eerdmans, 1992)

Brueggemann, Walter, *Praying the Psalms* (Winona, MN: St. Mary's Press, 1993)

Buttrick, G.A. (ed.), *The Interpreter's Dictionary of the Bible* (Nashville, TN: Abingdon Press, 1962/85)

Calvin, John (I. John Hesselink, intro.), *On Prayer* (Westminster John Knox 2006)

Carson, D.A. (ed.), *Teach Us to Pray* (Grand Rapids, MI: Baker Book House, 1990)

de Caussade, Jean-Pierre, S.J., *Abandonment to Divine Providence* (New York: Doubleday/Image, 1975)

Chase, Steven, *The Tree of Life: Models of Christian Prayer* (Grand Rapids, MI: Baker Book House, 2005)

LeClercq, Dom Jean, *Alone with God* (New York: Farrar, Straus and Cudahy, 1961)

Colliander, Tito, *Way of the Ascetics* (Crestwood, NY: St. Vladimir's Seminary Press, 1985)

Coniaris, Anthony, *Introducing the Orthodox Church* (Minneapolis, MN: Light and Life Publishing, 1982)

Coomaraswamy, Rama, *The Invocation of the Name of Jesus as Practiced in the Western Church* (Louisville, KY: Fons Vitae Press, 1999)

Cutsinger, James S. (ed.), *Paths to the Heart: Sufism and the Christian East* (Louisville, KY: Fons Vitae Press, 2002)

Daggy, Robert (ed.), *Thomas Merton in Alaska* (New York: New Directions, 1988)

Danielou, Jean, *Prayer: The Mission of the Church* (Grand Rapids, MI: Eerdmans, 1996)

de Mello, Anthony, S.J., *Sadhana* (New York: Doubleday/Image, 1984)

Dieker, Bernadette and Jonathan Montaldo (eds.), *Merton and Hesychasm: The Prayer of the Heart* (Louisville, KY: Fons Vitae Press, 2003)

Dister, John E., S.J., *A New Introduction to the Spiritual Exercises of St. Ignatius* (Collegeville, MN: Liturgical Press, 1993)

Endres, John C., S.J. and Elizabeth Liebert, *A Retreat with the Psalms* (New York: Paulist Press, 2001)

L'Engle, Madeleine, *Walking on Water: Reflections on Faith and Art* (Wheaton: Harold Shaw Publishers, 1980)

Forsyth, P.T., *The Soul of Prayer* (London: Independent Press, 1916/51)

Foster, Richard J., *Prayer: Finding the Heart's True Home* (San Francisco: HarperSanFrancisco,1992)

Freeman, Lawrence (ed.), *John Main: Essential Writings* (Maryknoll, NY: Orbis, 2002)

Freeman, Lawrence, *Light Within: The Inner Path of Meditation* (New York: Crossroad, 1987)

Fry, Timothy, O.S.B. (ed.), *The Rule of St. Benedict* (Collegeville, MN: Liturgical Press, 1981)

Goleman, Daniel, *The Varieties of the Meditative Experience* (New York: E.P. Dutton, 1977)

Graham, Aelred, *Contemplative Christianity* (New York: Seabury Press, 1974)

Gratton, Carolyn, *The Art of Spiritual Guidance* (New York: Crossroad, 1992/2000)

Green, Thomas H., S.J., *When the Well Runs Dry: Prayer Beyond the Beginnings* (Notre Dame, IN: Ave Maria Press, 1979)

Gregory of Nyssa, *The Life of Moses* (New York: Paulist Press, 1978)

Grenz, Stanley J., *Prayer: The Cry for the Kingdom* (Peabody, MA: Hendrickson, 1988)

Guenther, Margaret, *Holy Listening: The Art of Spiritual Direction* (Boston: Cowley Publications, 1992)

_____. *The Practice of Prayer* (Boston: Cowley Publications, 1998)

Gundry, R.H., *Soma in Biblical Theology* (Cambridge: Cambridge University Press, 1976)

Hall, Thelma, R.C., *Too Deep for Words: Rediscovering Lectio Divina* (Mahwah, NJ: Paulist Press, 1988)

Hart, Patrick, O.C.S.O. (ed.), *Thomas Merton: Monk* (New York: Sheed & Ward, 1974)

Hawthorne, Gerald and Ralph Martin (eds.), *Dictionary of Paul and His Letters* (Downers Grove, IL: InterVarsityPress, 1993)

Herman, E., *Creative Prayer* (New York: Harper & Bros., n.d.)

Holder, Arthur (ed.), *The Blackwell Companion to Christian Spirituality* (Oxford: Blackwell Publishing, 2005)

Jewett, Robert, *Paul's Anthropological Terms* (Leiden: Brill, 1971)

Johnson, William, S.J., *Christian Zen: A Way of Meditation* (San Francisco: Harper & Row, 1971/79)

_____. *Silent Music: The Science of Meditation* (New York: Harper & Row, 1976)

Jones, Tony, *Soul Shaper* (Grand Rapids, MI: Zondervan, 2003)

Kadloubovsky, E. and G.E.H. Palmer (transl.), *The Philokalia* (London: Faber & Faber, 1951/83)

Kavanaugh, Kieran, O.C.D. and Otilio Rodriguez, O.C.D. (transl), *The Collected Works of St. John of the Cross* (Washington, D.C.: ICS Publications/Institute of Carmelite Studies, 1979)

Keating, Thomas, O.C.S.O., (ed.), *Finding God at the Center* (Still River, MA: St. Bede Publications, 1978)

_____. *The Human Condition: Contemplation and Transformation* (New York: Paulist Press, 1999)

_____. *Open Mind, Open Heart: The Contemplative Dimension of the Gospel* (New York: Amity House, 1986)

Kelsey, Morton T., *The Other Side of Silence* (New York: Paulist Press, 1976)

Kirvan, John, *Raw Faith* (Notre Dame, IN: Sorin Books, 2000)

Lamott, Anne, *Traveling Mercies* (New York: Anchor, 2000)

Lewis, C.S., *Letters to Malcolm, Chiefly on Prayer* (London: Collins/ Fontana, 1964/66)

_____. *Reflections on the Psalms* (London: Collins/Fontana, 1958/ 61)

Malherbe, Abraham J. and Everett Ferguson (eds.), *Gregory of Nyssa: The Life of Moses* (New York: Paulist Press, 1978)

May, Gerald G., M.D., *Care of Mind/Care of Spirit* (San Francisco: HarperSanFrancisco, 1992)

_____. *The Dark Night of the Soul* (San Francisco: HarperSan-Francisco, 2004)

Merton, Thomas, O.C.S.O., *Contemplative Prayer* (New York: Doubleday/Image, 1969/71)

_____. *Love and Living* (New York: Harcourt Brace Jovanovich, 1985)

_____. *New Seeds of Contemplation* (New York: New Directions, 1961)

_____. *Praying the Psalms* (Collegeville, MN: Liturgical Press, 1956)

_____. *Seasons of Celebration* (New York: Farrar, Straus, Giroux, 1950/77)

_____. *Thoughts in Solitude* (New York: Farrar, Straus, Giroux, 1956)

_____. *The Wisdom of the Desert* (New York: New Directions, 1960)

Meyendorff, John (ed.), *Gregory Palamas: The Triads* (New York: Paulist Press, 1983)

_____. *The Orthodox Church* (New York: St. Vladimir's Seminary Press, 1981)

Michaelle, *Yoga and Prayer* (Westminster, MD: Christian Classics, 1980)

Murphy-O'Connor, Jerome, O.P., *Becoming Human Together: The Pastoral Anthropology of St. Paul* (Wilmington, DE: Michael Glazier, Inc., 1982/84)

N.A., *The Cell of Self Knowledge* (New York: Crossroad Press, 1981)

N.A., *The Cloud of Unknowing* (New York: Penguin, 1961/71)

N.A., *The Jesus Prayer* (Crestwood, NY: St. Vladimir's Seminary Press, 1987)

N.A., *Orthodox Spirituality* (Crestwood, NY: St. Vladimir's Seminary Press, 1978)

Newell, J. Philip, *Echo of the Soul: The Sacredness of the Human Body* (Harrisburg, PA: Morehouse Publishing, 2000)

Nhat Hanh, Thich, *The Miracle of Mindfulness!* (Boston: Beacon Press, 1975)

_____. *Peace Is Every Step* (New York: Bantam Books, 1991)

Norris, Kathleen, *The Cloister Walk* (New York: Riverhead Books, 1996)

Pascal, Blaise. *Pensées* (William F. Trotter, transl.) (New York: Washington Square Press, 1965)

Paulsell, Stephanie, *Honoring the Body: Meditation on a Christian Practice* (San Francisco: Jossey-Bass, 2002)

Peers, E. Allison (transl.), *Teresa of Avila: Interior Castle* (New York: Doubleday/Image, 1989)

_____. *Teresa of Avila: The Way of Perfection* (New York: Doubleday/Image, 1991)

Pennington, M. Basil O.C.S.O., *Centering Prayer* (New York: Doubleday/Image, 1982)

_____. *A Place Apart* (New York: Doubleday, 1983)

_____. *Lectio Divina* (New York: Crossroad, 1998)

Robinson, John A.T., *The Body: A Study in Pauline Theology* (Philadelphia: Westminster Press, 1952)

Rosen, Richard, *The Yoga of Breath* (Boston: Shambala, 2002)

Roth, Nancy, *An Invitation to Christian Yoga* (New York: Seabury Books, 1989/2005)

Ryan, Thomas, C.S.P., *Prayer of Heart and Body* (New York: Paulist Press, 1995)

_____. (ed.), *Reclaiming the Body in Christian Spirituality* (New York, Paulist Press, 2004)

Sehr-Sigel, Elisabeth (Fr. Steven Bigham, transl.), *The Place of the Heart: An Introduction to Orthodox Spirituality* (Torrance, CA: Oakwood Publications, 1992)

Senn, Frank C. (ed.), *Protestant Spiritual Traditions* (New York: Paulist Press, 1986)

Shannon, William (ed.), *The Hidden Ground of Love: Letters of Thomas Merton* (New York: Farrar, Straus, Giroux, 1985)

_____. *Thomas Merton's Dark Path* (rev. ed.) (New York: Farrar, Straus, Giroux, 1987)

Skinner, John (transl.), *Julian of Norwich: Revelation of Love* (New York: Doubleday/Image, 1997)

Slosson Wuellner, Flora, *Prayer and Our Bodies* (Nashville, TN: The Upper Room, 1987)

Steindl-Rast, David, O.S.B., *Gratefulness: The Heart of Prayer* (New York: Paulist Press, 1984)

_____. *A Listening Heart: The Spirituality of Sacred Sensuousness* (New York: Crossroad, 1993/99)

Thornton, Martin, *Spiritual Direction* (Boston: Cowley Publications, 1984)

Thurston, Bonnie, *Spiritual Life in the Early Church* (Minneapolis, MN: Fortress Press, 1983)

Ulanov, Ann and Barry, *Primary Speech: A Psychology of Prayer* (Atlanta: John Knox, 1982)

Underhill, Evelyn, *Abba* (New York: Vintage, 2003)

_____. *Concerning the Inner Life* (Oxford: One World, 2000)

_____. *Practical Mysticism* (New York: Dutton, 1960)

_____. *The Spiritual Life* (New York: Harper & Bros., n.d.)

de Waal, Esther, *Seeking God: The Way of St. Benedict* (Collegeville, MN: Liturgical Press, 1984)

Walker, Susan (ed.), *Speaking of Silence: Christians and Buddhists on the Contemplative Way* (New York: Paulist Press, 1987)

Ware, Timothy (Kallistos), *The Orthodox Church* (New York: Penguin Books, 1963/76)

Weaver, Mary Jo, *Springs of Water in a Dry Land* (Boston: Beacon, 1993)

Wicks, Robert, *After Fifty* (New York: Paulist Press, 1997)

Williams, Rowan, *A Ray of Darkness* (Cambridge: Cowley Publications, 1995)

_____. *Where God Happens: Discovering Christ in One Another* (Boston: New Seeds, 2005)

Zernov, Nicholas, *Eastern Christendom* (London: Weidenfield & Nicholson, 1961)